When Angels Wept

Jan S. Przybyła [signature]

When Angels Wept

*The Rebirth and Dismemberment of Poland and Her People
in the Early Decades of the Twentieth Century*

A BIOGRAPHICAL MEMOIR

Jan S. Prybyla
(PRZYBYŁA)

When Angels Wept: The Rebirth and Dismemberment of Poland and Her People in the Early Decades of the Twentieth Century

Published by Wheatmark®
610 East Delano Street, Suite 104
Tucson, Arizona 85705 U.S.A.
www.wheatmark.com

International Standard Book Number: 978-1-60494-325-2
Library of Congress Control Number: 2009933029

People die twice: first physically,
then again when they are forgotten

To the memory of
Jan Przybyła
and
Marta Przybyłowa

Killed in Auschwitz on
August 11, 1942
and
October 11, 1942

KL Auschwitz and Auschwitz-Birkenau
Polish Political Prisoners Numbers
39217
and
8561

Light be the earth upon you
Lightly rest

Contents

Acknowledgements

My daughter, Elizabeth, and her husband, Paul Hinderliter, have been of much help throughout this project, which included a trip to the town of Oświęcim, near where Auschwitz-Birkenau was located. The archival documentation division of the Auschwitz-Birkenau State Museum has been very cooperative in procuring copy extracts from the camp's *Sterbebuch* (Book of Death). Elisabetta Stangel-Grifoni's help in supplying family information and Polish-language sources was generous and indispensable. I express my deep appreciation of and thanks for all this valuable assistance.

I should like to add to the book's dedication, my wife Jacqueline, a good partner and companion of forty-eight years. She succumbed to pancreatic cancer shortly before the book began to be written.

Introduction

This book is first a memorial to Jan and Marta Przybyła, two ordinary people who perished in the hell of Auschwitz only because they were Polish and "political," loyal to and in love with their country—a capital crime in the eyes of their killers. It is also a recognition of efforts exerted by their brave but vulnerable daughter Maria (Marysia) to save them from unspeakable agony at the hands of Nazi barbarians and to prevent her brother, already imprisoned, from suffering the same fate.

Second, it is a memoir, not a history textbook. It looks from a distance at the people and the times they lived in. It also provides personal interpretations and judgments from what V. S. Pritchett called "the imaginative retrieval of memory," or what I see as "analysis with an attitude."

Third, the memoir combines microbiographies of individual and family lives caught in the whirlpool of state policies in peacetime and war. It starts with the life of a family and then branches out to the history of Polish Upper Silesia and of Poland itself in the years where the family lived and worked. Finally, it describes the destruction of the Polish state by Germany's war machine, its extermination of Jan and Marta, and dispersal of the family throughout Europe and the world. The viciousness of the process can best be understood by giving specific examples of the carnage, as well as profiles of individual victims and their killers.

Fourth, the coverage of the text begins with the Przybyła farm in Sierakowice in the late nineteenth century and ends with the death of Jan and Marta at Auschwitz in 1942. The focus is on the early stages of the German occupation of Poland (1939–1942), when Auschwitz transitioned from a concentration camp destined for Polish political prisoners (1940–1941) to a mass extermination industry of Jews from all over Europe—carried out mostly in state-of-the-art gas chambers, which came online in early 1943. Before that time, killing was done in less efficient gassing facilities, but first and foremost by incredibly hard labor, refined torture, perverted "medical" experiments, beatings, public lashings, mass hangings, firing squads, lethal injections, and hunger. These continued to the last day of the Third Reich.

When Angels Wept

Birth

Sierakowice

An oil painting of a quaint, unpretentious rural cottage shaded by a tall poplar in the midst of serene fields hung on the dining room wall of Villa Sixt—a mansion bequeathed at the turn of the nineteenth century to the city of Bielsko (then Bielitz) by wealthy German industrialist and merchant Theodor Karl Sixt—from 1935 until the outbreak of World War II on September 1, 1939. For close to five years I looked at that painting almost every day during family lunch while half listening to energetically patriotic political discussions around the table. However, my preteen interest in the fine arts was not strong enough to find out more about the picture. Then one day, out of the blue, my mother mentioned in passing that it depicted my sister Zofia's and my father's birthplace in the village of Sierakowice. The geopolitical appendage to this bit of private news—for there was always one—was that because of an early 1920s decision of the victorious World War I Western allies (the English and the French in particular) following a plebiscite and three Polish armed uprisings, Sierakowice remained in German Upper Silesia as it had been for centuries. The Nazis deemed the name too Polish-sounding and, in a form of cartographic aggression, changed it to Graumannsdorf in 1936.[1] As of 2008, Sierakowice was a suburb of the county seat Gliwice. Its population was around 1,300 spread over an area of 2,600 acres, almost two thirds of it wooded.

The owner of the modest Sierakowice farm—probably not more than low two-digit acres—was Teodor Przybyła, known in the vicinity of Gliwice (then Gleiwitz) for collecting Polish Silesian folk songs, many of them religious. His hobby seemed to be a harmless pastime, but it was actually dangerous in the combustible political climate of the time. Teodor married Karolina Franosz from nearby Sośnicowice, a small town long on history but short on growth that often changed ownership in extraordinarily convoluted ways and that was recurrently ravaged in whole or in part by religious and dynastic wars.[2] As for Karolina's maiden name, Franosz was one of the twenty thousand most common names in Poland in the 1990s (as was Przybyła), and while there was some romantic speculation in the family that it might have had a French connection (Franoche), research could not verify this claim.

Teodor and Karolina had five children: three boys and two girls. The boys were Jan (Janek in the diminutive), the co-subject of this memoir, born on October 18, 1884; Józef (Józek), born in 1886; and the youngest in the family, Wiktor, born in 1893. The two girls were Zefla (Józefa) , born in 1889, and the beloved Maria (Maryśka) who died of scarlet fever in childhood. Karolina was a good woman: strong, honest, hard-working, affectionate, and uncomplaining. She died a few years after the birth of Marysia. As a little boy, Wiktor would cuddle up beside his mother's sickbed. One morning, when he awoke, she was dead. After her death, Wiktor was brought up by his sister Zefla.

It can be assumed with a fair degree of certainty that all five children were baptized in Sierakowice's wooden Catholic church of St. Catherine of Alexandria built in 1675 by carpenter Józef Jozka, the same year in which the area was incorporated by Hapsburg Austria into the Bohemian crown domain.

Life of a large family on a small freehold became increasingly problematical despite long hours of work to which the children contributed as best they could, irrespective of age. Being a small freeholder is all very well in free market theory, but it is unheroic as a day-to-day practice on low-grade soil when you have seven mouths to feed, no savings, and zero political influence. Moreover, being a Polish Silesian, you were subjected to the Prussian *Kulturkampf* (culture struggle) within which you were a suspect national if instead just growing cabbage you collected Polish Silesian folk songs and worshipped in a Catholic church. It is fair to note that Teodor's decision toward the end of the 1890s or perhaps very early 1900s to sell his farm and take a manual labor job at the Donnersmarck steel mill in nearby Zabrze (Hinderburg) was also part of an industrialization wave sweeping through central Europe that involved large population displacements from lower- to higher-income areas, from agriculture to industry. These economically rational migrations. as well as the influx of refugees escaping oppression in the Russian-occupied eastern provinces of Poland, were made simpler by the development of railways. But when the rush was at its peak, authorities in Berlin saw to it that passenger trains did not stop at stations in the most congested Upper Silesian industrial cities of the German Empire.

Not long before that time, almost the whole adult male population of Sierakowice would walk to Zabrze on Sunday after lunch (a distance of some sixteen kilometers, or about ten miles) to work in the steel works all week and then return the following Saturday. The mill seemed to have made provisions for their housing in dormitories during working days. Józek and Wiktor probably did not work in the Donnersmarck mill; Józek went into the timber business early in life (and for life), and Wiktor attended and, after interruption for compulsory service in the German army in World War I, graduated from a Bytom high school.

When he completed primary school in Sierakowice—where instruction was exclusively in German and the curriculum was stolidly practical in content and culturally hostile in form: insistent on strict discipline, docility, conformity and knowing your place in society—Janek joined his father at the mill. That surely pleased Teodor, who wanted to see all his sons become steel workers for life. It made good sense to Teodor financially and socially: family income and living standards would rise compared with what they had been on the farmland, and the transition from farmer to industrial worker represented a step up on the social status ladder in a nationally class-conscious, urbanizing society that was separate and unequal.

At the time, two kinds of divergence in personal career aspirations emerged: one generational, between Teodor and his three sons, and one between the sons themselves. Not surprisingly, given his background and the pressure of short-term financial needs, Teodor's horizons stopped at industrial work on the factory floor, whereas the sons' ambitions went well beyond. They wanted to tack their way into the middle classes, preferably the upper-middle, the ranks of which, under Prussian rule in Upper Silesia, counted few Poles, who were generally debarred. Since they did not intend to become factory workers for the rest of their life, Teodor's sons had to figure out how to make the transition. They realized they needed to learn more than what they had learned in primary school—and unlearn a good many other things, such as the heavy-handed distortions about their national origin. Franz Graf von Ballestrem, an Upper Silesian grandee who became president of the legislative assembly of the German Empire from 1898 to 1906, once opined that "the Poles should be punched in the snout." Asked to explain this undiplomatic prescription, he went on public record that he saw no problem since there were no Poles in Upper Silesia but only Polish-speaking Prussians.[3] In any case, for many primary school pupils in the countryside, and for Poles especially, there was no secondary school in their future, either because they could not make the high, centrally set passing grade, they did not meet the requirements of the prevailing political correctness, or they could not attend due to financial reasons. But some did make it against the odds, including Wiktor. As we shall see, due to circumstances beyond their control but also through personal choice, Teodor's three sons interpreted the appropriate method of reaching their objective in different ways.

In 1903, at just under nineteen years of age, Janek quit his job at the steel mill and went his own way.

Notes

1.   It was about that time that I got to know visually my father's place of birth. By then he had already served a couple of years as government commissioner of Bielsko. Having untangled and sanitized the city's financial and sundry other ailments he was elected mayor by the City Council in March 1935. The second floor of Villa Sixt was the mayor's residence. When seventy years later I happened to get hold of a photograph of the Sierakowice cottage taken at the time of my father's boyhood, I realized it is true what they say about the difference between photo realism and the artistic license to embellish reality on canvas.

2.   One of those who passed through Sośnicowice on August 23, 1683, was the King of Poland, Jan III Sobieski with his army, including the much-feared winged hussars, leisurely en route from Warsaw to relieve Hapsburg Vienna, which was besieged by the Turks. Not feeling well that day, he stopped in Sośnicowice to get off his horse and into a small carriage, had a brief how-do-you-do with a local notable (a veteran of Turkish wars by the name of Jan Kozłowski) and after that went on his way to save the Holy Roman Empire and European Christianity. Then in May 6, 1921, Sośnicowice was the place through which Polish Silesian insurgents under the command of a captain Cyms passed on their way to wage battles with Germans, the idea being to persuade the members of the League of Nations in Geneva, Switzerland, to reunite this parcel of their homeland with a then reemerging Polish state. (The League did not reunite it).

3.   Helmut Neubach, "Origins and effects of the catchword 'One must hit the Poles on the mouth' [Man muss die Polen aufs Maul schlagen]: An exchange of letters between the Upper Silesian member of the Reichstag, Franz Graf von Ballestrem, and his colleague from Poznań, Josef von Kościelski (1891). *Zeitschrift für Ostmitteleuropa-Forschung*, vol. 54, nr. 2, 2005, 194–215. The article is in German. In that language the word "Maul" (mouth) applies to animals, and is offensive when used in connection with humans. http://cat.inist.fr/?aModele=afficheN&cpsidt=17166573

   H. P. Rosenthal, "National Self-Determination: The Example of Upper Silesia," *Journal of Contemporary History*,7, 1972, 231–241

Farm in Sierakowice. Early 1900s.

Maryśka, Jan, and Józef (Józek) in Sierakowice

Józefa (Zefla) in 1950

Interior of church in Sierakowice

Jan and Maryśka on the farm

Life

Youth
Internal Exile (1903–1919)

Insofar as it can be pieced together from what is known of his experience up to this time and his later actions, Janek's view of what had to be done and how was that although further learning was essential and desirable to attain his goals, it did not need to—and perhaps, at that stage of his life, could not—come in the form of organized, institutionalized, school education in Prussia. He wanted to be of the middle class, yes, but a middle class in a free, sovereign Polish nation-state reconstituted after consecutive three-way partitions from 1772 through 1795 by Prussia, Austria, and Russia. His long-range vision was romantically emotional, his short-term methods rationally down-to-earth. He and his kindred spirits were in a hurry, restlessly making their way through landmines of regulations laid down by Berlin's autocratic bureaucrats about *verboten* (forbidden) things. This was not the time, and there was no time, they concluded, to memorize prepackaged, selectively censored knowledge in classrooms and regurgitate it unchanged in return for grades, degrees, and parchment diplomas.

In 1903, the year Jan left his job at the mill, he joined the Zabrze branch of an outlawed Polish organization called Eleusis (Els for short) founded by internationally known philosopher and philologist Wincenty Lutosławski in Kraków (Cracow). The organization was located on former Poland territory that had been annexed during the partitions and renamed Galizien by the Austro-Hungarian Empire, an ally of Prussia but also a competitor that was comparatively more relaxed, moderate, and tolerant of ethnic, national, and religious diversity. Els was widespread in Galizien (Galicia)

and expanded rather quickly, given the virulence of the opposition, into the Prussian and Russian areas of dismembered Poland.
Its Zabrze-Gliwice branch was set up and managed by Silesian
activist Joachim Sołtys. The association's purpose was to raise
Polish national consciousness and awareness of Poland's history
and culture among the broad masses of Polish people in Silesia
(many of them recent arrivals from the countryside) through
lectures, seminars, discussions, and publications, as well as culti-
vation of character and abstinence from alcohol. It was, as its full
name indicated, one of several bourgeoning alternative but illegal
educational and self-help associations for national upbringing and
moral revival—if one was willing to take the risk. For support, Els
reached out overseas to Polish émigré communities in London and
the United States.

In 1903, the forty-year-old Lutosławski and a young man
named Kornel Makuszyński, who was just out of high school
in Lwów (then Lemberg, the intellectual epicenter of Austrian
eastern Galicia), were traveling incognito through Upper Silesia
and making *verboten* contacts with Sołtys's Els network. For several
months Makuszyński, later a prolific writer, theatre critic, and
poet, dodged the Prussian police and gave talks to many groups of
workers and miners in any place that would have him—and having
him took nerve. One such place was the Przybyłas' home in Zabrze.
Throughout this time Janek was Makuszyński's guide, adviser, and
protector, delivering him safely after each day's work to the Sołtys
household for the night. They hit it off right away. Makuszyński
found Jan to be of lively intelligence, outgoing, discerning, insight-
ful, and vigilant. They shared an optimistic outlook on life and a
keen sense of humor, Jan's being perhaps a trifle more trenchant
and satirical.

Later that year, Jan crossed the Prussian-Austrian border and
headed for Cracow. There he got in touch with Lutosławski, who
was about to leave for England to lecture at London's University
College from 1904 to 1906. As one story has it, Lutosławski brought
Janek and another young Silesian Els, Edward Rybiarz (who after
1918 became a member of the Silesian senate), to deparochialize
them and broaden their intellectual perspectives in a free Western
European country at the height of its power and international

renown. Another story states that for roughly four years, from late 1903 to 1907, the two young men attended the National Educa-tional Seminar in Cracow, a private, "alternative" Polish learning center created by Lutosławski and financed by Eleusis.

Because Janek was officially (though reluctantly) a German citizen, the German army drafted him when he was nineteen. Contrary to von Ballestrem's tactless, politico-linguistic comment, he was not a "Polish-speaking Prussian" but a Polish-speaking Silesian Pole, patriotic and fired-up, with perhaps at that age a mixture of local dialect and occasional departures from the classi-cal syntactic rules of a language that for almost six hundred years had been verbally preserved in Silesia. His crossing of the Rubicon from rigid Prussian occupation to the more laid-back, Austrian-governed provinces of carved-up Poland was more perilous than a simple migration in search of wider intellectual horizons and more education. It was a defiance of the *Reichswehr* (army) at the very heart of the Prussian-dominated, militaristic state decorated with a thin layer of neodemocratic judiciary and parliamentary proce-dures. For a young man whose travels thus far had been confined to the Sierakowice-Zabrze neck of the woods, it amounted to exile (territorial as well as cultural and political), with the added threat of deportation if and when the two overweight Germanic state bureaucracies got together.

That they might have done just that is suggested by Jan's fast exit from Cracow in 1907 for unexplained but apparently cogent political reasons. He moved to Lwów (today Ukrainian Lviv) in eastern Galicia, changed his name to Jan Sierakowski (more indica-tive of nostalgia for his birthplace than a reasonably foolproof cover of personal identity), and became a free auditor at the Agricultural Academy in nearby Dublany, whose director, an eminent agricul-tural chemist, became minister of religious affairs and public edu-cation in restored Poland in 1926. The Academy was established privately as a farmers' school in 1858 on land purchased a few years earlier by the east Galician Rural Economy Association and paid for by Polish nobleman Leon Sapieha whose family roots went back to Noah. In 1900 the school was granted academic recognition and gentrified its name from "advanced school" to "academy" so as to better reflect its new, more exalted standing. Jan studied there until

1909. But as we all know, "studied" is a pliable word with many meanings, from assiduousness to absenteeism.

In addition to agronomy, Jan pursued a trainload of other interests more congenial to his character and temperament in the company of old friends from Upper Silesia and Cracow. His roommate was Els member Tadeusz Strumiłło, a cofounder and nurturer in Lwów during this period of Polish scouting—a time-consuming job in which Jan was actively involved. His interest in scouting continued throughout the interwar years. Among his nonagricultural ventures during the years in Lwów, journalism was his favorite. Writing came easily to him, as it did later to his daughter Maria and youngest son Janusz. His occasional articles on current affairs, acclaim for Polish candidates running in elections to the German parliament, ideological commentaries and critiques, reports from Lwów and eastern Galicia, columns, letters, and the like appeared mostly in Silesian Polish newspapers, with a few in the Lwów academic periodical *Teka* (Portfolio). He used a bunch of aliases, for instance, "Jan Sier from Upper Silesia," which together with the pseudonym "Jan Sierakowski" were so transparent as to make one wonder whether they weren't picked on purpose to tweak his pursuers' noses. To cap it all, during the period 1907–1914 he frequently visited Upper Silesia, his "closer homeland," on clandestine Polish national business. These were times when in that restive, aggrieved part of Europe nationalistic politics, tinged with religion (Catholic, Protestant, Uniate, Orthodox, Jewish), intruded into just about everything, with cultural activities, high and humble, in the foreground. On both sides of every burning issue, journalism was expected to (and did) propagate the war of words. This also applied to the theater (Jan's second love, next to journalism), though with more circumspection. Lwów had a long and distinguished history of Polish theater that had been revived under Austrian suzerainty in 1842 by Count Stanisław Skarbek, who also put up, at his own expense, a fine, large professional building to house it. Between 1914 and 1918, its literary director was none other than Kornel Makuszyński, who also at the time held the position of artistic director of the Polish theater in Kiev. It seems that Jan's lifelong infatuation with the theater dated from this era.

At Dublany Jan met Marta Daisenberg, daughter of Antonina

Kownacka and Władysław Daisenberg. Władysław Daisenberg was a Cracow attorney, a doctor of laws and philosophy, and a lecturer at Jagellonian University (Poland's oldest seat of higher learning, founded in 1364). The Daisenbergs (originally von Deissenberg) were of German descent. The family had long been settled in the Cracow *voivodship* (province) and had become Polonized in spirit and in the spelling of their name. Marta was born in 1885 in Skawina, a few miles southwest of Cracow. For career reasons Władysław Daisenberg moved his family to Lwów. He opened a law office there but did not do well financially. Marta graduated from a pedagogical college in Lwów. For a time she taught the children of a landed family on the easternmost reaches of Austrian Galicia. When Jan met her, she was employed as a tutor to the children of the director of the Dublany Academy. They were married in Lwów in August 1913. There were three children: Zbigniew (Zbyszek), born in 1915; Maria (Marysia), born in 1917; and Janusz, born in 1922.

In the maelstrom of his extracurricular activities, Jan had evidently acquired enough proficiency in agricultural science to be appointed inspector of dairies and instructor at the Galician Rural Economy Association, a position he held from 1909 to 1919. Sometime before 1915 he traveled to Scandinavia and Switzerland for an on-the-spot study of advanced farm practices. It is fair to say that by then, farming was not his first preference for a profession. He had an avid interest in political journalism and activism, focusing on Silesia's peaceful reunion with a resurrected, sovereign Polish state. Starting in February 1915 and concurrently with his jobs at the Association, he was secretary of the Lwów delegation to the Kraków Committee of Aid to Victims of War (World War I). For his initiative in organizing food supplies and other aid to refugees and children orphaned by the war, he received from the delegates a warm letter of thanks signed by, among others, the Polish archbishop of Lwów.

Not one to be idle, in 1918 he edited a paramilitary Lwów periodical, *Pobudka* (Reveille), and then put together a forty-eight-page booklet dealing with the contribution of the first Polish air force squadron, piloted by young natives of the city, in the defense of Lwów from a Ukrainian-armed takeover attempt in November

1918. The book appeared in 1919 under the imprint of the reputable Lwów publishing house Gubrynowicz & Son.

Jan left Lwów as soon as he learned of the outbreak on August
17, 1919, of the Silesian uprising (the first of three). He headed for
Sosnowiec, a town on the Polish side of the provisional western
border that had been designated by the Versailles Treaty for the
reemergent Polish state in advance of a plebiscite that was scheduled to take place on the ferociously disputed Silesian side of that
frontier, then still in German hands. The operation was to be under
the direction of and monitored by an Interallied Plebiscite Commission headed by France, Britain, and Italy. In Sosnowiec, Jan was
put in charge of food supply by the Silesian branch of the Polish
People's Commission (KL), the executive arm in Silesia of the
Supreme People's Council (NRL) in Poznań, which was an organization of politicians from the three parts of Poland annexed by
Prussia, Russia and Austria, preparing the future government of
Poland while the country was being put together like a jigsaw
puzzle into a modern state. It took six borderland wars to get the
edges "right," though they were not to everybody's satisfaction.

Jan was back in Lwów on August 25, giving a speech in the
courtyard of the city hall to a rally organized by the Committee
for National Defense. He appealed to the Polish citizens of Lwów
(60 percent of the population) for solidarity with and material aid
to their insurgent Silesian compatriots. It was not as easy as it may
sound; the Poles in Lwów had their hands full trying to prevent
Ukrainian nationalists from seceding from the rickety Austro-
Hungarian Empire, carving out of it eastern Galicia, and forming
an independent Ukrainian state. For diplomatic and other reasons,
Polish authorities in Warsaw and elsewhere were cool toward the
idea of a Silesian insurrection at this time.

Back in Sosnowiec, Jan learned that the insurrection had collapsed on August 24 under the onslaught of larger, better trained,
better armed, and better coordinated German police, Border Patrol
(*Grenzschutz*), and regular army units, the last equipped with
machine guns, artillery, airplanes, armored trains, and armored cars.
The full complement of the German army on the disputed territory of Upper Silesia in mid August 1918 was between seventy and
eighty thousand men. The numerical strength of the insurgents is

not known, but it was certainly much less, consisting for the most part of scattered, uncoordinated, lightly armed small units high on enthusiasm but low on ammunition. Even at its height, the insurrection affected only the eastern segment of Upper Silesia. When defeat appeared imminent, to avoid falling into German hands, more than nine thousand insurgents and their families—twenty-two thousand people in all—began to cross the German-Polish border across the Brynica river to Sosnowiec, where they were given food, clothing, and shelter by several organizations, including the commission of which Jan was now a key member. Soon, other organizations of aid and defense for Upper Silesia sprang up throughout Poland, particularly in Poznań, the major city in what is known as "Greater Poland" (*Wielkopolska*), and in Warsaw, where hundreds of thousands of demonstrators turned out in support of Silesia's reunification with Poland. During his last months in Sosnowiec, Jan helped edit *Powstaniec* (*The Insurrgent*) a periodical produced by Upper Silesian refugees, publishing several articles and a series of topical narratives, the first of which, together with his address to the Lwów rally, were later reprinted in the collection *Struggle for Upper Silesia from Insurrection to Plebiscite.*

Return to the "Closer Homeland" (1920)

For Upper Silesia and the newly born but not yet delivered Polish Republic, the Treaty of Versailles (Article 88)—signed on June 28, 1919, and ratified by the League of Nations in January of the following year—meant plebiscite or referendum by the voters of the area. It was a compromise solution favored by British Prime Minister David Lloyd George and, more hesitatingly, by U.S. President Woodrow Wilson, for the vexed problem of an ethnically, nationally, linguistically, denominationally, socially, and economically divided people inhabiting 10,700 square kilometers of highly industrialized land. Such a cultural smorgasbord was not uncommon in Europe's border areas throughout history, but in Silesia it was worse than usual. The French, who lost Alsace and Lorraine to Prussia in 1871, were now among the victors and made sure that they would not have to go through a plebiscite to recover them. In Upper Silesia the plebiscite was to be supervised and its results implemented by the Interallied Governmental and Plebiscite Commission (IAGPC), which was staffed by representatives of France, Britain, and Italy and was headed by French general Henri Le Rond, who was well inclined toward Poland. The reason for a Frenchman at the top? One million two hundred fifty thousand French soldiers, as well as four hundred thousand civilians, were killed in World War I. Most of the western front battles were fought on French territory, causing widespread destruction.

The commission arrived in Opole (Oppeln) on February 11, 1920, and established its headquarters there. German regular troops were withdrawn, but German police (the *Sicherheitzpolizei*, or Sipo) and local levels of German civilian administration were left in place. The task of keeping the peace, which essentially involved keeping the two opposing sides completely apart, was left to thirteen thousand French, British, and Italian soldiers who came with the Interallied Commission and were assigned to different sectors of the plebiscite area. German and Polish plebiscite commissions were each accredited to the IAGPC.

The German commission, under Kurt Urbanek, opened its offices in Katowice (Kattowitz); the Polish-headed commission, led by Wojciech Korfanty resided in the Hotel Lomnitz in Bytom (Beuthen). Actual voting took place more than a year later, on March 20, 1921, and the final distribution of the plebiscite territory between Poland and Germany occurred seven months after that, on October 20, 1921.

For Jan Przybyła, the plebiscite meant that he could leave Sosnowiec and return to his Silesian "closer homeland" after sixteen years and without forged papers and fictitious names, even though the place was teeming with Sipos and irregulars better known in general parlance as the *Freikorps* (Volunteer Corps), made up of army veterans. This he did as soon as the Polish Plebiscite Commission opened its offices in Bytom in February 1920. He reported to Korfanty and was assigned to the press department, directed by Edward Rybarz. Additionally, on March 1 he was put also in charge of the Upper Silesian department of the Polish Telegraph Agency (PAT), the news media arm of the Polish government in Warsaw. Since early January 1919, this wrangling collage of competing political movements, personalities, and outlooks did its best to hold together a country—then still more a cherished idea than reality—

that had no recognized borders, no cohesive overall administration, and, if the truth be known, no modern army to speak of.

On August 12–25, 1920, near the Polish capital, the army faced Soviet Bolshevik hordes acting on Lenin's order. Modern or not, after heavy fighting in which 4,500 of its soldiers lost their lives, the small Polish army turned a massive communist revolutionary mission into an expeditious retreat. (Another painting in the Bielsko Villa Sixt dining room was a portrait of my mother's youngest brother, Janusz Hager, in a Polish lieutenant's uniform. He was killed in action in the August battle of Warsaw). Characteristically, the momentous victory would go down in Polish historical mythology as a miracle, only the second big national miracle since 1655, when the invincible Protestant Swedish army was made to give up up its siege of the Jasna Góra monastery in Częstochowa by a few poorly armed Polish defenders. There is no doubt that in whatever way one chooses to explain the outcome of the battle of Warsaw—Piłsudski's good strategic leadership, the rejection of arguable advice from French general Weygand to abandon the capital, the raw courage of the defenders, overconfidence combined with logistical overextension by the enemy, or heavenly intervention—it saved the nascent Polish republic from instant extinction, gave it twenty years to breathe, and kept out communist influence from middle Europe until 1945.

Working to Bring the "Closer Homeland" Back Home

A word about Wojciech Korfanty, an interesting and, in some ways, tragic political personality whose handling of his job as head of the Polish Plebiscite Commission has been both praised and questioned during the interwar years. He was born the son of a Silesian miner in 1873; studied philosophy, law, and economics at the Technical University in Charlottenburg (Berlin) and the University of Breslau (now Wrocław in Lower Silesia); and edited the paper *Górnoślązak* (Upper Silesian) in Katowice from 1901 to 1903. A German citizen, in 1903 he was elected to the German parliament, where he served until 1912, and had a second stint starting in 1918. In this position he led the Polish caucus, composed of parliamentarians of Polish nationality who traditionally supported the German Catholic Zentrum Party (the middle-of-the-right-of-center party of the unlovable Ballestrem) and in return received little else than contempt. Inevitably, as Benjamin Franklin warned the British of their disdainful attitude toward Americans in 1773, "though many forgive injuries, none ever forgave contempt." Prussian Zentrism tended to see Catholicism in nationalistic terms: a state agency to be used, when necessary, for purposes of Germanization, rather than as a supranational moral entity. In a climate of nationalistic intransigence, the Poles looked to their Catholic clergy for succor in preserving their national identity, and they got it.

Korfanty was also elected to the Prussian legislative chamber and served there from 1904 to 1918. On October 25, 1918, he delivered to the German national parliament an impassioned, irredentist speech that resonated through the world at war, demanding that all Polish lands taken by Prussia be returned, entire and undivided, to a new independent Polish state; this included West Prussia (with the port of Danzig / Gdańsk), the Masurian part of East Prussia, Greater Poland, and Upper as well as Middle Silesia. On November 12, 1918, he joined the Polish Supreme People's Council (NRL), a government-in-waiting in Poznań, and its executive commission, to which he was later elected as one of two representatives of Upper Silesia. He remained in Poznań through most of the successful Greater Poland Uprising (December 1918–March 1919). Then, in January 1920, he was appointed head of the Polish Plebiscite Commission in Bytom.

Among those working to bring their "closer homeland" back home, was the Silesian Stanisław Ligoń a member of the Polish Plebiscite Commission's press department. Ligoń was a man of many talents and, said some, unpolished language (the Germans disparagingly called it *Wasserpolnisch*—broken, diluted Polish), that others claimed was pristine Old Polish, going back to who knows when, spiced with Silesian dialect and a loose interpretation of syntactic recipes. In the interwar years, among his many activities was a series of broadcasts from Radio Katowice called *Bery i Bojki* (Silesian Polish for "Jokes and Fairy Tales"), which apparently many listeners found very funny for linguistic as well as contextual reasons.[1] He also broadcast several entertaining talk shows that made Rabelaisian but good-natured fun of the Germans—no laughing matter after 1932. In the spring of 1920, Jan Przybyła and Ligoń suggested to Korfanty that a satirical magazine targeting Upper Silesians might be launched and serve as a weapon in the propaganda war waged by both sides in anticipation of the plebiscite. Korfanty gave his approval. The first issue of *Upper Silesia's Cheerful Periodical*, as it announced in bold letters on its illustrated front page, appeared on June 10, 1920. According to my calculations based on data from the Silesian Digital Library, by the end of 1922, there were forty-three issues, then one in 1923 and two in 1928. It would seem that the magazine was run on a modest budget with one eye on the Sipo, informing its readers that it "appears whenever it wants and when it can." Like all satire, it expressed itself through irony, and its political *bery* were designed for the mines and factory floors, not the drawing room. It was called *Kocynder*, a name whose etymology best be left alone. Jan Przybyła, using the pseudonym Franciszek Miądowicz (a chilling omen of things to come two decades later), was the editor of the first four issues in 1920. Later, from 1921 on, *Kocynder* listed Stanisław Ligoń as art director and Jan Przybyła as editor. Both wrote, and Ligoń, a gifted illustrator, also drew for the periodical. Jan later used the pseudonym *Hanys z Kocyndra* ("Jan from Kocynder"); Ligoń appeared under the name *Karlik*. From the Polish standpoint, *Kocynder* apparently had a positive effect on the voting attitudes of Silesian workers because of its light approach to serious questions; its mockery of mirthless German bureaucrats; and its unpretentious, homey language with which the working voter base could identify.

The turbulent months between the arrival of the Interallied Commission in Opole and the final apportionment of Upper Silesian territories to the Second Polish Republic and the postwar German Weimar Republic witnessed two types of conflict: a battle of words and battles with guns. The first was conducted, directly or through outsourcing, by the two national plebiscite commissions, with strong support (Germany) and lukewarm support (Poland) of their respective governments. It included the organization of municipal, county, district, and village committees as well as an avalanche of speeches, meetings, rallies, mass demonstrations, parades, pamphlets, posters, press releases, strikes, dirty tricks, and, whenever possible, diplomatic overtures to the allied powers. The Poles put out feelers to the French and Americans, and the Germans courted

the British, who seemed to be concerned more about the hypo-
thetical future power of France than the likelihood of a resurgent
powerful Germany. Battles with guns preceded, accompanied, or
followed the exchange of inflammatory words.

In this setting the Germans had a distinct advantage for four
reasons: one, their police and militias were on the plebiscite ground;
two, the Polish military in Upper Silesia (POW) was a secret organization, badly shaken by the failure of the 1919 uprising, with
thousands of members in exile and the remaining units undergoing
reorganization; three, the bulk of the economy was under German
ownership and control, and therefore Germans could and did put
meaningful pressure on the voters, most of whom were employed
in their firms; four, the Polish government in Warsaw was preoc-
cupied with other problems and had other priorities, which some
of its influential leaders believed to be not only more important for
the long-term survival and good of the reemerging national state
but of immediate urgency, like the threat posed by the Soviet Bolshevik armies staring them in the face on August 16, 1920. On that
day the tricks department of the German press agency in Berlin
sprang to attention. It disseminated a story that the Polish capital
had fallen to the Bolsheviks. The next day German newspapers in
Upper Silesia picked up this fabrication in bold script on page one.
Jan's Silesian PAT branch, which he had built from scratch, kept
the Warsaw government and major Polish newspapers abreast of
the rapidly changing events in the plebiscite area and combated
the misrepresentations of its German counterpart. Later, on July
10, 1922, when their ways parted, Korfanty certified Jan's great
contributions to the Polish cause in Silesia as head of the Silesian
PAT branch, by describing his work at the Plebiscite Commission
as conscientious and efficient.

On the plebiscitary "gun, fist, and boot" front, the German
militia and the Upper Silesian *Freiwilligenkorps* (volunteer corps)
had been busy from the word "go," setting a precedent for the 1938
Kristallnacht (Night of the Broken Glass). They broke not only
window glass but tore up rallies, attacked the Polish Plebiscite
Commission in Bytom, vandalized several of the Commission's local
offices, and trashed the homes and businesses of those suspected
of leaning toward the Polish side. In Katowice they stormed the

residence of the Interallied Commission's county superintendent. French troops responded, killing ten of the assailants. In reply, the militias murdered Polish activist Dr. Andrzej Mielęcki and for good measure sacked the Polish Plebiscite Commission's municipal office in the hotel *Deutsches Haus,* mangling its occupants.

On August 17, when according to the German papers Warsaw had fallen to the Bolsheviks, more armed clashes occurred between the *Freikorpsmen* and the French troops. At this point a battalion of Polish insurgents from the Katowice area arrived in Sosnowiec demanding that the leadership of the POW distribute arms to start an insurrection. By the night of August 18/19, 1920, the Second Silesian Uprising unofficially began, a procedure that flummoxed the German side. When on August 19, representatives of Polish political parties met in Bytom under the chairmanship of Korfanty and gave their blessing to the insurgency, and the POW supreme command (which was transferred for the duration from Sosnowiec to Dąbrówka) issued the official order for it to start, almost the whole of Katowice county, the city excepted, was in the insurgents' hands. The disarming of the Sipos and the militiamen was well on its way, and the insurrection was spreading rapidly through ten of the twenty-two plebiscite counties. By August 24, when Korfanty called for its termination, it had nearly encompassed the whole plebiscite area.

The Second Silesian Uprising achieved its limited objectives by and large. These focused on removing what the Polish side considered to be the more intrusive obstacles to an evenhanded conduct of the referendum. The Interallied Commission ordered the Sipo units to report in three towns (Gliwice, Rybnik, and Opole). The commission disarmed and dissolved the Sipo, and the organization was replaced by a new police force, the Apo (*Abstimmungspolizei,* Plebiscite Police), manned equally by Germans and Poles. The disbanding of the militias was carried out more haphazardly, if only because of the slippery nature of the bands. Government business was henceforth to be conducted in both German and Polish, not exclusively in German, as had been the rule before. A Polish-German agreement was concluded to prevent future use of force and violence, and the POW was officially dissolved in the plebiscite territory. Its place was taken by a new outfit called Head Office of Physical Education, which operated out of the Lomnitz Hotel. The outfit was a phys ed sobriquet for signing up and training recruits for a future insurgent army in Upper Silesia. Its sworn membership at the turn of 1920–21 has been put at sixteen thousand, plus about the same number of volunteers ready to serve instantly when called. The organization was discontinued in January 1921, its assets being at that point transferred to department 1 of the Command of Plebiscite Defense, an organization formed the previous month in Kępno (Greater Poland) by Korfanty and General Kazimierz Raszewski. This one went by the name of Warsaw Industrial and Construction Corporation. Its assets were acquired through a friendly takeover, so to speak, on the first day of the third uprising by the Supreme Command of Insurrectionist Forces, which had at its disposal an estimated forty thousand Silesian shareholders and their kin from the Wielkopolska army. By April 1921 a plan for the third Silesian uprising was ready and endorsed by Korfanty. Of course, the Germans were not sitting on their hands either. Veterans of border patrols and self-defense units were being mustered, and job- and thrill-seeking *Freikorpsers* poured out of the bier halls of Bavaria.

Jan was a man of peace, but not a pacifist or an appeaser. He had an ardent love for his downtrodden Poland, a deep devotion to his native Silesia, and an unshakeable commitment to their reunification in freedom after centuries of forced separation. He was not a self-attentive academic intellectual, but he was a man of action and an ardent advocate, forthrightly putting his ideas and sense of ordinary decencies into everyday practice. He helped those in need to the full extent of his abilities. His chosen weapon in defense of what he fervently believed in was the pen. This he used often and skillfully, in prose and verse, passionately when needed but always with an undercurrent of cheerfulness. The last composition from his pen, shortly before his death, was a poem on Wawel, the ancient fortress and palace of Poland's kings in Cracow. During the first two Silesian uprisings, he was fully engaged in crucial battles on the front of information, propaganda, and counterpropaganda and in materially helping the victims of the battles with guns. Some of his ideas, especially those touching on his vision of the country's and his "closer homeland's" future, paralleled those of Korfanty. They both understood that a nationalist state needed a sense oneness.

They had a common national purpose but moved in different orbits; Jan's orbit was around Silesia, Korfanty's higher up in rank.

The plebiscite was held, as planned, on March 20, 1921. Of the 1.18 million valid votes cast, 707,000 (59.65 percent) went for Germany, and 479,000 (40.35 percent) were for Poland. The wrinkle in this was that generally in rural areas the majority of votes went for reunion with Poland, whereas the opposite was true of urban enclaves. Taken a bit aback by the numbers, the Polish side complained that the Germans carted into the plebiscite area masses of people who had been born in Silesia but had not resided there on a permanent basis at the time of the plebiscite—they were émigrés, or more loosely, "outsiders." This was indeed the case, but the argument lost some of its persuasiveness in the light of two facts: First, that it was the Poles who asked for the Paris (Versailles) Peace Conference of 1919 to include such migrant birds in the voting, presumably because of misgauged expectations about the national sentiments of numerous Silesian workers living outside Silesia, especially in the Ruhr; besides, some Poles who lived in Galicia also cast their votes. Second, there was an issue with the unreliability of political arithmetic. In round figures, of the reportedly 192,000 imported votes nearly 90 percent went for Germany. If the votes cast by the nonpermanent residents were to be ignored, the net difference between the two sides would have been significantly reduced but would not have changed the final winner. However, such tapering could have encouraged the loser to argue against any attempt by the powers in charge of the plebiscite to use the "winner take all" (or "as good as all") principle in finally deciding who gets what. This was a distinct probability because Britain's David Lloyd George, an obstinate minimalist where Poland was concerned, was ready to use the "winner takes (almost) all" electoral solution after seeing who had come out on top. He remarked that he would no more hand over Silesia to Poland than he would a watch to a monkey.[2] Also, in an insular moment, he confused Silesia with Cilicia, a large piece of real estate along the Aegean coast and bordering on Syria.

Apart from this issue, it was possible that not all the arrivals were actually born in Silesia—or organizations used the names of blessed departed citizens—and that according to some specialists on the topic, five hundred thousand Silesians voted for an autonomous Silesia. Be that as it may, with the balloting over, the war of words gave way to rampant rumors and hearsay about what the Interallied Commission, meeting in closed but apparently leaky sessions, would decide on the distribution of the plebiscite territories between Germany and Poland. The word on the street was that Poland would at best get two of the counties at play. There was less shouting but more tension, anxiety, uncertainty, and mistrust.

At a conference of delegates of Polish political parties and social groups (nongovernmental organizations) held on April 30, 1921, Korfanty proposed that, given the situation as he saw it—the apparent indifference of Warsaw to what might happen to Upper Silesia, plus the slanted attitude of Lloyd George—pressure had to be put on the Interallied Commission through a general strike on May 2. The proposal was accepted by the Warsaw government, but Prime Minister Wincenty Witos rejected any thought of yet another uprising, presumably in the belief that it would do more harm than good by further alienating the allied powers, the British in particular and the Italians a close second.

On the night of May 2 / 3, the uprising began with a series of big bangs. The insurgents blew up several railway bridges on the main railroad lines from Germany to Silesia, as well as the telephone network, replacing it with their own means of telecommunications. In contrast with the first two uprisings, the whole insurrectionist army was deployed that night. On May 3, celebrated as Poland's National Day in remembrance of the 1791 Constitution, Korfanty, who earlier had been inclined to wait for a diplomatic solution, issued through his press department and the Silesian section of PAT (headed by Jan) a "Manifesto to the People of Upper Silesia" in which he let the people know that he had been removed (or, as another version has it, removed himself) from the Polish Plebiscite Commissioner's post because of his inability to prevent the uprising from happening and that, as of that day, he would personally lead the insurrection.

In mid-May Jan was selected to head the press department attached to the supreme command of the insurgent army in Szopienice, near Katowice. Its major function was to win over public opinion to the cause of the uprising. He revived the periodical *Powstaniec* (The Insurgent) with which he had been associated in 1919 after the collapse of the first uprising and which, until this time, through seven issues, had been the organ of the political press department attached to the Insurgent Eastern Group Command. It was now published by the press department of the Supreme Insurgent Army Command, with Jan as the editor-in-chief. This same department, under the editorship of Augustyn Potempa, also put out a German-language periodical, "Free Speech for Upper Silesia," for German-speaking Silesian Poles—evidently a waste of ink and pulp as far as the holiday voters' opinion went. Jan's reports on Silesian affairs were frequently carried by the Polish press outside Silesia, including the elite *Gazeta Warszawska* (Warsaw Daily). Not infrequently *The Insurgent* berated the Warsaw all-party national defense government under the premiership of Wincenty Witos (July 1920–September 1921) for its ambivalence on the Silesian question. Witos had ordered Korfanty to prohibit the uprising. When the uprising did occur, the government took a neutral position and closed the border between Poland and the plebiscite area for the duration. But borders have been known to be porous. The angry tone of the *Powstaniec* censures, though within the broad limits of courtesy, echoed Kocynder's tonality in that periodical's more restrained moments.

The general strike of May 2, 1921, involved 190,000 industrial workers affecting almost all industrial firms. The initial results of the uprising were very favorable to the insurgents, who by May 6 controlled roughly two thirds of the plebiscite territory. A few days later Korfanty declared that the objectives of the insurrection had been achieved. The Warsaw government was inclined to leave the decision on the future of Silesia to the allied powers—the entente, if one could call it that by now. However, heavy fighting continued when German forces launched counterattacks on several fronts. One of the most intense battles took place between May 21 and 26, at Mount St. Anna, between the *Freikorps Oberland* from Bavaria and two Polish Silesian divisions and several battalions. Eventually, after a stalemate in June, the two warring sides were separated into inimical coexistence by allied troops. A truce was reached on July 5. The insurrectionist and German forces were evacuated from the plebiscite territory, and the Third Silesian Uprising came to an end.

Jan interpreted the evacuation order as not applicable to him, possibly because he had not been directly involved in the gun battles. He stayed put, even though with the Plebiscite Commission gone, there was not much word work to be done. During the calm interlude, he assumed the position of regional inspector for Silesian branch of the Polish Boy Scouts Association, which had been established in the spring of 1920 and financed by the Plebiscite Commission.

Most of the scouts from various parts of Poland who had come earlier to help the commission in its plebiscite activities were back home by then. Although it was expected that Bytom would not be given to Poland, Jan found accommodations in the Lomnitz Hotel for the scout troops that were left. With the help of three scoutmasters, the training of the first Silesian scouting cadres continued until spring 1922, when the meeting place was transferred temporarily to the PAT office in Katowice.

Try hard it as it might, the entente embodied in the Allied Supreme Council could not agree on how to chop up this part of the world on national lines that made any sense without widening inter-allied rifts, and to add to the tension the entente had on their backs Weimar, Warsaw, Polish Silesians, German Silesians, the *Freikorps*, *Selbstschutz*, *Kocynder*, and *Powstaniec*, not to mention those Silesians who opted for an autonomous Silesia and the "internationalist," one-proletarian-world communists roused by the Soviet October 1917. The Supreme Council did what such bodies do when they couldn't agree: they sent their problem upward to another body, the council of the League of Nations, which referred it to a commission of experts that gathered data, interviewed witnesses, and sent its findings back to the League Council. In closed session the League Council pondered the situation some more, and on October 10 it made a recommendation to the council of ambassadors, which approved it on October 20, 1921, exactly seven months after the plebiscite. Loose ends had to be tied in subsequent months by Polish and German negotiators under the chairmanship of League appointees regarding economics, minorities, and other outstanding matters. This took another seven months. The formal military and civilian takeover of the portion of Silesia assigned to Poland by the intricate protocol of the plebiscite after several centuries of separation was marked by the entry on June 20, 1922, of regular

Polish troops into Katowice. The reunion lasted less than seventeen years.

Twenty-nine percent of the plebiscite territory went to Poland, but due largely to the Third Silesian Uprising and French support in the decision-making couloirs of power, Poland received two-thirds of the industrial area. This translated into half of all the iron and steel works, 76 percent of coal mines, 80 percent of zinc and lead mines, and every iron mine located in Upper Silesia's four most urbanized and industrialized counties, all of which reverted to Poland. Remaining in Germany were roughly 1.2 million people (54 percent of the plebiscite area's population), including a significant Polish minority, mostly in the countryside. The part allotted to Poland had a population of about one million, including a big German urban minority. All in all, it may have been the only feasible compromise, but it was not the best prescription for amicable cohabitation in the overheated nationalistic climate of the times.

The nationalist mood was contagious. Locally, some Silesians claimed to ignore the criteria of language (Polish versus German) and religion (Catholic versus Protestant) and demanded, in the name of antinationalism, that Upper Silesia be recognized as a sovereign Silesian nation-state, flag and all. In early 1919 citizens formed the Union of Upper Silesians (*Bund der Oberschlesier*) to serve as an institutional vehicle for a drive that in the actual geopolitical circumstances meant unhooking Upper Silesia from the imperial German tractor-trailer. The Union became mixed up in riots at Królewska Huta (later Chorzów) and was promptly suppressed by martial law. Its leaders were marched off to jail charged with treasonous sedition against the German state.

Communist contagion presented a larger, more intractable problem. Communism was armed with a dynamic, all-embracing, fraudulent fantasy parading as philosophy that, after Lenin's terrorist editing, had been assimilated into a huge state whose revolutionary armies had just menaced Warsaw and the rest of Europe. Communist agitation and propaganda spiked soon after the defeat of the German Empire in the first World War, especially in Silesia. A twenty-five-thousand-strong Communist Party of Upper Silesia was formed under the direction of Antoni Jadasz, whose father had been an ardent supporter of the Polish line until he was converted to communism by his son. It stirred the witch's brew of imperfectly understood ideas, causing widespread confusion, and gave the Polish Plebiscite Commission no end of headaches by calling on the mostly Polish "working class" to boycott the plebiscite, to support the Soviet Union as the vanguard architect of socialist internationalism and its objective of establishing an Upper Silesian Soviet Republic. The last cost it twenty thousand desertions to the Polish insurgent side. The role of communism in the plebiscite period was not discussed much during the more than four decades of the communist Polish People's Republic (1947–89), and when it was, it was scripted by the communist party and absurd.

Caught in the national, linguistic, and religious whirlpool were the Jews, whose contribution to the services sector of the Silesian economy (especially commerce and finance) was more significant than their absolute numbers. There was also a visible population of poor Hasidic Jews in small towns whose primary language was Yiddish. At the time, the relationship between Jews and the rest of the population—German, Polish, Protestant, Catholic—was generally civil and business oriented but wary, distant, and awkward. This did not preclude personal bonds of true friendship and affection across the tacit taboo lines, or mutual prejudice, injury, mistrust, and even sporadic acts of brutality at the extremes. There was not much spontaneous assimilation of Jews and only a marginal consensual melting of cultures. Whether they thought of themselves as Jewish Germans or Jewish Poles, they remained aliens in the recesses of their neighbors' minds, and though German citizens, they were the stateless "other," scapegoats for anything that went wrong. In return, to many Jews, their neighbors remained the *goyim*, and anti-Polonism was not absent, culturally as well as linguistically. The Jews tried, when possible, to stay out of the fray, but by and large they leaned toward the German side, viewing attempts to resurrect the Polish state with surprise, disbelief, and skepticism but also with apprehension stemming from economic and civilizational motives. There was a lot of silent human hurt that never healed.

Notes

1.   I was one of those listeners who at age of eight or thereabouts had picked up a little Silesian dialect during our earlier life in Katowice. My mother who came from Wielkopolska (Greater Poland) tried to dissuade me from this habit on the grounds that some of the *bery* were not appropriate for children, and the *bojki* would not help me get a decent grade in Polish language at school. On reflection, I could have argued in self-defense that my grandfather had collected Polish Silesian folk songs, but I didn't know it then.

2.   *Rzeczpospolita online.* Maja Narbutt (14/05/2008) http://rp.pl. artykul/138481.html

Franciszek Kuczarek, "Zegarek dla Polski" (Watch for Poland), *Tygodnik Katolicki* (Catholic Weekly), Gość Niedzielny (Sunday Guest) Nr. 13, 2006. http://www.goscniedzielny.wiara.pl/index.php?grupa=68

Jan Przybyła in Lwów (1907–1920).

POLAND, 1938

Riga
Latvia
Klaipèda
Baltic Sea
Lithuania
Kaunas • Wilno
Gdynia
Danzig/Gdańsk • Hel
Germany
Suwałki
Germany
Grodno
Minsk
Pomorze
(Pomerania)
Białystok
Bydgoszcz
Poznań
Wielkopolska (Great Poland)
Warszawa (Warsaw)
Pruszków
Łódź
Brześć
Pińsk
USSR
Lublin
Wrocław (Bresłau)
Częstochowa
Germany
Opole
Zabrze
Sosnowiec
Małopolska (Nether Poland)
Gliwice
Katowice
Bohumin
Oświęcim (Auschwitz)
Lwów
Ostrava
Bielsko-Biała
Cieszyn
Czechoslovakia
Hungary
Romania

Later Years

Return of the Larger Homeland (1921–1939)

When Polish army units entered Katowice on June 20, 1922, Jan was there to greet them as member of the presidium of the citizens' welcoming committee, chaired by Wojciech Korfanty in an honorary capacity. Jan had been in the city since November of the previous year setting up the Upper Silesian branch of the Polish Telegraph Agency, which he still headed. Jan found new offices for it, with some of the floor space made available, temporarily and somewhat informally, to the Inspectorate of the Polish Boy Scouts Association in Upper Silesia since the spring of 1922. Beginning in September 1922, he worked under contract with the press department of the Silesian Provincial Government, concurrently serving as city councilor of Katowice, the capital of Poland's most industrialized province. He became a full-time government official in charge of that press department on January 1, 1925. In 1924, Marta and the children—Zbyszek now nine years old, Marysia seven, and Janusz two—joined him from Lwów and settled in downtown Katowice at 6 Kochanowski Street, not far from the Polish Theater in the center of the city. Coincidentally, he was on the directorial board of Friends of the Polish Theater and was, for a time, the theater's literary director. Four years later he was on the managerial board of the Silesian Literary Society.

In October 1924 Jan's youngest brother, Wiktor, obtained a degree of doctor of laws from the leading Jagiellonian University in Cracow and moved with his wife, Anna, to Katowice. In 1924 Wiktor became head of the personnel department of the Katowice Region National Railways Administration, and in 1926 he was director and treasurer of the Department of Public Welfare of Katowice municipality, as well as a city councilor.

The middle son, Józef, totally apolitical and the most entrepreneurial of the three brothers, worked his way from the bottom up in a lumberyard at Oleśnica (Oels) near Wrocław, (Breslau) where, as he put it, he learned all he needed to know about the lumber avocation. He married Luta Lepiosch (Lepiorz in Polish) from a Silesian German family in the Gliwice area, and after the plebiscite they moved to Katowice, where Józef started his own timber firm. They lived in a top-notch apartment in a house they owned within walking distance of Jan and Wiktor. His family knew he was a helpful, good man with a deceptively gruff exterior, and Luta was a vivacious lady who brought her nephews and nieces wonderful toys from her trips to Germany. With only a hitch here and there, Józek concentrated on his workaday wits, leaving higher, conventional learning to others. He ran his business nonstop from the mid 1920s until his illness and death in 1959, through some of the most frightful decades of the twentieth century. However, he was imperturbable, puffing on his cigar and buying and selling logs while navigating under three incompatible, inimical political regimes: interwar Polish, Nazi exterminatory occupation, and postwar communism.

In 1905, when she was sixteen, Zefla left home (by then in Zabrze) for Zakopane in Austrian Galicia (today Poland's skiing and artsy resort in the gorgeous Tatra mountains near the Slovak border) to attend a finishing school for young girls. The school was founded in 1882 by a branch of the noble Zamoyski family, who were deeply involved in Polish history and, like many others of their breeding, were well-positioned and willing to serve as trustees of Polish traditions and promote the preservation and imparting of Polish culture from generation to generation. It was located in Zakopane's outskirts, under the name of School of Women's Household Work. In later but already dated academic language, one would call it School of Home Economics, with the original meaning of the word "home" as family, and "economics" as household management. Originally, the curriculum covered cooking, sewing, embroidering, and related household arts, in addition to social refinement, good manners, and most important, religiosity. It was developed and directed by the countess Jadwiga Zamoyska with help from her son Władysław Zamoyski (1885–1924) who owned much land in the area.[1]

For the three sons of Teodor Przybyła, early hopes had been fulfilled for the most part. Together in the capital of their native Silesia, each in his own way had helped to bring to life the independent, hopefully peaceful, lawful, and democratic country after nearly a century and a half of burial and national humiliation. They were comfortable in their professions and family life, and the future looked promising—challenging, as one would expect, but bright. They had arrived.

Sober Realities: The Large Picture

In 1926 issues developed within the reborn country that cast a shadow over the celebrations and dampened early hopes. These problems had been building up during the years of struggle against external foes but had been put aside, airbrushed by the need for solidarity in a time of mortal danger. Before, in the ranks of the fighters for independence, there was, if not seamless unity, at least a sense of togetherness and comradeship; that sense was now gone.

Domestic Affairs

In the early to mid 1920s, the country experienced fractionalization, an excessive splitting apart that poisoned personal and social relations; atomized political parties; caused policy gridlock; and replaced civil conversation and the search for compromise with shouting, wagging of reckless tongues, nastiness, ad hominem attacks, hate, and the search for personal revenge. The phrase *trzeba go wykończyć* (he has to be finished off, as in "put away") entered—or reentered—the political vocabulary. This jinx did not fall from the sky or erupt from the ground on national independence day; it dropped from an old family tree and made it easier for three voracious, neighboring empires on the move to help themselves to a lavish feast in 1772, 1792/3, and 1795. Now, in the mid 1920s, after being divided by force, the new Poland was being fragmented by habit. Restraining runaway talkativeness can be ticklish business. Almost certainly it will be seen by well-thinking people as an infringement of free speech, the bedrock of democracy. Besides, national self-determination and the establishment of democratic states were key postulates of the Versailles Treaty that, with the help of four uprisings and a few local wars, gave the Poles back their statehood. Moreover, verbal exuberance was to be expected from a recently freed people who for decades had been warned by the imperialists that their *Maul* was fit only for a Prussian iron fist or the Russian taiga. The future chief of state and marshal, Józef Piłsudski, experienced both of these during his imprisonment in the Magdeburg fortress and his deportation into the depths of Siberia.

Also, in the years between the Polish-Soviet Peace Treaty of Riga (March 1921) and May 12, 1926, despite all the difficulties and the blunders committed by newcomers to the ways of democracy, much good work had been done in laying the foundations for a democratic state, though regrettably on the constitutional model of the French Third Republic. It considerably circumscribed the executive power of the country's president, elected by a national assembly representing both houses, and vested it in a two-chamber legislature, the lower house (*sejm*, seym) and the upper senate, filled to the brim with umpteen bickering parties elected by a system of proportional representation. These parties were unable to agree on the formation of a government without resorting to odd, often mismatched, and always fleeting coalitions.

The hyperinflation and consequent mass worker disturbances of 1923–24, put down only by force, did not help any, nor did Piłsudski's cat-and-mouse game with the new constitution approved on March 17, 1921. The inflation was brought under control in 1924 through budgetary restraint and monetary reform. A central bank was created, and a new currency called the *złoty* was put into circulation. *Złoty* means "golden," but there was little gold in the central bank's reserves. No matter; the very idea, based on trust that there might be some solid backing for the new coins and bills, boosted public confidence in the *złoty* for a while. In 1925 hyperinflation struck again, this time provoked by the German-Polish tariff war, which adversely affected Poland's exports of coal from Silesia, played havoc with the balance of trade, contributed to unemployment, and caused yet another change of government. There were thirteen such government changes during the first seven years of independence, with many of the same political faces showing up again and again in the revolving door. In this, Poland was not alone.

From the end of the war until 1923, the contemporary German Weimar Republic, built on similar foundations, had eight government changes in five years. In December 1922, after five voting rounds of the brand-new but still bitterly splintered parliament's national assembly, Gabriel Narutowicz, a distinguished engineer and former Swiss citizen of Polish origin, became the republic's first president under the March 1921 constitution. Five days after taking office (December 16, 1922), he was assassinated by an extreme rightist influenced by an unprecedentedly virulent campaign of vilification unleashed against Narutowicz by the far-right National Democracy movement, led by Roman Dmowski.

Piłsudski, who in May 1923 retired from politics and, as he put it, "emigrated" to Sulejówek just outside Warsaw, was shocked and disgusted by the murder and what he called "partyocracy" messing with the nation's destiny. On May 12, 1926 he immigrated from Sulejówek back to Warsaw, and in the company of just enough troops to make his point, he headed for the Poniatowski bridge over the Vistula, where he had a brief "Do this, or else" conversation with the president of the Republic and then unleashed a coup d'état that lasted three days, cost several hundred lives, and, with fairly wide popular support of a citizenry tired of political infighting and the resultant stagnation, marked the beginning of the end of attempts at parliamentary democracy in interwar Poland.

The president, Stanislaw Wojciechowski, resigned. He was replaced by a Piłsudski man, Ignacy Mościcki, who served in that office until Poland was again erased from the map by the combined onslaught of Nazi Germany and the Soviet Union in September 1939. Prime Minister Wincenty Witos gave way to Kazimierz Bartel, a Piłsudski supporter.[2] To keep the lid on a volatile capital, Felicjan Sławoj Składkowski, was appointed as government commissioner, a rank equivalent to provincial governor (*wojewoda*), from the second day of the coup until October 1926, at which time Składkowski became minister of internal affairs and administration, a powerful job he kept for three years. Foreign affairs were given to August Zaleski, who remained head of this ministry from June 1926 to December 1932. The presidency (Mościcki), the premiership of government (Bartel), the bureaucracy and police (internal affairs, Sławoj Składkowski), and the army (Piłsudski) were all in safe hands. Now came the turn of the legislature, the judiciary, education, and the media.

On August 2, 1926, the constitution was, for lack of a better word, amended. It greatly restricted the role of parliament in national affairs and substantially increased that of the country's president by vesting in him the right to issue edicts with force of law and to dissolve both houses at the request of the government. The new regime was backed by the army and energized by a new movement, *Sanacja* (meaning cure, healing, improvement), which welcomed to its ranks members of any political party as well as nonparty people who shared Piłsudski's vision of strengthening the state by enlarging the power of the top executive. This policy divided the left, right, and middle political parties into followers and opponents of Piłsudski 's political ideas and his persona. The same was true of the civil service, the army, social organizations, and every politically conscious family in the nation. At this stage the parties were not silenced but were debilitated. Nevertheless, from 1926 to 1929, the economy of the Second Republic prospered as never before or after. This was due partly to international economic recovery from World War I but also because at home, before a counterattack, the incapacitated political parties took time to recover from the shock of the coup and from the follow-up, hit-and-run raids on the March 1921 constitution and parliamentary procedures by Piłsudski's commandos.

The party politicians came to in November 1929, refreshed by the realization that they had to hang together. Distasteful as that was, it was better than the electoral setback they had suffered in an election held on March 4, 1928. The leaders of six center and left parties formed within the parliament an anti-*Sanacja* coalition for the defense of democracy as they understood it. It was called *Centrolew* (Centerleft) and was an answer to the creation the year before of the Nonparty Bloc of Cooperation with the Government (BBWR), led by a Piłsudski person, Walery Sławek. On January 19, 1928, the BBWR issued a programmatic declaration of action for the attainment of *Sanacja*'s longer-term aim of introducing and passing a new constitution that would further reform—that is, restrict—parliamentary prerogatives. In the shorter-range view of its authors, the BBWR was a nonparty vehicle festooned with

Piłsudski's political notions for taking voters by hook or by crook, irrespective of party affiliations, race, sex, creed, religion, language, or national origin, to the voting booths on March 4, 1928, where they would elect, "as required," a more compliant seym and senate.[3] The election went as planned but not quite as required. The BBWR received the largest share of votes of all competing political groupings, but not enough to change the constitution in the way its leaders had in mind. The biggest loser was the right-wing National Democracy movement (popularly called *Endecja*). Moreover, the BBWR's candidate for speaker of the seym (Bartel) got only 141 votes to the 206 received by Polish Socialist Party's (PPS) leader, Ignacy Daszyński. In April, following a mild stroke, Piłsudski's health began to decline. He dissolved his cabinet in June, when the office of prime minister devolved for the second time on the "now you see me, now you don't" Bartel. But it did not devolve for long.

On June 30, 1930, after more governmental reshuffles, a Centerleft rally in Cracow promised more than twenty mass demonstrations for September 14 demanding the resignation of the government and the president. At this time, the country was suffering from the Great Depression, which hit Polish agricultural exports particularly hard. The government, by now headed by Walery Sławek, did indeed resign on August 23, but its place was taken by a cabinet headed by Piłsudski. Six days later, at now Prime Minister Piłsudski's request, both chambers were dissolved by the president of the Republic (Mościcki). Parliamentary elections were held on November 16 and 23, 1930. *Sanacja* received 56 percent of the votes cast for seym deputies and 69 percent for senators—still not enough to change the constitution. The election went down in history as the "Brześć election," also known in more satirically or theologically inclined circles as the "miracle of the ballot box" (*cud nad urną*).

In accordance with the amended 1921 constitution, deputies and senators could be and were stripped of parliamentary immunity. It was now no longer a question of silencing the opposition or removing them from office; it was about finishing them off. Henceforth the opposition, or at least their party leaders, were just ordinary, out-of-office has-beens who could be arrested and put away, without judicial fuss and bother, by the minister of the interior, Felicjan Sławoj Składkowski, and housed in the old Russian fortress at Brześć (Brest Litovsk), at the time a Polish military prison. Among the first to be shipped to the prison was Wincenty Witos and nineteen former Centerleft deputies, and later Wojciech Korfanty, who since 1922 had been a Christian Democratic Party seym member and since 1924 had been publisher of two national newspapers, *Rzeczpospolita* and *Polonia*. In 1935 he went into exile in Czechoslovakia—a more democratic country than Poland, unless you asked the Slovaks. A letter of protest alleging brutal and demeaning treatment of the Brześć prisoners was signed by the faculty of Jagiellonian University.

Sławoj Składkowski was an obsessive micromanager. As a former medical doctor, he correctly noticed that the sanitary condition of restrooms in Polish eateries left much to be desired. On his frequent travels on official business through the country as prime minister and minister of the interior (1936–1939), he personally inspected the latrines. When word got out that he was on the road, panic seized the restaurant industry, as well as millions of peasants who had been ordered to erect outhouses where there were none. The wits soon named the facilities *sławojki* in honor of his name. Shortly before the Nazi invasion, he issued an order that all fences in the Polish countryside were to be painted green for purposes of military camouflage, perhaps even aesthetics. To reduce their costs, the peasants smeared their fences with cow dung. When my father, in his capacity as mayor of Bielsko, took Składkowski on a tour of a new dam in Wapienice near the city, the prime minister pointed to a toolshed and ordered that it be immediately removed because it spoiled the view. In exile in London a decade later, Składkowski accidentally met my father and asked whether the eye-offending shed had, in fact, been removed. Składkowski was not extraordinarily philosemitic, but during the war he had to take refuge for five years in Palestine.

On August 23, 1935, with the help of adroit procedural maneuvering, an authoritarian constitution was finally adopted. One of its provisions was that a third of the senate's membership be appointed by the president of the republic, who also had veto powers over bills passed by that chamber and was "responsible to God and history." On May 12, 1935, exactly nine years after the coup, Piłsudski died of cancer at age sixty-seven. His funeral was the occasion for an elaborate patriotic display of national unity and mourning.

There was unity among the Poles—a tough, individualistic, emotional, impulsive and quixotic people—on one fundamental issue: they wanted a free, strong, stable, independent, just, prosperous, modern nation-state of their own. They were nationalist, some more than others, but all Poles young and old (especially those born after the foreign tripartite occupation ended) had an ongoing love affair with their homeland. The exception were the cadres of the Polish Communist Party and their fellow travelers; they saw the world through the Marxist prism of historically inevitable class conflict, fantasized about a proletarian paradise, and owed their loyalty to the Soviet Union. His allegiance to the Soviet Union notwithstanding, Polish Communist Party (KPP) activist Adolf Warski was arrested and shot in Moscow by the Soviet secret police on July 9, 1937. By the time Stalin was through with them, all the KPP leaders who had sought refuge in the workers' paradise met the same fate. The Polish domestic quarrels and mudslinging were about the way a good state should be built: what materials to use (how much democracy, how much diktat; how much market, how much administrative planning), who were to be the architects and administrators (that is, of power), and above all, how to protect the infant republic from harm by ill-wishers within and outside its borders.

A third of the country's population was made up of national, ethnic, linguistic, and confessional minorities: German, Ukrainian, Ruthenian, Belorussian, Russian, Lithuanian, Czech, Slovak, Roma (Gypsies), Jewish, Protestant, Eastern Orthodox, Greek Catholic (including Uniates recognizing papal supremacy). These minorities were resentful, unassimilated, antagonized, irreconciled, and increasingly assertive. In the context of organic nations and integral nationalism (unity within a sovereign nation-state) that Poles and others in eastern Europe and the Balkans fervently believed in and practiced, the problem could be addressed, but not necessarily solved, by assimilation of the minority in the dominant majority culture—peacefully by mutual consent, or better still, on the uncoerced initiative of minority individuals, like in America. This takes at least a generation, as evidenced in the early 2000s by the troubles experienced by France and Germany with their second-generation Muslim citizens. Another way is assimilation by force, which, as we have seen in Silesia, tends to produce a round of greater coercion by one side and armed resistance by the other. The cycle gets more vicious when forced assimilation is applied to minority religions and languages. It becomes life-threatening to the nation when minorities, by reason of geographical location, live next door to their national compatriots in bordering states that support and encourage their demands. It jeopardizes national existence when one or two of these neighboring states—say, Germany and the Soviet Union—are in the hands of fanatical dictators equipped not with rickshaws but panzer divisions and lethal doctrines that large segments of your minorities find attractive. Under those circumstances, solution of the minority quandary through assimilation, nicely or ugly, is not possible. Interwar Poland saved herself the trouble by having no meaningful minorities policy beyond the right of representation in the quarrelsome seym and pious generalities before mid 1926—the time of "seymocracy" as Piłsudski liked to call it. When heavy-handed efforts at forced Polonization began that, even allowing for intense provocation by those to be Polonized, were unworthy of a country that itself had suffered a similar process, in reverse, at the hands of czarist Russia and imperial Germany.

The most violent minority acts were committed by a militant Ukrainian nationalist movement, the Organization of Ukrainian Nationalists (OUN), cobbled together in 1929 in Vienna from various Ukrainian activist groups operating in Poland in the 1920s. Its objective was the creation of an independent Ukrainian state (which didn't happen at the time) by rejecting compromise with the Poles or anyone else holding a square inch of what the OUN deemed Ukrainian territory. The OUN resorted instead to "nationalism by deed"—terrorism for short. In August 1931 they assassinated Tadeusz Hołówko, a high-ranking member of the BBWR and a seym deputy who was a Polish proponent of a moderate course and Polish-Ukrainian reconciliation. The OUN's paramilitary West Ukrainian Territorial Executive (UVO) launched a campaign of terror by arson against Polish landowners in former Galicia and Volhynia. Piłsudski's response in September 1930 was pacification by cavalry, in the course of which several Orthodox and

Greek Catholic churches were torched. In January 1931 the OUN formally complained to the League of Nations, which opined a year later that the pacification was justified by reason of the "disloyalty of citizens to the state."

On June 15, 1934, in Warsaw, a member of UVO shot to death Poland's minister of internal affairs, Bronisław Pieracki. Two days later the Polish government opened at Bereza Kartuska an internment camp ("place of isolation") for persons representing danger to the security of the state, in which suspects could be held for three months by simple administrative decision. Its original purpose was to act as a "toy gun"—a disincentive. The camp was closed and all detainees were released in September 1939, shortly after the Nazi invasion. By then they were a politically diverse and multicultural group comprising members of the OUN, Polish communists, and right-wing activists—mainly young people of the neofascist, antisemitic National Radical Camp (ONR) formed in May 1934 and banned in July but countenanced after 1936; the group had severed relations with the rightist National Democracy movement. Also released from the camp were members of opposition parties, writers and journalists critical of the government, and common criminals, with recidivists in the lead. In Bereza, the ONR split into two factions. One of them was popularly known as ONR-Falanga (a name parroted from Franco's Falange) and officially known as the National Radical Movement (RNR). The RNR was led by Bolesław Piasecki, who after World War II, in conformity with the law of the unity of opposites, switched to the communist regime subservient to Moscow and organized for them a satellite Polish Catholic movement named PAX. Despite risk to their persons and careers, many ordinary citizens criticized the presence of the Bereza camp. The total number of prisoners during the five years of the camp's operations was between fourteen and seventeen thousand; the number of deaths was twenty, with four of them in the camp and the rest in outside hospitals.

In the portrait gallery of strongmen, many of Piłsudski's compatriots thought he deserved to be hung in the benign room, or better. His death when Poland was only sixteen raised the question of succession to which monocracies, benevolent or otherwise, have no institutionally satisfactory answer. His legacy remains contro-

versial, but not his patriotism or strength of personality. He was
a military man who understood hierarchical discipline better than
parliamentary democracy—or at least the querulous special education democracy he saw at home. He was a liberator but not a
libertarian. His socialist background made him prefer a heavily
state-regulated and state-run economy, and he was suspicious of the
profit-oriented, capitalist way of creating wealth, which he never
quite understood and found a trifle un-Polish, and perhaps un-
Christian. He wished the new Poland to be a federation of diverse
peoples living amicably within extensive eastern and northern
borders under the Polish "crown," the way it had been before the
partitions—a vast land between the Baltic and the Black Sea that
would be Europe's bulwark against the aggressive intentions of
Russians and Asiatic tribes farther east.

Apart from its romantically imbued remembrance of placid relations between Poles and others within the prepartition Commonwealth of Poland and Lithuania, Piłsudski's vision assumed that in
the meantime national consciousness had not sprouted or gained
strength in peoples other than the Poles. He was appalled that in
his day and age there were a lot of people who preferred to have
their own state, or just a statelet, rather than live in Poland; these
people had to be dealt with. This only made them more reluctant
and rebellious, adding to the ranks of malcontents. Others left and
besmirched the country abroad. Piłsudski's eyes, however, remained
for a while longer on the east and on what he saw as "middle" Lithuania with Wilno (Vilnius) at its center. Like Silesia for others, it was
his place of birth and closer homeland. He took it and incorporated
it in the Polish Republic between October 9, 1920 and February 20,
1922, by concocting a flimsy ruse and sending in the army. In the
end, intentionally or unwittingly (and evidence seems to point to
the former) he laid the foundations of an authoritarian state.

What he left behind was not, as is often said, a void, but an
increasingly centralized, personality-driven political system
without the personality; this was a reason to mourn for some, a
sigh of relief for others. There were many candidates for succession in the ruling top coteries, and glimmers of new hope among
those still in organized (if not always legal) opposition at home or in
exile abroad. There existed three nodes of mild intraclan election-

eering: the presidential palace, the military, and the people around Walery Sławek, the right-wing ideologue, cofounder of the BBWR, and three-time prime minister. Seemingly the differences between the three nodes, mostly of degree and emphasis, were papered over. The actual transition was therefore relatively quick, smooth, and predictable in its personnel and direction. Most of the mates were already on the top deck of the ship of state, and the rudder had been set in a direction chosen by the now defunct captain. The remaining question to be answered, other than how to handle the muffled hollering from the lower decks, was one of personality: who among the contenders was to be given the helm and be trusted to keep the ship sailing on the same course, avoiding collision with his fellow officers and foreign vessels?

The name of that person, if not personality, was Edward Rydz-Śmigły (or Śmigły-Rydz, whichever one prefers). Born in Austrian Galicia, he became a good portraitist and landscape painter. As an officer in the Polish Legion (Piłsudski's First Brigade) in the Austrian army during World War I, he fought the Russians in Galicia, rising to the rank of colonel. While Piłsudski was incarcerated in the Magdeburg fortress, Piłsudski made Rydz-Śmigły commander of the Polish Military Organization (POW), and on Piłsudski's release, not long after becoming provisional head of the Polish state on November 11, 1918, he confirmed Rydz's rank of brigadier general. Rydz-Śmigły fought valiantly in the Polish-Bolshevik war (1919–1921), particularly on the crucial central front of the Battle of Warsaw, and he led the troops that successfully encircled the Bolshevik armies, forcing them to retreat.[4] After the war he was appointed inspector general of the army in the Wilno district. A few years later he backed the May 1926 coup d'état by dispatching some of the troops under his command to shore up Piłsudski's forces against the pressure of army units loyal to the government. In 1929, back in Warsaw, Piłsudski delegated him to deal on his behalf with military matters in the troubled east of the country.

On May 13, 1935, within twenty-four hours of Piłsudski's death, Rydz-Śmigły was appointed inspector general of the armed forces by President Mościcki and the cabinet, apparently in accord with the late marshal's wishes. On July 15, 1936, a government circular decreed that Edward Rydz-Śmigły was to be treated next to the president as the prime person in the state hierarchy. On November 11, 1936, Rydz-Śmigły was promoted to marshal of Poland, Piłsudski's former rank. The rest is tragic history, for him personally and for the country. However, Poland's fall was not, as is sometimes suggested, largely due to Rydz-Śmigły's actions, inactions, or overall limitations. Much of what happened in the few remaining years of Poland's independence had to do with *Machtpolitik* (power politics) by the near-abroad to the west, over which Polish diplomacy had little if any control, no matter who was in charge of it, or how finessed.

Foreign Affairs

Patient, well-mannered, prudent behavior and reasoned dialogue, associated in the olden days with aristocratic refinement and, in the language of foreign affairs, called diplomacy, played a material role in bringing Poland to the sympathetic attention of the American people, the U.S. Congress, and President Woodrow Wilson, thus putting the country again on the agenda for redrawing the map of Europe. Instrumental in this was Ignacy Jan Paderewski, an internationally renowned Polish pianist and composer with just the right looks, distinguished personality, flair, elite connections throughout the world, mass appeal, and eventual wealth (which he enjoyed but also generously donated to Polish and international cultural, humanitarian, and social causes, including aid for Jewish refugees from Hitler's Germany in Paris).

In 1913 Paderewski made his home in America, where he gave numerous piano recitals to overflowing, enthusiastic audiences in every state of the union. He became prime minister of Poland and concurrently minister of foreign affairs on January 16, 1919. Two weeks later the United States recognized the Paderewski government, followed by France, Britain, and Italy. He and Roman Dmowski were Polish delegates at the Versailles Peace Conference, putting their signatures to the Peace Treaty on June 23, 1919, to which was attached a treaty for the protection of minority rights—dubbed the "Small Versailles Treaty" and applicable to newly established countries with large national minorities, Poland being one of them. Paderewski was also involved in the preparation of Poland's temporary constitution, adopted in February 1919. The following year, partly for financial reasons, he withdrew from all political offices and resumed his musical career. On the tenth anniversary of Polish independence (1928), U.S. presidents Coolidge, Taft, and Hoover sent Paderewski a message of congratulations commending his statesmanship. He died in New York in 1941. By presidential decree he was laid to rest in Arlington cemetery. His remains were returned to postcommunist Poland in 1992 for burial in Warsaw's St. John's cathedral. It should be added by way of warning that to the extent that the diplomacy exemplified by Paderewski contributed to Poland's resurrection as a sovereign political entity in the crucial years (1918–1919) was because it found a positive response with civilized, if sometimes crotchety and vulpine, Western counterparts (Wilson, Lloyd George), the very opposites of the monstrous species with apocalyptic designs that was then incubating in Germany and Russia.

That two men, very different in style, manners, temperament, and political philosophy, should have been conjoined to represent and explain the Polish position at Versailles may seem puzzling. The reasons were domestic, centering on the bitter rivalry between Piłsudski and Dmowski, almost unresolvable because of the pigheadedness of both when it came to their respective conceptions of what the future Poland should be. Since both men had strong support at home, there was cause to fear an outbreak of civil war that would have ended all hopes of Poland emerging from Versailles as an independent state. Paderewski stepped into the breach, persuading the warring parties that in the national interest he and Dmowski should be sent as Poland's representatives to the Peace Conference while Piłsudski would mind the store at home.

Piłsudski was distrusted in certain entente quarters because, with Austria's consent, he had formed his Polish legion on Austrian-held territory and fought on the Austrian side against czarist Russia, then allied with the Western powers. The mistrust was not wholly erased by his refusal to take a pledge of allegiance to his Germanic sponsors in 1917, a piece of insubordination for which he was dispatched to the Magdeburg fortress. On the other hand, Dmowski wanted Poland to be a "healthily egoistic," self-maximizing state, as he once put it, compact, uniethnic (minorities free), monoglot; in his later formulations he also added to the list religious homogeneity (meaning Roman Catholicism), modern (industrialized), and science oriented. Pre-1914 Germany, which he disliked, could serve as useful reference. In his appearance before the Supreme Allied Council at Versailles on January 29, 1919, he earned grudging nods of approval from Poland-allergic Lloyd George and Wilson for his lack of interest in absorbing colossal chunks of territory inhabited largely by Ukrainians, Ruthenians, Belorussians, and Lithuanians that were once ruled by Poland, as well as for his emphasis on pragmatic rather than historical, not to say archaeological, reasons why Germany should give up parts of eastern Silesia that had mines and steelworks in them in order to provide Poland with an infrastructure for future industrial development. He argued that for commercial reasons, which the British Prime Minister understood better than central European geography, Poland should be given access to the Baltic Sea through Danzig Pomerania. All this pleased French Prime Minister Clemenceau, anxious as he was to prevent Germany from economically outstripping France and from turning ploughshares into swords in Silesia for as long as possible. Dmowski's supporters told all who would listen that with his nostalgia for "*Litwo! Ojczyzno moja!* (Lithuania! My homeland!), Piłsudski simply wasn't all that interested in the Danzig issue.[5]

Piłsudski's dislike of Dmowski, fully reciprocated, was lifelong. Woodrow Wilson could not stand him. On the cultural side, Dmowski told Paderewski that music was mere noise. He was convinced that Lloyd George was an "agent of the Jews," corrupted by an anti-Polish international Jewish conspiracy. He was seen by British diplomats as clever, in the sense of glibly facile. His advice to the Jewish minority in Poland was for all of them to emigrate. He was convinced that President Mościcki surrounded himself with Judeo-Masonic confidants (Sławek was a freemason).

Dmowski was a seym deputy in 1919 and minister of foreign affairs for three months in 1923. As time went on his views became too tame for some of his young followers who, as we have seen, left his Party in 1934 to form the National Radical Camp (ONR), pollute the political atmosphere, and further poison minority relations and undermine Poland's reputation abroad.

At an ungodly hour early one morning, during an international conference on European economic reconstruction and international cooperation held in Genoa in April 1922, a staff member of the Soviet delegate to the conference, People's Commissar for Foreign Affairs Georgii Tchicherin, telephoned the hotel suite of Walther Rathenau, the German delegate and minister of foreign affairs, to suggest that since they were in the neighborhood anyway, why not get together the next day in little Rapallo nearby to inhale the fresh sea air and converse over a glass of wine about issues of mutual interest to the USSR and postwar Germany? The implied understanding was that a consensus would shake the Western powers out of their condescension, make them stop acting like the two countries had the plague, and do a lot of short- and long-term good to the consensors as well. The suggestion was accepted, and the next day, Easter Sunday, April 16, 1922, Soviet Russia and Weimar Germany signed a treaty of friendship and commerce, renewed full diplomatic relations, cancelled all their outstanding prewar debts, signed trade agreements with most-favored-nation clauses dangling from them, and forever put Rapallo on the map. The treaty was followed by a flurry of secret compacts on military cooperation, specifically on training German army and airforce personnel, as well as the production and use of heavy military equipment that, under the Versailles Treaty, Germany was forbidden to have.

The Europeans were shaken, the Poles shocked by what they perceived to be not just a weakening of the Versailles peace arrangement but a direct diplomatic, political, and economic move of German and Russian irredentist revisionism made by the same partition partners who had done this before. Clearly the Rapallo agreement was not made in one day; there must have been thorough, undetected preparation. The Poles did not know then about the military addendum but suspected that it was either settled already or would be soon. But there was nothing, diplomatic or otherwise, they could do about it. Rathenau (a Jew) was murdered on June 24, 1922, by the German far-right terrorist Konsul organization, which a year earlier had killed Matthias Erzberger (a Catholic) who had signed the Armistice Agreement on behalf of Germany on November 11, 1918.

By 1925 the League of Nations had practically talked itself out of the business of solving disagreements between nation-states. Its Geneva Protocol of 1924, a project for the peaceful settlement of international disputes by submitting them for arbitration to a supranational Tribunal of International Justice and the League's Council, required more than a slight trimming of cherished national-state sovereignty rights. Even though the League passed it unanimously, the project of collective security died on the vine. By then comradely relations between former wartime allies had cooled down considerably as they pursued their competitive, often divergent, and conflicting national interests.[6] The two tainted outsiders' Rapallofest by the sea marked a return to the classical but flawed method of dealing with disputes directly between nations, concealed defense packages included.

Around that time it dawned on the French that what with the late war and all, France was no longer a great power in the sense of being able to defend its border by itself now that the resurgent and aggrieved Germany and Soviet Russia had patched up their relations. The British knew that too and became firmer than ever in their resolve not to be snagged again by the French into another war on the European continent, especially in exotic places like Poland's Silesia (Lloyd George's Cilicia) and Czechoslovakia, which they found hard enough to spell, never mind protect from harm. America, the emerging great power that helped design the Versailles settlement, had not ratified the peace treaty, thereby undermining the treaty's legitimacy (in the eyes of its German and Soviet critics on the lookout for legalistic excuses to ignore it) and contributing to the stillbirth of the League of Nations. Moreover, by 1924 America had turned inward, and Italy became fascist.

The awareness of virtual weakness and fear of another war encouraged France and Britain, the remnants of the entente, to try another foreign policy tactic. Instead of isolating Germany, the entente thought they should take a page out of the Rapallo book and bring the Germans, and eventually the Soviets, into the family of nations before they did something worse than just "whittle away their assurances and introduce new conditions as they have done up till now," as British Foreign Secretary (1924–1929) Austen Chamberlain remarked. The simplest way to do this was to give whining Germany economic concessions on the amount and schedule of reparation payments and stabilization loans. This was done in 1924, but Germany kept complaining about not being treated on an equal

political footing with the other nations. The 1925 Locarno conference, arranged by the French and the British, was intended to put
the situation right once and for all.

The conferees met at the picturesque Swiss town of Locarno
on Lago Maggiore. Seven countries were involved (France, Britain,
Belgium, Germany, Italy, Poland, and Czechoslovakia): four in
terms of substantive contribution to the outcome of the proceedings (France, Britain, Belgium, Germany); one who didn't care
much about attending (fascist Italy); and two wallflowers, both
French protegés (Poland and Czechoslovakia) who were not asked
to attend the plenary sessions and the informal conclaves, including
the privileged cruise on the lake on October 10, at which much of
the sensitive work was done. Each state, whether of first or second
rank on the conference's unwritten political Who's Who, was represented by its minister of foreign affairs, with Germany adding its
chancellor for good measure.

The Pact of Locarno consisted of three separate but fore-
bodingly interrelated parts: the Treaty of Mutual Guarantee
(commonly referred to as the Rhineland Pact), four arbitration
agreements, and two treaties of reassurance. The Treaty of Mutual
Guarantee concerned what could be called "level one" countries:
the victors in World War I (France, Britain, Belgium, and Italy)
and Germany, which signed the treaty with France and Belgium on
October 16. It solemnly confirmed the inviolability of the existing,
Versailles-drawn German-French and German-Belgian borders—
and by implication, the permanent return to France of Alsace and
Lorraine, and the abandonment by Belgium of its former posture
of neutrality—and of the Versailles-ordered demilitarization of
the Rhineland zone (DMZ), where as of then some allied troops,
mostly French, were still stationed. France, Belgium, and Germany
pledged not to go to war with each other, except in legitimate self-
defense. In the event of flagrant violation of any of these border
reaffirmations and war forswearings, Britain and Italy would jump
in and punish the treaty-breaker without waiting for time-consuming investigation by and permission from the League of Nations
Council (the predecessor of the UN Security Council). British public
opinion took a sanguine view of the guarantee, partly because it
was not a second *entente cordiale* with the French and also because it

suggested a departure of France from that country's earlier policy
of military sanctions against those disturbing the hard-won and
still fragile Versailles new order.

The jubilation surrounding the Locarno Pact as a whole was
confined to Western Europe, specifically to level one countries.
The celebrations afterward, Sir Harold Nicolson noted later, were
"scenes of orgiastic gush." There was little celebration in Germany
despite the fact that "on every major issue raised at the Conference
the German viewpoint was the one that found acceptance."[7] Signed
in Locarno on October 16, 1925, the pact had to be ratified by the
parliaments of all the affected countries, then officially signed in
London on December 1, 1925, a ceremony that Mussolini chose not
to attend (Italy's representative was Scialoga). The implementation
of the pact had to await Germany's formal admission to the League
of Nations. This occurred on September 8, 1926, by unanimous
vote. Germany also joined Britain, France, Italy, and Japan as a permanent member on the League Council. Poland, after some hard
bargaining and a threat of withdrawal from the League, obtained a
semipermanent seat on the Council for three years, with possibility
of reelection at the end of each three-year period.

The arbitration treaties fell into two classes. The first two—
between Germany and France, and Germany and Belgium—
spelled out detailed procedures for the peaceful resolution of
disputes between level one states of the Rhineland Pact. The other
two treaties were concluded by Germany with level two countries:
Poland, which the Weimar Republic always regarded as a "seasonal
state," and Czechoslovakia. The arbitration treaties did not confirm
the inviolability of Germany's Versailles-approved eastern borders
with Poland and Czechoslovakia, the way the Rhineland Treaty
did for Germany's borders with France and Belgium, because the
Germans had no intention of signing any such thing, and neither
France nor Britain were in a mood to press them on that point.
Locarno thus created the concept of two kinds of European borders:
first-class, set in concrete in the west, and second-class, on roller
skates in the east.

What the Poles and Czechs got from France were treats: treaties
of reassurance containing hedged promises of mutual armed assistance, pursuant to article 16 of the League Covenant in the event

of unprovoked attack by Germany. In plain language France could take military action against Germany if the League decided that such military response was appropriate. Stresemann insisted that no mention be made of these in the text of the Rhineland Pact, for the Pact and the treaties of reassurance were quite different.

The spirit of "peace through appeasement" was released in Locarno the same year that the first volume of Hitler's *Mein Kampf* was published (and pooh-poohed by the *bien pensants* everywhere as the ravings of a madman). A few years later, Hitler, now master of Germany, diagnosed his opponents' insecurities and put to the test their habit and record of preemptive concessions; he put the Locarno genie back in the bottle and then smashed it.

Looking west, Polish foreign policy makers could see heavy storm clouds forming soon after the diplomats had left sunny Locarno. Between January 1926 and June 1930, all allied troops were withdrawn from the Rhineland, five years earlier than scheduled by the Versailles Treaty. In 1927, the Interallied Control Commission, empowered by that treaty to make on-site inspections of German disarmament efforts, was disbanded. War reparation payments, a huge bone of contention between Germany and France, were progressively reduced by various write-downs, write-offs, and loans to the subprime debtor and were finally eliminated in 1931 by the Great Depression that had been playing havoc with world economies since the stock market crash in New York on October 24, 1929. On September 14, 1932, Germany informed the chairman of the Conference for the Reduction and Limitation of Armaments, sponsored by the League of Nations, of its intention to withdraw, which it did a year later. In December 1932, at a conference in Lausanne, the major Western powers acknowledged Germany's right to rearm.

On January 30, 1933, Adolf Hitler became chancellor of Germany, and within a few months he was the supreme leader (*Führer*) of the country. On October 21, he let the League of Nations know of his intention to withdraw Germany from that body, and he did so two years later. To compensate for the expected loss of a big-power member, in 1934 the League, with French encouragement, admitted the Soviet Union (then in the midst of bloody purges) and elected it to a permanent seat on the Council. In March 1935,

Hitler rejected all restrictions imposed on German rearmament by the Versailles Treaty and introduced compulsory enlistment in the German army, all the while reassuring everyone of his peaceful intentions. No action was taken by the supine League or anyone else, beyond some tut-tutting from Geneva. A year later (March 7, 1936), several companies of the German army entered the Rhineland and settled down for good, while Germany rejected the international status of the rivers Rhine, Oder, and Niemen and of the Kiel canal. The League of Nations censured Germany for violating the Versailles Treaty; Britain and France also did nothing. On March 8, 1936, the Führer denounced and repudiated the Locarno Pact. On January 30, 1937, he cancelled Germany's recognition of Article 231 of the Versailles Treaty, wherein Germany accepted responsibility for all losses and damage which the Allied and Associated Governments suffered as a consequence of the war imposed upon them by the aggression of Germany and her allies—and, by extension, any war reparations imposed on it, which anyway had been wiped out by the Great Depression.

For Poland, the diplomatic elbow room in which to handle Germany's rapid return to international political influence, military might, and old territorial appetites was limited and constrained, and sharply so after the Stresemann era (1923–29) of the postwar drama. Arguably squeezed by the miseries of the Great Depression, the Germans were ready for a savior, but so were Americans, who elected Roosevelt when the Germans got themselves Hitler. In the Weimar Republic's November 1932 elections to the Reichstag, the National Socialist German Workers Party (NSDAP, the Nazis) picked up the largest number of deputies of any party, more than one third; the Social Democrats (SPD) came in second with 121 seats (nearly 21 percent); and the communists (KPD) were third with 81 places (16 percent). Of course, there is always the historical "if." If the socialists had cooperated with the communists, the outcome could have been different, but Stalin forbade the communists to do this. What if those *German* communists had disobeyed him...? But they didn't. When the Locarno spirit was drifting about, relations between Germany and Poland were strained at best, even though Weimar Germany, unlike its Nazi successor, did not consider armed force to be the appropriate way of dealing with territorial and other disagreements with its neighbor to the east. For one thing, they did not have the armed force to do it.

Piłsudski read the Locarno playbook to mean that neither Britain nor France cared enough about Poland to guarantee that her borders with Germany remain as fixed and unalterable as France's and Belgium's, and this despite France's 1921 agreement of cooperation with Poland in international affairs (and a secret codicil that in the event either country were attacked by Germany or the Soviet Union, the other would come militarily to its aid). That was before France lost its will. Great Britain wished not to be distracted from her primary interests: protecting her future commerce with a well-off Germany; attending to her vast empire, which was showing now and again signs of restlessness; and maintaining her rule of the waves. On June 18, 1935, the British entered into a naval agreement with Hitler, which set the tonnage ratio of the German fleet to the Royal Navy at 35:100, exceeding the limits on the German navy placed by the Versailles Treaty. The ratio was good enough for Nazi Germany to control ship movements in and out of the Baltic Sea. Hitler seemed to have believed that the agreement would bring Britain into his projected Anticomintern Pact directed against the Third Communist International and the Soviet Union, which it did not. The British wanted to believe that Hitler had changed for the better since his belligerent *Mein Kampf* days, which he had not.

After Locarno, Poland pursued a two-pronged external policy, first under foreign affairs minister August Zaleski (May 15, 1926, to November 2, 1932) and followed by Józef Beck (November 2, 1932, to September 30, 1939). On the one hand, Poland tried to be a responsible member of international organizations, the League of Nations in particular, but she insisted on being treated as an equal of the Locarno level one powers by being granted a permanent seat, not a folding one, on the League Council. In this she was rebuffed and relegated to the status of apprentice. Poland noticed that the postwar European masters, France and Britain, were demoting themselves to the rank of journeymen by their ill-conceived complaisance and humoring of a Germany that never, other than on paper, accepted responsibility for the outbreak and damage inflicted on the Allies and their associates in World War I or the consequences to itself of the war's outcome, including loss of territory in the east. Poland in the early 1930s tried a neutralist, balance-of-power bilateralism—a personally invested insurance policy—that was very short lived, as it turned out. She was not alone in this. Having taken a good look at the record of the League of Nations, governments in eastern Europe scrambled to sign two-way pacts, treaties, agreements, and declarations of reciprocal respect, cooperation, and nonaggression with anyone who had a pen. Hitler's Germany joined in by having a ready pen as well as top officials willing to travel abroad and not blabber about their people's need for *Lebensraum* (living space) in the east. The entrails of the League of Nations were put in a canopic jar, just in case.

In a speech to the Reichstag in March 1933—three weeks after the Reichstag fire and the disposal of what was left of civil and human rights in the country, and three days after the opening of the Dachau concentration camp—Hitler offered his hand in friendship to any nation that desired, on principle, to bring closure to a sad past. Now, the principle of Piłsudski's equal-balance policy was Poland's identical treatment of Germany and the Soviet Union, a sort of armed neutrality between the two, with equal understanding and equal distance. In line with with its neutralist balance-of-power bilateralism, on January 26, 1934 Poland signed a nonaggression declaration with Hitler's Germany valid for ten years, and in March the two states made an agreement to terminate the tariff war that had begun in 1925. During the German charm offensive that followed, several topmost Nazi officials visited Poland, among them Hermann Göring, Josef Göbbels, Hans Frank, and Heinrich Himmler. They were there not just to hunt wild boar in the Białowieża forest or shoot craps with Sławoj Składkowski, but to lobby (unsuccessfully) for the Anticomintern Pact. The Polish position on this was consistent throughout and included rejection of invitations to join regional, multilateral pacts in which the Soviet Union was included, such as the Eastern Pact, described as an "eastern Locarno."

On July 25, 1932, Poland and the Soviet Union entered into a nonaggression pact, valid for three years, which in addition to the usual renunciation of resort to force to settle prickly problems bound both countries to remain impartial in the event one of them was assaulted by a third party. In May 1934 the validity of the document was extended to December 31, 1945, and, to make clear that all was well and good, reaffirmed in November 1938. But then, in compliance with another agreement concluded with Hitler in August 1939, the Soviet Union invaded Poland on September 17, 1939, and at the end of 1945 still held onto all it had earlier taken from Poland—this time with the approval of the Western powers. "Paper," Stalin once said, "will put up with anything written on it."

By the end of 1937, the season of smiles was finished, and Germany's *Drang nach Osten* (penetration of the east) shifted into high gear. Darkness set in on Europe. Disarmed by paper-thin promises of nonaggression and disoriented by unmet assurances of peace and goodwill, the West was not ready. Neither was Poland. Germany was.

Notes

1.   Zefla married Stefan Święcicki, a geodesic engineer. They lived in Poznań until the 1960s when—following her husband's death—Zefla moved to Warsaw to stay with her daughter Danusia. Zefla's son Jurek was a medical doctor in one of Warsaw's hospitals. She died in Warsaw in 1973.

2.   Kazimierz Bartel was a geometrician. Born in Lwów in 1882, he served in the Austrian army during World War I. In 1919, he defended Lwów from the Ukrainians as commander of Polish railroad troops. In 1919–20 he was minister of railroads. Elected to the national seym in 1922, he served as a representative until 1929. He abandoned the left-wing *Wyzwolenie* Party in 1925 and, with several other parliamentarians, formed a new Labor Party. In Piłsudski's first government he served as vice premier, and as premier five times thereafter, until 1930, when he left politics and returned to academic work. He became president of Lwów Polytechnic. From 1930 to 1932 he was chairman of the Polish Mathematical Society, and from 1938 until the outbreak of World War II, he was a senator of the republic.

3.   Andrzej Garlicki. "Wybrać jak trzeba" ("Elect as required"). *Polityka*, nr. 36, September 8, 2007, 75–78.

4.   The encirclement of the Red army was Piłsudski's idea, well carried out by Rydz-Śmigły and others. Polish cryptographers had broken the Soviet codes and were able to block Tukhachevsky's radio orders to his units. Cryptography was well advanced in Poland due partly to the high level of mathematical logic research in Warsaw and Lwów.

5.   'Litwo! Ojczyzno moja!' First line of the first stanza of Adam Mickiewicz's masterly poem "Pan Tadeusz" (1833–34).

6.   The core of the Geneva Protocol was immediate aid by all members of the League of Nations to any member that was attacked. British opposition scuttled the project.

7.   United Kingdom, Office of Foreign & Commonwealth Affairs. "Locarno in Diplomacy." http://www.fco.gov.uk/servlet/Front?pagename=OpenMarket/Xcelerate/ShowPage&c=Pag

INTERWAR POLAND

1921–September 1939

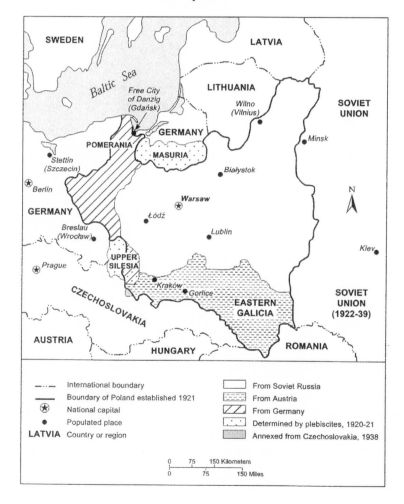

Legend:

- – ·· – International boundary
- ——— Boundary of Poland established 1921
- National capital
- • Populated place
- **LATVIA** Country or region

- From Soviet Russia
- From Austria
- From Germany
- Determined by plebiscites, 1920-21
- Annexed from Czechoslovakia, 1938

0 75 150 Kilometers
0 75 150 Miles

Last Years
In Silesia

On June 20, 1922, in Katowice, the military bands stopped playing, gabby officials ended their inspirational speeches, the streets were cleared of flags and richly decorated triumphal arches, the Te Deum was sung at the High Mass of thanksgiving, and the altar erected for the occasion on the market square in front of the Polish Theater was removed. At this time, the task of smoothly and efficiently incorporating the geographically small but economically important Upper Silesian region should have been among the higher priorities of reborn Poland. Officials certainly intended to incorporate Silesia, despite political discord among the parties and the executive, if only because the newly acquired, heavily industrial, natural resource–abundant region was generating close to three quarters of the country's national income. Of course, good intentions are one thing, but the realization of that goal was another—and not always because of premeditated ill will. Sometimes it is a question of luck, good and bad. More often, the obstacles to good intentions are predictable, embedded in restrictions imposed on policymakers by international conventions and other legal instruments that raise delicate and complex questions of congruity between, say, civil rights and national security. One such was the Versailles- and plebiscite-related condition embodied in the constitutional seym's statute of July 15, 1920, that granted Silesia broad autonomy within the borders of the Polish Republic, which included having its own legislative body and an executive, as well as endowing the provincial council with a bunch of competencies exclusive of international relations, national defense, the judiciary, and tariff policy. The underlying idea was to assuage the fears of sizeable and nervous German minorities in several plebiscite counties by pledging respect for the tradition of local self-government in the province, even though under the former Prussian militarism the local self-government tradition was somewhat less than advertised. The autonomy did not prevent skirmishes before and became a battleground after Piłsudski's May 1926 coup d'état. Piłsudski himself visited Silesia only once during the lifetime of the Republic, in August 1922, to award decorations to former insurgents and others who had worked, as he put it, "on the Silesian question." Inevitably, hardcore Silesians interpreted this as lack of concern and dwelt on his reputation among critics as a freethinker, a neosocialist centralizer, and a "man of Wilno" always gazing east

With the celebrations over, the three Przybyła brothers, Jan, Wiktor, and Józef, all now in Katowice, rolled up their sleeves and went to work: the first two in the regional state sector (building local institutions), and Józek in private business (supplying wood to build houses). Their sister Zefla Święcicka settled in Poznań, raised her two children (a son, Jurek, and a daughter, Danusia). It was a comparatively and superficially calm and routine period—testing, often tense, but productive and satisfying, a pioneering exploration of uncharted nation- and culture-building in the wake of tectonic shifts brought about by World War I and its aftershocks.

Following the May 1926 coup, Poland's early attempts at parliamentary democracy were trimmed not without resistance. The political structure became authoritarian and the influence of the military increased, but nothing like what happened in totalitarian Russia under Lenin and Stalin, and was to to be done in Germany under Hitler. However, from now on one had to make an "as required," crystal clear decision about which side you were on, and do so openly and publicly, particularly if you were already part of, or wanted to be (and stay) in, a government service that represented a significant share of total white-collar employment. For those who had fought in their youth to liberate their country from the degrading yoke of occupation—and not just around negotiating tables—it was important, now that they had reached middle age, to solidify the republic's construction without delay rather than engage in factional hairsplitting about how best to do it. Hence the decision to get along with the regime was often made on mixed grounds under conditions of few alternatives. The opposite end of this situation was the danger of opportunism, careerism, cliquishness, waste of scarce professional talent, creeping authoritarianism, and having the wrong professions in the wrong positions—in Poland's instance, a surfeit of colonels.

The May 1926 coup officially arrived in Katowice on September 3 when Mieczysław Bilski, governor of Silesia since May 1924, was fired. During the coup he had resolutely supported the government of Prime Minister Wincenty Witos and, by the same token, had opposed Marshal Piłsudski. Three days after Bilski's recall, Michał Grażynski, a Piłsudski supporter of long standing and a left-wing *Sanacja* man, replaced him as the province's fifth governor since June 1922. He remained in that job for thirteen years, until the German invasion in September 1939, and ruled with a steady, sometimes iron hand.

Jan, together with many of his Els colleagues and plebiscite co-workers, former Silesian insurrectionists, and founders of the Polish Scouting Organization (ZHP), opted without hesitation for Piłsudski's programmatic model and the *Sanacja* movement. Temperamentally making clear-cut decisions when in his judgment it was time for action was not new to Jan. For all its imperfections, this being still a democracy of sorts, others chose to join opposition parties. Rifts long in the making never really healed. What formerly had been lively, sometimes harsh, disagreements among acquaintances, friends, colleagues, and family members turned into a tribal cold war that even in foreign exile was waged for years after Poland had been wiped off the map.

Early in 1923, Jan took part in the formation of the Silesian Insurgents Association (ZPŚ) founded by Alfons Zgrzebniok, commander of the First Silesian Uprising of 1919. Its membership consisted of veterans of the 1919, 1920, and 1921 Silesian uprisings. It soon became an influential organization in the politics of the province, and in the hands of Grażyński—its honorary chairman and "spiritual leader," as he was referred to by some members—it was a weapon in the governor's struggle with the opposition, specifically in his take-no-prisoners vendetta with Wojciech Korfanty, who since 1924 owned and edited in Katowice a Christian Democrat–oriented daily *Polonia* (Poland), as well as *Rzeczpospolita* (Republic), a paper of nationwide circulation bought from Paderewski. Both men were partial to being praised and deeply resented criticism. Before the takeover by Grażyński of the voivedship's top office, Korfanty was widely regarded as the uncrowned king of Upper Silesia whose word counted in the staffing ("stuffing," his opponents claimed) of the administrative apparatus with people, mainly Christian Democrats, who shared his views. In February 1925, the administrative board of the ZPŚ in Katowice began publishing a daily newspaper, *Polska Zachodnia* (Western Poland), with Jan Przybyła as managing editor. In early December 1926, he was replaced by Edward Rumun, a friend from the days of their work in the press department of the Polish Plebiscite Commission in Bytom, but Jan continued to contribute to and exert influence on the paper's editorial policy in the subsequent years. In 1927 he joined the Union of Journalists of Silesia and the Dąbrowa Coal Basin (SDŚiZD).

On May 21, 1926 in his capacity as first vice-chairman of the Association of Silesian Insurrectionists (ZPŚ) and together with other members of the governing board, Jan signed a declaration in favor of *Sanacja*'s program for the Polish state. In essence the program approved the changes to the constitutional structure of the Polish state envisaged by Piłsudski. These amendments, passed by parliament on August 2, 1926, strengthened the powers of the executive branch of government at the expense of the legislature. The three major changes were: (1) the president of the republic was given the power to dissolve both parliamentary chambers (the seym and senate) before their prescribed term, at the request of the council of ministers (cabinet), while concurrently the right of the seym to dissolve itself on its own initiative was rescinded; (2) with approval of the seym, the president could issue decrees having the force of law; (3) the executive was given the power to pass the national budget in the event the seym was unable to do so.

The very day the ZPŚ Governing Board passed its resolution, a group of center and right-of-center ZPŚ members, most of them Korfanty supporters, were rankled by what they regarded as the organization's too leftward a course and, even worse, its unacceptable and overt political sponsorship by Grażynski. The group seceded and formed the governing board of a separate and compet-

ing body, the National Association of Silesian Insurrectionists and
Former Soldiers (NZPBŻ), and appointed Korfanty as chairman.
Sadly, the die was cast. Running on the ZPŚ ticket in the municipal
elections six months later, Jan was elected municipal councilor of
Katowice, a city in which 57 percent of the votes went to candidates of a combative German minority People's Party (*Volksbund*),
perhaps because of the Grażynski-Korfanty rift on the Polish side.

A word of explanation is in order. What was it that estranged,
often for a lifetime, families, friends, neighbors, colleagues, former
comrades-in-arms, and fellow citizens, increasingly poisoning their
relationships as time went by? It certainly wasn't lack of patriotism, even though the attitude and behavior of those branded
was often perceived as being not far from treason. Nor was it a
dearth of national consciousness, in its best sense of belonging to a
large group of compatriots who shared, not without bellyaching, a
common history and culture, and preserved that feeling of oneness
even when their nearer homeland was separated from the mother
country against their will.

In Silesia the division was personified by Wincenty Korfanty and
Michał Grażynski (the stand-in for Piłsudski) in their acrimonious,
personal, and political struggle, which was unresolved and unrec-
onciled to the bitter end. They both came from families of modest
means. Korfanty, born in 1873, was the son of a Silesian coalminer;
Grażynski, seventeen years younger, was a teacher's son in Gdów,
Galicia, by the name of Kurzydło (which in Polish is unappealing to
the eye and ear and was changed, apparently at the insistence of his
mother, to one of literary renown and more mellifluous tonality).[1]
Both men were well educated. In 1895–1901, Korfanty studied philosophy, law, and economics (*Staatswirtschaft*, state economy) at the
Technical University in Charlottenburg (Berlin) and at the University of Breslau (Wrocław) under the internationally-recognized
sociologist, historian, and political economist Werner Sombart.
Grażyński earned two doctorates from the Jagiellonian University in Cracow, one in philosophy (1913), the other of law (early
1920s).

They both had extensive experience in politics and upper-
level state administration under trying conditions that tested their
executive and, for Korfanty, legislative proficiency. Before World

War I, Korfanty, a German citizen, had been elected to the German Reichstag as representative of Polish national minority, and to the Prussian legislative provincial assembly (*Landstag*). In both of these he tried to combine firmness on national principles with a measure of conciliation, compromise, and networking, appearing to some to meander in search of proper timing and the golden mean. In November 1918, the day after the Armistice, he became part of the executive commission of the Polish Supreme People's Council in Poznań. On February 8, 1919, during the prime ministership of Ignacy Paderewski, he was appointed by decree of the chief of state, Józef Piłsudski, to the legislative assembly in Warsaw, which passed the temporary Constitution of the Second Polish Republic (Korfanty delivered the first speech of the event). In January 1920 Korfanty was designated by the government then under centrist prime minister Leopold Skulski the successor of Paderewski to head the Polish Plebiscite Commission in Upper Silesia.[2] We know that Korfanty stepped down from headship of the plebiscite office on the night of May 2/3, 1921, when the Third Silesian Insurrection began. There is disagreement on whether his resignation was voluntary or whether it came under pressure from the central government in Warsaw; it was probably both. Regardless, he concurrently appointed himself absolute leader of the uprising—"dictator" was the word bandied about. In point of fact, this meant putting his signature, albeit hesitantly, on a document that sanctioned the insurrection; he also had to keep as much control as possible over the insurgency's political development, specifically to prevent its takeover by "undesirable elements," hotheads included. Actual warfare was in other hands, among them those of the chief of staff of Combat Group East, by the name of Borelowski, an officer of the Silesian POW, otherwise known as Grażynski, a volunteer from Nether Poland (*Małopolska*) of all places: the "backward" Galicia where they still had goat trails for roads.[3] He had the reputation of cutting knotty political entanglements with military tools, which involved not just getting rid of the problematic knot but offending people, including innocent bystanders, in the process.

As mentioned in chapter two, the POW of Upper Silesia was formally dissolved under the Polish-German Agreement after the Second Silesian Uprising and was replaced by the Head Office of

Physical Education (CWF), which recommended a healthy lifestyle and fitness through plenty of exercise. The CWF was lodged in the Hotel Lomnitz in Bytom, and its real purpose was to protect people on the Polish side engaged in preparing the plebiscite, as well as their rallies, outposts, and voting places, from German guerrilla hit squads belonging to the *Kampforganisation Oberschlesien* (Combat Organization of Upper Silesia). The highest organ of the CWF, which was subordinated to the Polish Plebiscite Commission headed by Korfanty, was composed of POW officers whose chief of staff was Captain Alfons Grzebniok, the leader of the first and second Silesian insurrections. The deputy chief of staff of this so-called physical fitness outfit was Captain Michał Grażynski.

Not getting the support they believed they needed from the Warsaw government to equip, train, reorganize, and modernize the Polish underground army in Silesia, the leadership of the CWF issued an emotive memorandum and in January 1921 joined an organization formed only a few weeks before that was originally devoted, in name only, to promoting industry and construction but that reinvented itself in 1921 as the Command of Plebiscite Defense (DOP). To placate the Interallied Governmental and Plebiscite Commission, the DOP was set up across the border from the plebiscite area in Sosnowiec. It had close ties with the commanders of two Polish military regions (Poznań and Cracow) that, despite the Warsaw government's reluctance to foment the Silesian situation and risk losing what minimal goodwill Poland could count on with the British, were sharing intelligence and under-the-table arms and ammunition with the DOP. The head of the organization's six geographical inspectorates and future battle groups was Karol Grzesik, who had also been the Polish representative to the joint police established after the Second Silesian Uprising.

When the Third Silesian Uprising began (May 2 /3, 1921), the DOP became the Supreme Command of the Insurgent Army (NCIA) in Szopienice, a suburb of Katowice, where it remained until July 5, 1921. Of interest here is the composition and strategic placement at the beginning of the crucial Third Uprising of the pieces on the political-military chessboard, because there was always the possibility that in trying to checkmate their enemy, the insurrectionists might disagree on how best to do it and perhaps would even be tempted to knock some of their own side's pawns off the board. It looked like this: Korfanty, head of the supreme council for Upper Silesia, in charge of civilian affairs, to which the Supreme Command of the Insurgent Army (under Colonel Maciej Mełżyński) was formally subordinate; Grzesik, commander-in chief of Combat Group East; Grażyński his chief of staff; Jan Przybyła, head of the Supreme Command's press media and editor-in-chief of *Powstaniec*, for a time the press organ of Combat Group East and now of the Supreme Command of the Insurgent Army; and Wolny, a Christian Democrat activist, long-time friend of Korfanty, coauthor of the 1920 draft statute on Silesian autonomy, and the man who, according to rumors, in the early hours of May 3, 1921, dispelled Korfanty's second thoughts about signing the order authorizing the insurrection. Standing by was an interfering but not particularly successful kibitzer, the Communist Party of Upper Silesia, which tried to turn Korfanty's nationalist call for a general strike on May 2, 1921, into an anticapitalist class war. They incited Silesian factory workers and miners, most of them Catholic, to keep striking and take over their workplaces by force in the name of Leninist, revolutionary, internationalist, proletarian solidarity, irrespective of the nationality of the owners—in short, they wanted to plunge the nationalist insurrection into anarchy. On May 4 and 8, 1921, the Communist Party held two congresses of "work councils," the Bolshevik euphemism for industrial collectives. Those who went along, many out of material desperation, were treated harshly by both sides to the conflict.

Under continued pressure from the central government of Prime Minister Wincenty Witos not to stretch the patience of the British and Italian representatives on the Interallied Plebiscite Commission and higher up, Korfanty was anxious to put an end to the uprising at an early but appropriate time—that is, when things were going well for the insurgents. This was the case in the first week of the uprising. On May 7, he met with French General Henri Le Rond, head of the Interallied Commission. Two days later they arrived at an agreement specifying the status quo, at that time favorable for Poland, as being the demarcation line for the cessation of hostilities. On May 10, Korfanty issued a manifesto declaring that the insurgency had accomplished its ends and fulfilled the aspirations of the Silesian people.

But as they say, it takes two to tango. The German government flatly rejected the invitation and looked the other way as military reinforcements in guns, munitions, and *Oberländische Lederhosen* (Upper Bavarian leather pants) poured into Silesia while the leadership and strategy of German armed forces on the spot was being reorganized with a view to spirited counterattacks. These were launched on May 21 and resulted in the retaking by the Germans of the strategically important Mount St. Anna, but they subsequently failed to break through the new Polish defense lines. Torrents of snobby vituperation directed at Poland and the Silesian uprising came from Britain. On the Polish side, Korfanty's manifesto caused confusion and undermined discipline in the ranks of the insurgents, including in one instance a mutiny in a battalion from the Tarnowkie Góry region, a Christian Democrat stronghold and an area that included Korfanty's birthplace, Siemianowice. The reason for the mutiny was that the battalion had not been satisfactorily led and had suffered heavy combat losses. However, one unintended consequence of Korfanty's declaration was the exodus of some insurgents and volunteers from outside Silesia, including from Greater Poland (the area around Poznań and Gniezno), who took the manifesto literally, packed up their belongings, and headed for home. As a matter of fact, the most intensive and bloody fighting of the insurrection took place after Korfanty's victory declaration, from May 21 to June 6, during what is now called by historians the second phase of the Third Silesian Uprising, when much of the territory earlier occupied but not yet fully consolidated by the insurgents was lost.

But that was not all. In the first week of June 1921, the more unbending, fight-to-the-end officers in Combat Group East, led by the group's chief of staff Borelowski-Grażyński, decided to give the putsch to Korfanty because they were convinced Korfanty was too vacillating, skeptical, shilly-shallying, accommodating, and prone to search for an elusive quietus. and the officers therefore compelled him to nominate Karol Grzesik, the supreme commander of the Insurgent Army (SCIA) in place of Maciej Mełżyński, who was just then being recalled to Warsaw. For whatever reasons, the intrigue never got off the ground, and on June 6, a new commander, Lieutenant Colonel Kazimierz Warwa-Zenkteler, got the job, heralding the third noncombat phase of the uprising (June 6–July 5, 1921). The phase consisted mostly of negotiations intended to put an end to the fighting, create a neutral zone occupied by allied troops separating the two opponents, and craft an agreement on a complete withdrawal of both German and Polish armies from Upper Silesia. This undertaking would have been a plateful were it not for the exhaustion of both sides to the conflict, especially in Weimar and Warsaw, where those in charge of their respective countries had other fish to fry. The Poles accepted this solution on June 11, the Germans on June 25. Even if it fizzled, the attempted Combat Group East putsch had injected at an early date a toxic ingredient into the long-term relationship of two ambitious personalities. Grażyński never forgave Korfanty for allegedly threatening him with arrest and a firing squad if the rebellion were not put down at once. Sometime later, when Korfanty extended his hand to him, Grażyński refused to take it. In a symbolic sense, the first blow of battle had been struck.

The break, which at first was personal and regional, with overtones of something much larger, spilled over dramatically to the national scene in 1922, the year Upper Silesia became a province within the Polish state. The political aspirations of the adversaries were never exclusively local. Both men fervently and genuinely desired to see Silesia reunited with Poland, using armed force if necessary, but for Korfanty only as a last resort. Whether by birth or adoption, their affection for and identification with the province were not feigned. At loggerheads all the way, it was not tactical opportunism for each of them to use Silesia as a stepping stone to nationwide political power, but a fall from this slippery stone was as good as fatal for the unwary climber.

In contrast, Jan Przybyła's political horizons were, by his own choice, circumscribed by the geographical frontiers approved by the entente's council of ambassadors on October 20, 1921, even though he remained emotionally committed to the land of his forebears (Sierakowice, Zabrze), which were on the "wrong" side of the border. As head of the Silesian branch of the Polish Telegraph Agency in Korfanty's Polish Plebiscite Commission, he kept Warsaw informed of the fast-changing situation in Silesia before and during the Second Uprising, refuting the factual inaccuracies spread by the German press about the alleged fall of Warsaw to the Bolshevik armies on August 17, 1920. He was involved in the preparation and analysis of data for Korfanty's presentation at an international conference in Spa of a Polish White Paper that charged the German government with tolerating terrorism committed by freebooters and demoralized soldiery against the Polish population before, and especially after, the collapse of the First Silesian Uprising. As head of the press department of the Supreme Command of the Insurgent Army, he excoriated on the pages of *Powstaniec* the indifferent attitude of the Warsaw post-plebiscite Witos government to the measly allocation of Silesian territory to Poland. Jan never seemed to have intended to translate his past involvement in national politics into a national-level career.

A little more than a year after the miscarried putsch, in July 1922, Korfanty accepted the invitation of the Christian Democratic and National Democratic parties (the right-of-center and right-wing parties in the seym, respectively) to run for the office of prime minister of the republic. Within a few days he was elected to that office by majority vote of the legitimate seym commission, albeit against the opposition of the Polish Socialist Party (PPS), which in protest called for a general strike. At this point Chief of State Józef Piłsudski expressed his opposition to the seym commission's choice, giving his reason with Hemingwayesque brevity: "There will be no Korfanty cabinet." By the end of the month, the commission withdrew its earlier designation of Korfanty for premiership, and the chief of state appointed a person of his choice to be premier, who lasted about four months. For Korfanty, the hope for a national political career began to evanesce, and the downslide began. There was one little bump on the way down. As the leader of the various carousel governments of those days, Witos was back on the rotating conveyor belt in May 1923. His second choice for vice premier and minister without portfolio (on October 27) was Korfanty, and for foreign affairs he chose Dmowski. That combination was out—Witos included—after a month and a half. The day the government fell (December 14, 1923), Korfanty went back to Silesia. However, he retained his post of Christian Democratic delegate to the national seym (1922–1930) and the Silesian seym (1922–35), which gave him legislative immunity from prosecution.

Over the next few years, Korfanty concentrated on journalism to propagate the Christian Democratic agenda, founding *Polonia* in Katowice, acquiring Paderewski's equity in *Rzeczpospolita* in Warsaw, and later becoming a partner with Jan Teska, the founder of the Pomeranian daily *Dziennik Bydgoski*. The *Rzeczpospolita* purchase in 1924 for allegedly fifty thousand dollars (a large sum for its time) raised eyebrows in the Piłsudski camp, who were curious about where all that money came from. The transaction disconcerted the co-owner of the paper, Stanisław Stroński, a prominent National Democrat, seym deputy, and vociferous opponent of the chief of state and of Piłsudski's candidate for the first president of the republic, Gabriel Narutowicz. He apparently knew nothing about the sale, was unhappy about the finagling that he thought was going on, and was concerned by what he suspected would be an ideologically diluted future for the paper once the National Democratic hand was no longer on the tiller. Stroński and the whole editorial board resigned, and subscriptions declined. It should be added in all fairness that allegations of financial impropriety in Poland and other central European countries at that time, while often not wrong, should be taken with a grain of salt; allegations were frequently motivated by a desire to destroy political opponents. The twisted logic that a person who made a bundle in the market *must* have done it by dishonest means was, and remains, part of the social psyche of a good many countries, big and small.

Shortly after Korfanty had completed building his journalistic fortifications from which he launched every day a barrage of vitriolic criticism at Piłsudski's positions, his nemesis, Grażyński, quietly slipped into Katowice to take up the governorship of Silesia on September 3, 1926. After the insurrection Grażyński had moved to Cracow to bone up for his doctorate in law, and he worked for military intelligence on matters affecting treatment of the Polish minority in the Opole region, a delicate assignment that involved traveling under imaginary names in Germany, where he was not exactly welcome. In 1924 Grażyński was a department head at the Ministry of Agricultural Reform during the premiership of economist Władysław Grabski, who created the independent Polish central bank in 1920 and who in 1924 was instrumental in the currency reformation that curbed the hyperinflation devastating the nation's economy. On returning to Katowice, Grażyński's moves were covered, his rear well protected by Warsaw on the principle that, for all the misadventures, this was still pretty much Korfanty's chessboard, and because in these iconic atmospherics Grażyński did not expect to be welcomed with an extended hand, but more likely with the tip of the foot. His quantum bounce up to the powerful position of governor of Poland's richest province was not accidental given his vitae, connections, the changed balance of power in Warsaw after the May 1926 coup, and the constitutional corrections made a month before his arrival. Through the intermediary of the Association of Silesian Insurgents (ZPŚ), he became a cofounder with other like-minded groupings of the Association for Improvement of the Republic (ZNR), an attempt to round out Piłsudski's personal appeal to a very sizeable segment of the population with a coherent *Sanacja*-oriented political philosophy and policy platform—a coming-together of concerned citizens, as one might call them today, crossing party lines in the national but not ultranationalist (à la the National Democracy) interest. In the seym election year 1928, the ZNR became part of Sławek's Nonparty Bloc of Cooperation with the Government (BBWR). After the results came in, the power balance in the capital shifted more in Grażyński's favor.

In the meantime, with a view to impeachment, Korfanty was charged with cozying up to German big business, as well as financial misconduct. The first had to do with Korfanty's trying to reduce taxes on Silesian heavy industry, most of which was owned by German capital, allegedly in order to keep the plants and the jobs they provided for Polish workers expanding rather than fleeing to Timbuktu. The second was about funds provided by the Upper Silesian mining and steel employers' federation, which the indictment alleged were transfused into *Polonia*'s bloodstream. The case was heard before the seym court, which in November 1927 returned a misty verdict. It censured Korfanty for acting in a manner inconsistent with the dignity and professionalism of a member of parliament and a journalist, but it stopped short of impeachment, providing ample material for doubt and idle speculation. Korfanty lost a measure of credibility and support among his followers and those sympathetically inclined toward him. As always happens in situations where the line between prosecution and persecution is blurred, even were it proved beyond a reasonable doubt that the charges had been unfounded, the accused can never fully get back his good name, for in the popular mind a question mark remains.

Toward the end of August 1930, after four more governments led by *Sanacja* premiers (Bartel, Świtalski, Bartel again, and Sławek); in face of Centerleft's June 1930 threat, which was made in Cracow during a Congress for the Defense of Law and People's Freedom to paralyze the system by recurrent mass demonstrations; and due to the world depression affecting the economy, President Ignacy Mościcki used the competency accorded him by the August 2, 1926, constitutional amendments to accept the resignation of the Sławek cabinet, dissolve both chambers of parliament two years before the expiry of their tenure, and select a new premier to clean up the mess the best way he knew how.

It came as no surprise that he picked Marshal Piłsudski. First off, Wincenty Witos and several other former opposition delegates, no longer covered by parliamentary immunity, were arrested (night of September 9/10, 1930) by simple fiat, without court warrants, and sent to the Brześć military penitentiary to be interrogated in preventive detention. About two weeks later, the second Silesian Autonomous Seym was also dissolved, with its former member Korfanty arrested and sent to join his colleagues in the bogs of Brześć. On this particular interpretation of constitutional law, they were now no longer special individuals but ordinary Wincentys, Wojciechs, and other plebeians who should have known instinctively how to behave themselves in the interest of national strength and stability, instead of raising Cain. Having cleared the decks, with the mutineers safely under lock and Sławoj Składkowski's key in the marshy wilderness of Brześć, new elections to the national parliament and the Silesian Autonomous Seym could be held, and so they were in November 1930. The BBWR came up with gratifying results in both houses: 149 seats out of 444 for the seym, and 75 seats out of 111 in the senate—but without plaudits for electoral fairness, even from those who shared the disquiet about the parliamentary three-ringed circus. The BBWR was dissolved by its founder, Walery Sławek, five years later.

Contrary to the best-laid plans, Korfanty was reelected to the

Silesian seym on November 23, 1930. Once more shielded by parliamentary immunity, he was released a few days later from prison as law required, and in 1931 he was elected chairman of the National Christian Democratic Union. The third Silesian seym was inaugurated on December 9, 1930, by Governor Grażyński. Konstanty Wolny was reelected as speaker.

On December 4, 1930, Piłsudski resigned for serious health reasons, handing over his office to Walery Sławek, but not before he had referred the case of the eleven leading personages of the Centerleft opposition to the Warsaw District Court for trial by a panel of three judges. The proceedings, known as the "Brześć trial," opened on December 26, 1930. At the end of November, the ten remaining accused had been released on bail from their preventive detention for the duration of the trial and were free to hire defense attorneys of their choice. In summary, they were charged with plotting and taking steps to unseat the government, but not the republican state system, by force—something like what Piłsudski had done a few years back. They came close but failed. Ultimately, they got on the marshal's nerves and unbuckled his dangerous temper. The verdict was read on January 13, 1932. All but one of the accused were found guilty as charged. The sentence: one and a half to three years of incarceration plus court costs and financial fines. Witos got one and a half years. The verdict was not unanimous, however. In his dissenting vote, one judge argued that the activities of the accused did not constitute a criminal offense under the law and asked that the case be dismissed. The verdict was sustained on appeal and confirmed by the supreme court. Of the ten sentenced, five actually served their terms. The others left the country: two, including Witos, for Czechoslovakia; the others for France, pursued by prosecutorial orders of arrest on sight. All were amnestied on October 31, 1939, by the first Polish president in exile, Władysław Raczkiewicz, after the destruction of the Second Polish Republic by Nazi Germany and Soviet Russia.

While Korfanty was in prison (about two months, from late September to late November 1930), his daily *Polonia* in Katowice kept up its wholesale attacks against *Sanacja* and ad hominem assaults on Piłsudski, most of which fell to the sensor's eraser. However, his photograph with accompanying eulogies was prominently displayed in each issue. On his return, besides serving in the national and Silesian parliaments, he continued editing the paper and sparring with *Polska Zachodnia* (Western Poland). Year by year he witnessed the decline of his paper, and after June 1935, he watched the dismemberment of his party from afar, despite the Party's efforts to save itself through merger and implants in 1937. Anticipating arrest in the event of another loss of parliamentary privileges, he emigrated to Czechoslovakia in June 1935, about three weeks after the death of Piłsudski. From abroad, together with other exiles, he carried on resistance to the regime's domestic and foreign policies, editing *Polonia* from a distance but by and by losing touch with the pulse and zeitgeist of his land and the readers of his paper. From 1936 to 1938 he helped organize a political lobby of compatriots living abroad—exiles and emigrés, including Ignacy Paderewski and Wincenty Witos. It became known as Front Morges, from the name of the Swiss town on Lake Léman near Lausanne, where the group met in Paderewski's villa and drew up alternative concepts for post-Piłsudski Poland. He moved to France in March 1939 when Germany took over what remained of Czechoslovakia. The French were willing enough to give people refuge so they could immerse themselves in French culture, but they drew the line on having the refugees run around their country stirring up political trouble for the government's foreign policy. On April 28, 1939, Korfanty returned to Katowice, was arrested the next day, and was sent to prison in Warsaw. Released for health reasons on July 20, he died on August 17, two weeks before the German invasion of Poland. His funeral in Katowice was attended by a large number of admirers.

The Constitutional Act of July 15, 1920, granted broad legal powers to the single-chamber Silesian seym in areas such as the official language (Polish, German, or both) to be used in legislative, administrative, and judiciary proceedings; the extent of the autonomy exercised by local governments (cities, counties, districts, or *gminy*); police; control over construction, education, and religious affairs (except matters falling within the purview of the concordat concluded with the Vatican); relief of poverty; and local public works and transport. The seym was entitled to levy regional taxes and public charges, borrow money, and pass its own budget. It also had a treasury, about one tenth of whose revenues was transferred to the central government. The president of the republic could dissolve the seym during its statutory session, but not before it had passed its budget for the next fiscal year and he was required to order the holding of new elections within seventy-five days of the dissolution. The problem, of course, was to implement all this to the satisfaction of all concerned through some sort of compromise or consensus with little help from historical precedent and in an environment where everything was challenged at every step by various political groups, by people in the street, by the press, by municipal and regional councils, and even on the floor of the seym itself by ill-disposed foes venting national animosities. There were also increasingly troubled relations between the legislature and the executive. This was allegedly democracy, except for the national / linguistic / upbringing question that inserted itself with persistence in a scarred borderland to bedevil the best intentions, which were few and far between in these feverish times.

On September 14, 1922, the first Silesian seym, elected by 74 percent of those eligible to vote, consisted of forty-eight deputies; under the system of proportional representation, thirty-four of them were Polish, and fourteen represented the German minority. This seym lasted until February 12, 1929, when it was dissolved by the president. It passed over three hundred laws and resolutions, including three hotly debated ones: Polish became the official language of Upper Silesia's government; the złoty became the legal tender of the province; and Silesian residents were subject to Poland's military draft. The question of Polonization—vexed from the beginning, as evidenced by the raucous debates about official language—became more incensed after September 6, 1926, the day Governor Grażyński arrived on the scene, especially in matters of schooling, budgetary allocations, and the division of prerogatives between the legislature and the executive. The apparent inability of the legislators to stop talking and actually address the growing industrial unemployment led President Mościcki to shut down the seym on February 12, 1929. Questions were raised about the constitutionality of that step.

After a long abeyance, the results of the second seym election on May 11, 1930, were sobering for the Poles who had fought as much among themselves as against the German candidates during the election campaign. The Germans united in a single association, the right-wing German Electoral Union (DWG), and with about one third of the votes, won fifteen of the forty-eight seats, more than any single Polish party. Korfanty's Catholic People's Bloc (KBL) got thirteen seats. *Sanacja*'s newly born National-Christian Union of Labor (NChZP) picked up ten. The turnout of those eligible to vote was 91 percent. The Germans promptly claimed that this election, like an earlier municipal one (November 1926, in which the German list had come away with 41 percent of the votes), was a more accurate indicator of the Silesian people's will than the original plebiscite of 1921. They also argued it was a reflection on the inept policies not only of the *Sanacja* but of the Polish state as a whole.

The NChZP was a regional Upper Silesian organization, the product of a meeting held by eighty political figures in Katowice in September 1928. It was modeled on Walery Sławek's nationwide Nonparty Bloc of Cooperation with the Government (BBWR) and had an almost identical purpose: to propagate and bring into being Piłsudski's vision of a strong, independent, and prosperous country that was able to solve the problems confronting it with patriotic unanimity, an authoritative (some would say authoritarian) administration, and a minimum of parliamentary wrangling. Jan Przybyła was elected to the organization's three-person control commission. On February 28, 1930, in advance of parliamentary elections scheduled for later that year, the council of the NChZP passed several resolutions clarifying the organization's leadership position on the economic, social, and political challenges facing Polish Silesia and the systemic reforms proposed by *Sanacja* that the nation needed. Jan was one of the sixty-one councilors who signed the document. This came as no surprise, for already early in November 1927 he had been active on behalf of a BBWR regional group in preparing the March 1928 national electoral campaign in Silesia.

Korfanty presided over the first meeting of the second Silesian seym, on May 27, 1930. The seym elected the regional executive council and discussed measures to be taken to alleviate the plight of the unemployed.[4] It also wrestled Governor Grażyński to a standstill about the budget. After seven meetings and thirty-five days, the second session of the Silesian seym was closed by the president on the very day (July 1, 1930) the debate on the budget was scheduled to resume. Resuscitated on September 10, it met three more times only to be shut down on September 25, 1930.

Jan's brother, Wiktor, had been elected to the second seym and, among others, served as the seym's secretary for the National Workers' Party (NPR), which had three seats in the assembly. Wiktor was also a municipal councilor of Katowice city in charge of the department of social welfare and had authority over its funds. The NPR emerged in 1920 from an amalgamation of two Polish parties that had been active in the formerly Prussian-ruled parts of Poland. After the 1926 coup, members favoring Piłsudski's program broke away and created a separate wing that came to be known first as NPR-Left and later (1932) as the National Labor Party (NSP); the original NPR became part of Centerleft and in 1937 merged with the Christian Democratic Party to form the opposition Labor Party run by Karol Popiel. It should be noted that in those days the designation "Left" referred primarily to a political party's positive, vaguely neo-Keynesian attitude to government activism in the country's economy; "National" referred to a party not being of a Marxist-Leninist, internationalist, class-warfare persuasion.

The November 1930 election for the third Silesian seym was held against the background of the Brześć arrests. Unlike the national contest, it was not so much another miracle of the voting booth (which in Grażyński's aspirations meant absolute majority for his camp) as a draw between the KBL of the Christian Democrats and *Sanacja's* NChZP, each of which won nineteen seats (including a KBL seat for Korfanty's wife). The PPS (Polish non-Marxist Socialists) got one seat, and the German minority parties picked up the remaining nine. As a result, Grażynski's top priority of Polonizing Silesia's government within the existing constitutional framework had to be achieved through imaginatively interpreted administrative instructions combined with legislative action in the seym by *Sanacja's* representatives (the NChZP) and its allies (the NPR-Left)—in other words, by unrelenting parliamentary struggle against both Polish (Christian Democratic, KBL) and German minority opposition parties. From 1933 on, the German parties were given new self-assurance and financial support by the Nazi regime next door. Grażyński's method of Polonization consisted of conservatively interpreting the autonomous status of Silesia. This was stubbornly resisted even in its milder, pre-1926 form of attempted cultural assimilation by most of the Germans who had stayed in Polish Silesia after the plebiscite because they had been confident that the law of nature would take care of Poland's seasonal sovereignty.

Germans would not become Polish in less than two decades anymore than Poles, over several centuries, would become German; and German Protestants would not convert to Catholicism anymore than Polish Catholics would turn Protestant. The separation of church and state, of religion and government, was seen as an alien concept thought up by heathens. It could be paid tribute, if necessary for the sake of international relations, but in actual practice, it was honored mostly in the breach. Those were the days in another age, before supranational and secular ideas of accommodation took root in European soil.

There was in those days a German politician in Silesia, now almost forgotten, who tried to bridge the national and religious chasm of animosity and prejudice. His name was Eduard Pant. Born in 1887 in a farming family of Austrian Silesia near the vicinity of Moravska Ostrava (then *Mährisch Ostrau*), he studied philology and German language and literature at Prague University; taught in various German-speaking schools in Prague, Linz, Vienna, and Bielsko (then *Bielitz*); and obtained a doctorate in philosophy in 1913. During World War I he served in the Austrian army. With the war over, he returned to his teaching job at the Bielsko high school and remained there until 1930. Between 1920 and 1926 he was a city councilor of Bielsko, the deputy mayor, and a member of the German minority Catholic People's Party (KVP) in Silesia, the religious minority of a national minority later known as the German Catholic People's Party (DKVP) of which he became the chairman in 1927 after the death of its founder, a German Silesian named Thomas Szczeponik. Until 1930 he was the editor in chief of the party's press organ, *Oberschlesischer Kurier* (Upper Silesian Courier). In August 1933, to compete with other German minority parties either leaning toward Hitler's national socialism or unabashedly supporting Nazis and being generously financed by the German government, the DKVP changed its name to German-Christian People's Party (DChVP), the idea being that this would bring under its umbrella other German Christians, the Lutherans in particular, and thus form a united front of German moderates in Poland. At the inaugural session of the renamed organization in Katowice in January 1934, Pant advocated a policy of negotiations that would replace the ongoing confrontations with Polish authorities about minority rights and would, for reasons of the moral irreconcilability of Nazi Weltanschauung with Christian teaching, Catholic and Lutheran alike, bring about resolute opposition by the DChVP to the unfolding attempt by the Nazis to take over the German minority in Poland. In February 1934, Pant came out with a weekly *Der Deutsche in Polen* (The German in Poland, 1934–1939), which in its pages excoriated the Nazi system.

Despite reservations on the Polish side about hidden agendas, it would have seemed reasonable at first glance that the presence of a man like Pant at the head of a relatively important German-minority political party would bode well for at least a measure of conciliation between the adversaries, if only because of the offices Pant held within the Polish legislative system at both the provincial (Silesian) and national levels, as well as the energy with which he performed his duties. He had been elected to the first, second, and third Silesian seyms (1922–1935) and was one of the deputy speakers during all three terms. Before 1928 he regularly found himself at sharp odds with Polish delegates on questions concerning the operative meaning of Silesia's autonomous status. Later, together with the Polish parliamentary opposition (the Christian Democrats, NPR-Centerleft, and Polish socialists), he opposed Grażyński's attempts to administratively constrict the constitutional prerogatives of the Silesian legislature, more specifically the governor's Polonization drive. He had also been elected to the national senate in 1928 and 1935 (its second and fourth terms).

Because of his actions, Pant was barred from access to the Upper Silesian Courier; was branded by his compatriots as an enemy of the German nation; was forced to resign his chairmanship of the DChVP, which he expected would bring together all Christian Germans of goodwill in Poland; and witnessed membership of the DChVP plummet from seven thousand in 1935 to nine hundred in 1937, tottering on the brink of collapse while the Hitlerite minority parties thrived. He founded in April 1937 a new organization, the

Association of Germans in Poland (VDP), and kept writing articles critical of the Nazi system in his *Der Deutsche in Polen*. His support of the Polish opposition parties made it impossible for the Polish government to support him. He died in Katowice in October 1938.

It must be said that in the interwar years, the window of opportunity for Polish-German reconciliation was very narrow. The fact that Göring regularly climbed through that window after January 26, 1934 (the date of the German-Polish joint nonaggression declaration) to shoot bison in Białowieża forest and eat them afterward at Warsaw state receptions made things more difficult for those like Pant and Korfanty, who tried to build bilateral understanding based on Christian moral codes. For example, Pant's articles were frequently expurgated by Polish government censors for offending the head of a "friendly" foreign state that had signed a promise not to aggress Poland until 1944. As for Christians, the Catholic and Lutheran establishments would not deliver because, with few exceptions, each hierarchy identified itself, culturally and emotionally, with its own nationality. They were, one might say, nationalized de facto, if not de jure. Neither, were the bonds between Polish and German Catholics very strong or effusive since the late 1840s and the rebirth of the Polish state. Both nationality and the associated living standards (social "class") obstructed close relations.

During the third term of the Silesian seym (1930–1935), the fulfillment of governor Grażynski's agenda involved not only the prickly questions of language and minority education but many bread-and-butter issues covered by the regional budget. In the ongoing confrontation, the KBL, consisting of Christian Democrats and allied groupings, sided with the German parties for reasons of rule of law (and also to get a workable majority in parliament). The convention (a component of international law) laid down guidelines for the treatment of German minorities in Polish Upper Silesia and Polish minorities in the German part. To monitor compliance, the League established an Upper Silesian mixed commission in Katowice and an arbitration tribunal in Beuthen (Bytom). The commission and tribunal were quickly swamped with complaints, overwhelmingly from the German side: more than seven thousand of them were lodged with the commission by the German Upper Silesian People's Federation for the Defense of Minority Rights (DOVzW), mercifully abridged in everyday usage to *Volksbund* (People's Party). The People's Party was tied by an umbilical cord to authorities in Berlin. It was run by Otto Ulitz who in the early 1920s had been active in the German plebiscite office in Katowice and since 1933 was a follower of Nazism as well as a member of the Silesian seym during the first three terms of that body.[5]

Jan Przybyła had to deal with the *Volksbund* and Ulitz ever since Jan served on the Polish Plebiscite Committee in the early 1920s. Ulitz would have had to have been close to negligent not to have included Jan's name on his enemies list.

Another specimen was Rudolf Wiesner, the founder of probably the most important and effective German minority organization in interwar Poland, the Nazi *Jungdeutsche Partei für Polen*, or German Youth Organization in Poland (JdPP). Born in Aleksandrowice near Bielsko in 1890, Wiesner finished the local German secondary school and graduated with a degree in architectural engineering from the Polytechnic in Graz (Austria). In 1922, he was elected municipal councilor of Bielsko, a position he held concurrently with the leadership of the JdPP from 1931 until the outbreak of World War II in September 1939. His professional career focused principally on deconstructing the Polish state. After the occupation of the city by German forces (September 3, 1939) and its incorporation, together with its sister city Biała, into the German Third Reich, he was appointed mayor of the whole municipality, a job he held until his preemptive move to safety in West Germany to avoid approaching Soviet troops in February 1945. He had apparently expected a higher position, perhaps the leadership of the Silesian *Gau* (Nazi Silesian Province) created after the German invasion, if only because under his leadership the JdPP extended its activities from Cieszyn and Upper Silesia to include Greater Poland (*Wielkopolska*), Pomerania, (*Pomorze*), and the country's second largest city, Łódź. Its mostly young, urban membership in the mid-1930s has been estimated at fifty thousand, compared with Ed Pant's German-Christian People's Party peak of seven thousand. Its press organ, the daily *Der Aufbruch* (Break Away) published in Bielsko, accurately reflected the JdPP's central aim of breaking up Poland, but not its overt strategy of formal loyalty to the Polish state and its tactics of taking full advantage of existing laws. These enabled it to participate in the country's political process, such as elections for the national parliament and for regional (e.g., the Silesian seym) and local legislatures. The party opposed the boycott of such attractive opportunities by other German minority parties, a "the absent are never right" procedure that, in the view of the JdPP, did not advance the overriding purpose of bringing about the breakup of the Polish system from within through access to insider information and internal sabotage. In 1935 this pro forma cooperation earned Wiesner an appointment by President Mościcki to the Polish national senate during the improvement of neighborly relations following the conclusion of the German-Polish nonaggression declaration and the normalization of economic interactions, especially in the field of tariffs, between the two countries. He remained a senator until the last days of August 1939 when, to avoid arrest, he moved to Danzig (Gdańsk), from where he loudly and angrily denounced Poland and its works via radio.

Since 1935 he had also been one of two deputy mayors of Bielsko (the other being a Polish Silesian) and had occupied a spacious mansion known by passers-by as Wiesner's Villa, a few blocks from the mayor's residence. During his term as mayor (September 1939–February 1945), Nazi racial and nationalist policies of ethnic cleansing by destruction and death were implemented: the synagogues in Bielsko and Biała were burned and razed (October 1939); a Jewish ghetto was set up in Biała in 1940; and except for a few dozen married couples in which one party was a German Aryan, by 1943 the entire Jewish population of the twin cities had been dispatched in packed railroad cattle cars to extermination camps. Whenever a Polish resistance fighter was caught by the gestapo, SS, *Einsatzgruppen* (death squads), or the Wehrmacht, all family members were executed on the spot. It is conceivable that in the perspective of relativistic legal and nihilistic moral philosophies, Wiesner was not personally responsible for, and hence guilty of, the crimes of racial and national extinction committed during his term as mayor by the system he believed in, faithfully served, and helped to implant on the ashes of the Second Polish Republic. It is inconceivable, however, that he was so distracted as not to know or be unaware of what was going on. He died in Fritzlar, Hessen (Federal Republic of Germany), in 1974.

Not unlike his brother Jan, Wiktor Przybyła—governmental commissioner from 1933 to 1935, and from 1935 mayor of Bielsko— had to cope on a day-to-day basis with a progressively better financed, aggressive, and obstructionist JdPP that claimed to represent all of the city's German citizens, close to 60 percent of the total population. This population increasingly included nazified German residents of Greater Poland, Polish Pomerania, and Łódź. When the sizeable Jewish minority caught in the middle is brought into the equation, governing and promoting harmony in what in today's terminology would be called a "multicultural" community became a tightrope balancing act not made any easier or less dangerous as 1939 approached, which saw intensified systemic centralization, decline of willingness to compromise, and a groundswell of military intrusion into the city's nominally self-government.

By an unprecedented, nearly unanimous agreement of those who had known him during his years as a knowledgeable, capable governmental commissioner and mayor, Wiktor Przybyła, resolved Bielsko's financial plight, managed the city well, modernized and beautified it beyond compare, and most important, maintained reasonable civic peace in times of general turmoil. He succeeded in keeping the ethnic, linguistic, confessional, and ideological mix away from histrionics and hollow abstract nouns, and he transformed city council meetings into something resembling rational and civilized conversation to an extent thought impossible in those days. By his personal example, he channeled energies into providing mundane urban services that inhabitants of modern cities expect. One such project was the construction of an Olympic-sized, state-of-the-art swimming pool. He dealt calmly with the controversial problem of secular and religious education and the associated issue of the language(s) to be used in admissions and instruction. He also had trees and flowers planted, improving the quality of life by making an already attractive, historic city (known by some as the"Little Vienna") still more pleasant to the eye.

A kind and gentle man, his tolerance and inborn sense of fairness earned him the respect of those not impaired by diseased ideologies of the right, left, and cabals in between. He did not hesitate to prove his resolve in times of crisis. When in 1937 anti-Semitic riots, fanned by ultranationalists, erupted in the city, and mobs recruited in the surrounding countryside to riot in the streets, he asked for and received from his friend and colleague Adam Kocur, the president of Katowice, a detachment of disciplined cadet riot police who dispersed the inebriated crowds.

In 1939 he let it be known that he would not be available for another term of government office, having accepted a position in the private industrial sector that was to take effect at the end of that year. Half a century later, after the removal of the communists from power, the Bielsko-Biała city council named a street after him.

On January 16, 1930, Jan Przybyła took leave from his work at the press bureau of the Silesian voivodship office in Katowice to become district manager (in this case roughly equivalent to a burgomaster) of Chropaczów, a coalmining and heavy industry administrative unit (*gmina*) on the German border. The Donnersmarck steel mill was just a few miles on the other side of the frontier, subjectively a world away.[6] He was confirmed in his new position on July 31, 1931, and served with distinction and plaudits from the inhabitants until the German invasion in September 1939. In 1934 he joined the board of the Silesian Institute, an educational and research foundation, and in September 1935 he was elected to the fourth term of the Silesian seym. The election was conducted within the framework of the newly adopted authoritarian national constitution. The number of deputies was reduced by half (from forty-eight to twenty-four), and they were elected by majority vote in two-seat electoral districts. Boycotted by the opposition, all seats went to *Sanacja*-related contenders (twenty-one of them to the ZChZP). Although the outcome of the triage was predictable, in some districts *Sanacja* candidates who were critical of the new electoral procedures were elected. There were no representatives of the German minority parties. Ironically, at about the same time Rudolf Wiesner was made a member of the national senate by the president of the republic. Karol Grzesik of NChZP, the current mayor of Chorzów and the 1921 commander in chief of the insurgent Silesian Combat Group East, became the seym's speaker. After the Polish occupation of a slice of Czech Cieszyn Silesia in October 1938, President Mościcki appointed four more persons to represent the newly incorporated area in the Silesian seym, bringing the total number of deputies to twenty-eight. The bottom line is that the fourth and last Silesian Autonomous Seym (from September 1935 to September 1, 1939) became an arm of the governor's executive council, which included Grazyński, the deputy governor, and five other members.

In 1936, with proceeds from the sale of their former home in Lwów and a loan from a municipal savings bank in Katowice, Jan purchased a house on Kłodnicka Street in Ligota, a suburb of Katowice. The family referred to it in the affectionate diminutive "Pzybyłówka."

By then the children were grown: the oldest son Zbigniew (Zbyszek) served in the army in Warsaw, and Maria (Marysia) was pursuing studies at Warsaw's Higher School of Business. Only Janusz, the youngest, still lived at home, attending the mathematics and physical sciences division of the Mikołaj Kopernik (Nicolas Copernicus) High School in Katowice. In 1938, on the occasion of the twenty-fifth anniversary of Jan and Marta's marriage, a picture of the whole family was taken in Katowice. It was to be the last.

Notes

1.   During the wars of Polish independence he used several pseudonyms, as did many other fighters. Among his adopted names were Borelowski, Smyrda, and Sowa (Owl). The literary reference is to Adam Mickiewicz's poem "Grażyna: Powieść Litewska" (Grażyna: A Lithuanian Novel). Grażyna was the name invented by Mickiewicz for the heroine of his poem. To this day the name change is used by Grażynski's detractors to tarnish his memory in Web logs (blogs) that could use literary assistance.

2.   After the Soviet invasion of Poland on September 17, 1939, Skulski was arrested by the Soviet secret police and executed in the Brześć prison.

3.   Although no doubt imperfect, a population census held in Poland in 1931, which excluded the heavily urbanized Upper Silesia as well as the area around Wilno (Vilnius), showed a total population of close to 25 million, with 67 percent residing in villages. In the 1930s when Fiat began manufacturing cars in Poland, its advertisement stressing the resilience of their product read: "Polish Fiat for Polish roads."

4.   In 1933 the number of unemployed in Polish Silesia was about 130,000, and 445,000 in German Silesia. Alicja Galas, Artur Galas, *Dzeje Śląska w Datach* (History of Silesia in Dates). Wrocław: "Cadus'" 2004, 232.

5.   Between 1922 and 1927 the number of German minority schools in Polish Upper Silesia, financed partly by the Silesian treasury and in part by the *Volksbund* and a German bank in Beuthen (Bytom), rose from sixty-eight to ninety-five. Nevertheless, after the arrival of Grażyński, the Bund continued sending its complaints, irrespective of the commission's and arbitration tribunal's decisions, to higher instances: directly to the League of Nations and, when rejected, via the German Weimar Republic government to the International Court of Justice in the Hague (1927–28).

6.   Today it is an administrative component of the Ruda Śląska industrial complex in Upper Silesia. I wish to acknowledge the information contained in this and the subsequent section to Tadeusz Czylok *Geneza i Powstanie Katowickiego Harcerstwa: Inspector Harcerski Jan Przybyła, Informator historyczny nr. 3* [The Genesis and Development of Scouting in Katowice, Scout Inspector Jan Przybyła, Historical Source Nr. 3]. Katowice: Komenda i Komisja Historyczna ZHP w Katowicach, 1991 [Katowice: Headquarters and Historical Commission of the Polish Scout Organization in Katowice, 1991].

Dr. Wiktor Przybyła Government
Commissioner
and Mayor of Bielsko
(1933–September 1939)

Józef Przybyła, businessman
(1930s)

The Przybyła's house in Katowice-Ligota (1936–38), Jan in front

Party in garden at Katowice-Ligota on the twenty-fifth anniversary of Jan and Marta's wedding (1938). First Row: Left to Right: Alfred Dąbrowski (Marta's cousin); Zbigniew (Zbyszek) Przybyła (in military uniform); Mrs. Franosz (Marysia's aunt); Mrs Ligoń (wife of Stanisław Ligoń of Chapter 2);Marta Przybyłowa; Jan Przybyła; Mr Franosz (Marysia's uncle); Gustaw Daisenberg (Marta's brother); Maria (Marysia) Przybylanka; Wiktor Przybyła (holding sunflower); Anna Przybyłowa (Wiktor's wife); Luta Przybyłowa (wife of Józef Przybyła); Zosia Nowotna (Marysia's cousin).

Second row: Stanisław Ligoń (hiding); Janusz Przybyła; Józef Przybyła; Hela Franosz (Marysia's cousin).

*Last photograph of the family taken on the twenty-fifth anniversary
of Jan and Marta's wedding in Katowice (1938)*

On the Brink

From 1936 through August 31, 1939, on the eve of Germany's invasion of Poland from the west, north, and south; from the skies and the sea; and from within with the help of fifth columns like Wiesner's JdPP and Ulitz's Volksbund, Poles lived with tension, anxiety, and foreboding. With these feelings came an imitative domestic authoritarian response to the foul totalitarianism of Hitler, whose contagious, fascist disease spread through Europe and gave rise to second-hand, second-class authoritarian governments of various degrees of severity. Most of these—for example, Franco's Spain, Portugal, Greece, Yugoslavia, Romania, Bulgaria, and the Baltic States—were more repressive than Poland's authoritarian government, which operated alongside legal, albeit needled, political parties. The communist party was the only one banned outright. Since no single party could get sufficient votes in elections to form by itself a viable government, governmental party coalitions had to be formed. These coalitions broke apart with bewildering speed, to the disgust of many Poles. Piłsudski chose to call this system "partocratic seymocracy." Watching this catch-as-catch-can parliamentary politics, many Poles came to think that an authoritarian government was the lesser of two evils, the other being political chaos—this at a time when their country's very existence was threatened by Nazi Germany and the Soviet Union, while the democratic West, Britain in particular, could not care less, self-deluded by their trust in the efficacy of appeasement. With few exceptions, British statesmen wanted to avoid any commitments in Eastern Europe and considered the Polish Corridor (Poland's narrow territorial access to the Baltic Sea squeezed in between German Pomerania and German East Prussia) and the Free City of Danzig as the most asinine parts of the Versailles Treaty. The French, realizing that they needed British help in the event of a future war, began to look for ways to reduce their commitments to Poland.

After Piłsuski's death, Poland's top civil authorities interwoven with the army's high command (the "government of colonels," as it was often called) thought it essential for the nation to be "strong, unified, and ready." Given their personal backgrounds as brave soldiers in the war of independence, the slogan suggested soldiers standing shoulder to shoulder and awaiting the command to pounce on any aggressor. Quite naturally, strength meant to them obeying orders from above, and unity was to be arrived at through unquestioning obedience to a higher national cause rather than by discussion, explanation, and consensus. As for being ready, the first trial flight of a prototype Polish bomber took place in Okęcie (where today Warsaw's modern airport is located) in June 1936, just thirty-eight months before the outbreak of the war. A prototype of a modern fighter plane, the "Hawk," which could compete with German Messerschmitts in speed and firepower, was being tested as late as May 1939, three months before the war. It was still not in production in July, nor was the slower and generally more antiquated P-11. Many of the Polish military pilots who managed to reach England after September 17, 1939, equipped there with British Hurricane and Spitfire fighter aircraft, fought valiantly and effectively in the Battle of Britain a year later.

The bottom line is that by 1936, except for Nazi Germany, no country, not even the richest in Europe and North America, was militarily ready for what was to come: The tsunami of iron, steel, and brutality that engulfed Poland less than three years later. The sixteen-year-old republic, with frontiers that after 1918 no German government had recognized and with an emerging, developing economy, was certainly not in a position to be ready, no matter who had been in charge. The domestic political system and the April 1935 Constitution on which it rested—or perhaps more accurately, which was used to strengthen central authority and its accompanying restrictions—could not be even remotely compared to the totalitarian dictatorships of Nazi Germany and Stalin's Russia. Nor can Piłsudski be called a dictator of the Hitler and Stalin genre, armed with a dogmatic philosophy with hatred at its core and terror as its principal means. He said that he did not want to be a dictator and kept his word. His wish was to make Poland as strong as possible and thus to safeguard her independence the best he could.

When dealing with Poles, appealing to patriotism is a guaranteed strategy. By 1936–37, the appeal for national unity of resolve and policy concentrated on the need to arm the country so that it could defend itself from the rapidly growing military might and increasingly expansionist appetites of Hitler's Third Reich, which by 1938 had Poland practically encircled, except on that country's eastern border, beyond which lay the lands of Stalin's gulags then in the throes of show trials, executions, and purges. Who better suited to provide that leadership than the army's high command, working hand in hand with a single-minded civil government largely staffed by reserve generals and colonels recruited mostly from Piłsudski's 1914–1918 legionnaires.Hardly anyone in the world envisaged the blitzkrieg in its full horror, except perhaps the Chinese with their experience of imperialistic Japan's brutality.

Misgivings

During the reshuffling of personal power influences within the top inner circle following the death of Piłsudski, the Nonparty Bloc of Cooperation with the Government (BBWR) was dissolved by its founder Walery Sławek (October 30, 1935), who, after serving ten months as prime minister in 1935, lost ground in the discreet succession elbowing among politicians. Even though from the onset the BBWR was more an election tool designed to bring together disparate voters who sympathized with the late marshal's intentions than a cohesive political philosophy, ideology, or permanent organization, its abrupt withdrawal from the scene left *Sanacja*'s motley assembly of factionalized supporters without an institutional home and updated guideposts, notwithstanding the efforts of recently formed regional movements such as the Silesian National-Christian Union of Labor (NChZP).

On Rydz-Śmigły's initiative, the void was to be filled by the formation in February 1937 of the Camp of National Unity (OZN), pop-

ularly known as Ozon. It was organized on military lines, as befitted
the locale, times and ambiance, by a retired colonel and chairman
of the Polish Central Bank, Adam Koc who was soon replaced by
General Stanisław Skwarczyński. Ozon's overall aim was to rally
the nation around the army and its leader (Rydz-Śmigły) so as to
defend the country and the 1935 Constitution. Aside from criticism by professional politicians now out of the loop, the details of
how this was to be accomplished were criticized by people at home
and abroad, by those knowledgeable of the workings of Western
democracies as well as by ordinary people worried about their
pocket books. The peasants responded to a call from the People's
Party (SL) and went on a nationwide strike August 15–25 that was
put down with bloodshed.

Here are a few samples of how the Ozon aspirations infiltrated
national policy.

The OZN took a page out of Dmowskism on its bad day and
moved its laundry list (its politico-ideological manifesto) more to
the right. The list contained items such as nationalism (from narrow
to narrower), with substantial cribbing from unsavory organizations such as the National Radical Camp ONR and its twins, the
ONR-ABC and RNR *Falanga*, born in the swamps of Bereza after
the government had outlawed their parent. They regarded the
rank-and-file members of Dmowski's National Democratic Party
(ND), the "endeks," as fuddy duddies ripe for retirement, what with
their talk about parliamentary procedures and the like, while the
OZN demanded change and power right now, preferably by resorting to force.

Then there was on Ozon's list the question of national minorities policy: accelerated Polonization effort; denial of autonomous
status to national minority areas; and the role of Roman Catholicism in the polity, which was to be protected and treated as state
religion, the opposite of the notion of separation of church and
state. Keeping in mind the pitfalls of political arithmetic, especially
in convulsive times, OZN membership has been estimated at forty
to fifty thousand in 1937, and double that in 1938.

There was also anti-Semitism, which still awaited a dispas-
sioned, balanced presentation. Emigration of Jews to Palestine and
Madagascar was encouraged. In April 1937, the Polish state airline

LOT extended its Warsaw-Athens route to Lidda (near Haifa) in Palestine, the longest nonstop air route in Europe. In reaction to Britain's decrease of emigration visas to their Palestinian mandate, intended to calm down Palestinian Muslims, the Polish government in the late 1930s gave secret military training to future fighters for an independent state of Israel, among them Moshe Dayan. The "New Zionist Organization," led by Włodzimierz Żabotyński, an admirer of Piłsudski, was active in Poland during this period.

In October 1937 university chancellors began to implement prescribed admission quotas for Jewish applicants, the so-called *numerus clausus* based on the ratio of Jews to the total population of the country. During the 1938–39 academic year, the proportion of Jewish students at Warsaw University fell from 25 percent to the newly required 8 percent. Moreover, as an attempt to control disruptions of lectures by fights between extreme right-wing nationalist elements on the one side and Jews and their defenders on the other, Jewish students were confined to specified places in lecture halls, which came to be known as "ghetto benches." This was to the disappointment of radicals among the National Democrats, who had hoped for a *numerus nullus*.

There was another side to it, as evidenced by the actions of young Poles who came to the defense of their Jewish fellow students because, among other offensive stupidities, they found the ghetto benches a human and moral abomination. Years later, the former Israeli Prime Minister Yitzak Shamir, born in 1915 in Russian-occupied Poland, made a sweeping, difficult–to–refute bloomer worthy of an RNR Falangist. The Poles, he said, "imbibe anti-Semitism with their mother's milk."[1] A law graduate of Warsaw University, Shamir emigrated to Palestine in 1935, becoming a radical member of the nationalist underground *Irgun* movement, and when this broke up, he established himself as one of the leaders of the terrorist *Lehi* splinter responsible for attempted and actual assassinations of high British officials in Mandate Palestine. He ended his political career as a hardliner of the *Likud* party. What with every Pole being diagnosed a DNA anti-Semite, it is not surprising that little is known in the West or anywhere else about those Poles who regarded anti-Semitism as an infirmity of the spirit. *The Economist* puts it as well as it ever can be in an obituary of Irena Sendler, née

Krzyżanowska, a Polish Catholic who saved thousands of Jewish children from the Nazi's Warsaw ghetto during World War II at the risk of instant execution if caught; and she did it out of simple humanity.

She was nominated for the Nobel Peace Prize in 2007. Al Gore got it.

Official discrimination spread to the private sector, taking among other impediments to equal opportunity the form of an "Aryan paragraph" (refusing membership to Jews) in the bylaws of social and professional organizations, associations and clubs. Although many Polish cities hosted large-scale demonstrations protesting anti-Jewish excesses committed on March 9, 1936, in the town of Przytyk, attacks on Jews continued sporadically, fanned by far-right doofus led by one Adam Doboszyński in response to invented provocations and encouraged by what they took to be tacit approval of those responsible for public order. Lesser outrages mul-tiplied in the following months and into 1938. As crowds roamed the streets in search of Jewish homes, Christian homeowners lit candles in their windows and displayed pictures of Jesus or the Virgin Mary to avoid having their homes smashed by cobblestones. Riots erupted in Częstochowa right under the eyes of the Black Madonna of Jasna Góra Monastery,venerated by Catholics throughout the land. Boycott of Jewish shops and a shift of buyers' purchases to uncompetitive stores run by Christians—preferably Polish Cath-olics—in the name of patriotism was encouraged by no less a dig-nitary than the prime minister. In an address to the seym on June 4, 1936, Premier Feliks Sławoj Składkowski approved an economic combat but without hurting the Jews (presumably physically)—as if it were possible to subsidize competition and humiliate people with ghetto benches and Aryan paragraphs without hurt. Accord-ing to Jewish sources, the Jewish share of commerce in 1939 was 52 percent, with 40 percent in industry and crafts. Ironically, the culture handed down over the centuries by the social reference class, the "well-born" nobility high and low, did not regard commerce (*handel*) and its profit-making mentality (economic calculation) to be an appropriate occupation for a Polish gentleman. The Polish Catholic Church was on the side of patriotism, appearing ambiva-lent about capitalism.

On April 8, 1938. the seym unanimously passed a statute to protect the name of Józef Piłsudski from derogatory usage.[2] Disparagement of the memory of the deceased was punishable by up to five years in prison. As another slap at freedom of speech, the statute also offended, but not altogether strangled, the Polish sense of humor, which tends to revel in political irony. In the interwar years several satirical magazines, the printed equivalent of the Parisian *chansonniers*, appeared in the country, including the right-leaning *Mucha* (the *Fly*), *Szpilki* (*Pins*), and *Wróble na Dachu* (*Sparrows on the Roof*), the last given to nationalism, liberally depositing its products on the heads of Russians and the Czechs. When the inaugural issue of the leftist *Pins* (associated with the Polish Socialist Party and just about the only opposition satirical magazine during the interwar years) was severely bowdlerized in 1936, it put the censor's massive white blobs in between what little remained of the original text for its readers to see. Correctly interpreted by the government expurgators as an effective sales pitch, the blobs too were erased, the editors told never to do it again. Just twenty days before Hitler's assault on Poland, when *Pins* printed a caricature of Adolf as a knight-in-armor, the Łódź county sheriff (*starosta*) confiscated the magazine, citing the relevant article of the 1935 Constitution dealing with defamation of foreign heads of state. The intended byproduct of all this was journalistic self-censorship. It should be added that there was no preliminary censorship as in totalitarian states, but the government could and did threaten the major dailies with confiscation if certain words or sentences were not removed in the afternoon edition.

One may also have misgivings about Poland's foreign policy in the period 1936-1939: Since the annexation of what the Poles called "middle Lithuania," including the city of Wilno (Vilnius) in the early twenties, Lithuanian governments protested by refusing to enter into diplomatic relations with Poland and actually cutting off all communications. Lithuania made do with provincial Kaunas (Kowno) for the country's capital and, at an opportune moment at the end of World War I, appropriated some real estate in and around the German-speaking coastal town of Memel (Klaipèda), the only port at that latitude usable in winter.[3] On March 17, 1938, six days after Hitler's ultimatum to Austria and five days after his takeover of that country, the Polish government demanded that the Lithuanian diplomatic and communications oversight be corrected forthwith. In mid-March, allegedly spontaneous demonstrations bubbled up in Polish cities, the crowds pleading with Rydz-Śmigły, the commander in chief of the armed forces, to lead them against Kowno by March 31. Synchronized with this ultimatum were movements of Polish army units toward the closed Lithuanian frontier. Within two weeks diplomatic relations between Lithuania and Poland were established. By implication this was regarded in some Ozon quarters as equivalent to Lithuania's recognition of the legitimacy of her border with Poland, which it wasn't. Even if the Lithuanian government had taken such a step, it would have been recognition by ultimatum, a short-legged foreign policy long on bitter memories and desire for revenge by the loser. Hitler, busy with solidifying his takeover of Austria but also to reassure the Poles tacitly of his continued friendliness to them as per the 1934 German-Polish nonaggression declaration, which had still nearly six years left, sat on his hands for another year and then sent the Lithuanians an ultimatum demanding the return of Klaipèda to Germany, which Lithuania did immediately. The Poles watched nonplussed as a mighty fleet of German warships with Hitler on board sailed across the Baltic to Klaipèda in a display of one more annexation by resort to threats.

Another Pyrrhic victory was the takeover by Poland of a part of Czechoslovak Silesian territory (*Zaolzie*) across the river Olza that occurred at a politically unfortunate time, just three days after the Munich Agreement (September 29, 1938) concluded between Nazi Germany, Fascist Italy, and democratic France and Britain. By the terms of that compact, to the making of which—as distinct from just signing on the dotted line—the Czechs were not invited, the two democracies agreed to the immediate occupation by German troops of roughly forty-one thousand square kilometers of Czechoslovakia's western regions known as the Sudetenland, inhabited by a majority of three million ethnic Nazified Germans led by Konrad Henlein, who took his orders from Berlin and became head of the local Nazi Party, the *Sudetendeutsche Partei* (SdP), or Sudeten German Party. Neville Chamberlain, the mastermind of the British Foreign Office and a believer in the illusory healing powers of appeasement in exchange for megalomaniacal Hitler's promise of peace on earth and no more territorial demands, had given in to German demands, as did the French Foreign Affairs Minister Édouard Daladier three days later, though with less exuberance. On September 30, the day the Czechs agreed to abide by the Munich diktat, Polish Minister of Foreign Affairs Józef Beck demanded from the beleaguered Czechs the cession to Poland of Zaolzie with its preponderantly Polish-speaking population, coal mines, and heavy industry. The Czechs accepted that too. For some days already crowds in the streets of Polish towns had been demonstrating in support of this demand, chanting in unison for the commander in chief to lead them against the Czechs.

On October 2, Polish troops entered Český Tešin (the Czecho-slovakian part of the divided Cieszyn city) and began to occupy the rest of Zaolzie to the welcomed cheers of Polish schoolchildren rushing across the border bridge over the Olza river.[4] By November, when the border between Polish Zaolzie and Germany was final-ized, Poland added about one thousand square kilometers to its ter-ritory, a few mines and steel mills, less than two hundred thousand people, and a bad press for kicking a fellow country when it was down. Most Poles who agreed with the return of Zaolzie to the mother country argued that the Czechs had kicked them when *they* were down: On January 23, 1919, when Poland was distracted else-where by Bolshevik Russia and the Greater Poland Uprising, Czech troops invaded and occupied large areas of Cieszyn Silesia between the Olza and Vistula rivers that previously had been allotted to Poland, although later they had to give up some of their conquest by a Polish counterattack. In 1920, even as Tukhachevsky's Bolshe-vik armies were pushing toward Warsaw, and Poland's existence hang by a hair—and with it that of the Baltic states and potentially democratic west Europe—Czech railway workers, with a nudge, a wink and a nod from the Beneš government, refused to allow French military supplies to Poland to pass through Czechoslovak territory.

Originally a plebiscite was to be held in western Cieszyn Silesia, but in the end the decision was left to the Conference of Allied Ambassadors, who on July 28, 1920, cancelled the proposed plebiscite favored by Poland and gave Zaolzie to Czechoslovakia. Paderewski's reaction to the ambassadors' decision was that it

created an "abyss" between the two countries. One could argue it
had merely deepened the canyon that had divided them in the past.

Controversy on this subject continues to this day. That Polish
public opinion of the time saw the takeover simply as a payback
for past wrongs is probably understandable. Moreover, all political parties, except the Polish Communist Party decapitated by
Stalin's purges, insisted on the return of Zaolzie to Poland. General
Sikorski of the opposition Front Morges offered Beneš an alliance
in exchange for Zaolzie; Beneš refused.

What is more difficult to understand is what prompted the
Polish government to pursue a policy that would, and did, look to
average outsiders like an opportunistic grab that made them think
of Poland as switching sides to Hitler's corner. Combined with
the success of the Czech government in portraying Czechoslovakia as the only economically enlightened, tolerant, and democratic
country in central and eastern Europe (despite the protestations of
the Slovaks) was sure to make Polish strategy look bad.

The explanation provided by many Polish historians runs
counter to this instinctive outside judgment. It is a little convoluted,
but based on verbal and written information provided by leading
Polish actors in the Zaolzie performance, that the Polish acquisition
of Zaolzie, like the somewhat later Hungarian takeover of Subcar-
pathian Ruthenia, was not the result of the Munich Agreement but
an action taken *against* it. The Poles were not beneficiaries of the
Agreement that expected them to quietly wait until Germany got
what it wanted. But what if Germany also wanted Zaolzie, with
its mines, steel mills, and Polish-speaking population? The Polish
government reasoned that this was very likely to happen. Foreign
Minister Beck expected Poland to be invited to the Munich Conference as one of the great powers. Mussolini had promised his
support, but Hitler and Chamberlain wanted the gathering limited
to only four: Germany, Britain, France, and Italy. The Poles, of
course, remembered that they had also not been invited as negotiators to the Locarno Conference and had been summoned only to
present their case to the real conferees. They were treated throughout as representatives of "second level" countries. But that was
thirteen years ago. Perhaps things had changed. Foreign Minister
Beck wanted to make sure that the reunification of Zaolzie with

Poland was not a gift from Germany, which unfortunately is what it looked like to many outside observers not privileged to know the Beck's thinking. He wanted Poland to take Zaolzie back at a time of her own choosing and not have it handed on a plate by Germany as leftovers from the Munich banquet. If the well-armed Czechs did not accept the German demands concerning the cession of Sudetenland and decided to fight, the Polish ambassador to Prague was to remain with the Czechoslovak government. In such a case, France would have had to go to war with Germany, and Poland would not be on the German side in a European war. On the other hand, the Polish government assumed that if the Czechs did not fight, France and Britain would not oppose Poland from reuniting Polish-speaking Zaolzians with their mother country, having in 1938 accepted Hitler's use of force in Austria to reunite German-speaking Austrians with the *Vaterland*. Beck had warned Hitler that if German troops took the town of Bogumin, which Poland claimed, there might be conflict. Poland did get Bogumin, though it lost the town to the Germans eleven months later.

Granting the accuracy of the cool-headed explanation, the Polish payback cum sudden urge for national reunification with fifty thousand Polish-speaking compatriots, while mildly therapeutic for the Poles in times of Brobdingnagian stress, was in historical perspective an imprudent step.

That bigoted, hatemongering, scapegoating ideas should have been aired by militant groups, youthful naïfs, and political camps operating on the wrong side of sanity in hard times is unfortunate and sad but not surprising; neither were they limited to the Poland of the late 1930s. That such ideas were made into law and embodied in state policies by some important public officials is more disturbing. It had something to do with what responsible parents tell their offspring as they are growing up: "Watch what company you keep. It rubs off on you." This assumes that there is a choice, which in private life is most often the case, unless it's already too late. The young Poland was in the latter position. She wanted to make friends with the "good guys" (France, Britain, Belgium) at Locarno and was told to mind her place; she tried to have an equal say and permanent chair in the League of Nations' Council but got a stool. It also wanted a colony in Africa, something normal and fashionable in those days; Togo or Cameroon, former German protectorates administered in the interwar years by France and Britain for the League of Nations, would have been just fine.[5] However, Poland was rebuffed. In the meantime the two bullies on her western and eastern frontiers had got together in Rapallo for a friendly chat, a shot of vodka, and a stein of beer on a round table—with a military assistance pact under it. It was not so much that the Poles were hurt in their *amour-propre* by the conduct of their friends or were blinded by emotion politics or indelible ethnic/political prejudices, but they came to realize that they could not rely on the Western democracies for the security of their borders, or on their southern neighbors, the Czechs and Slovaks, who had border agendas of their own. This being so, Piłsudski sought to find a way for Poland to navigate between Nazi Germany and Soviet Russia, whose 1922 Rapallo spirits had by the early '30s gone the way of the spirit of Locarno, and the Nazis were scouring the neighborhood looking for volunteers to sign an anti-Comintern pact, while the Soviets concluded a five-year mutual assistance treaty with Czechoslovakia in 1935 and Belgium was released from its security obligations under the Locarno Treaty in April 1937. The upshot was Piłsudski's policy (continued after his death) of friendly but aloof evenhandedness, an armed neutrality vis-à-vis a couple of no good characters next door. It began with the left hand signing a three-year nonaggression pact with Stalin in July 1932 (which in 1934 was extended for ten more promissory years) and the other hand initialing a non-aggression declaration with Hitler in January 1934, also valid for a decade but torn up by Germany in April 1939. The stratagem has been criticized, often unfairly, given the constricted geopolitical, demographic, and economic aspects that Poland had to accept in the thirties. Regrettably, like all stratagems, this one came with a price, one much inflated after the death of its inventor. The price was contamination from exposure to the reprehensible qualities of those Poland tried to keep at arm's length but at the same time impress them with what might be called "me too–ism."

On January 7, 1937, in the spirit of the 1934 Polish-German nonaggression declaration, an agreement was signed between Poland and the Danzig (Gdańsk) government to try to resolve, or at least reduce and cool down, the heated disagreements between

Poland and Germany over the Free City's day-to-day status, which was far from being as free as the Versailles Treaty had envisaged it to be. This was especially so after the municipal elections held in May 1933 in which German national socialists (the Nazis) won a majority of the votes. From then on Danzig goose-stepped to the tune of the *Horst Wessel Lied*, the anthem of the Nazi Party.[6] Polish presence was thenceforth practically limited to post office workers, soldiers on the Westerplatte peninsula, and after-hours visitors from the nearby Polish port of Gdynia diligently losing their money in the casino of Sopot, a pretty resort suburb of a city drowning in Nazi flags and pushy Prussians.[7]

To give the 1934 nonaggression declaration a personal touch, Nazi dignitaries, most frequently Hermann Göring, were invited to Poland and hosted with impeccable hospitality. In the primeval forests of Białowieża unsuspecting bison, with help from Polish forestry personnel, regularly appeared in the crosshairs of fat Hermann's rifle, and lost their life in the interest of nonaggression and to assuage the gluttonous appetite of the *Reichsjägermeister* (Hunting Master of the Reich)—the latter with more success than the former.[8] On November 5, 1937, the two countries signed a declaration guaranteeing various civil rights to their respective minorities. Already in 1935 and again in 1938, in a gesture of goodwill and reward for his opposition to the German minority's intent to boycott those years' "nominated" Polish elections, Rudolf Wiesner of the JdPP was appointed to the senate of the Polish Republic by President Mościcki, where he sat (with Hitler's permission, naturally) until August 1939 when he was arrested by the Polish police, released just in case his arrest might cause a war, and promptly headed for Gdańsk. In sum, from 1935 until April 1939, when Hitler ordered the preparation of a plan (*Fall Weiss*, White Destruction) for the invasion of Poland and two weeks later announced that the 1934 Polish-German nonaggression declaration was null and void, the Polish side had carried out the declaration almost to the letter. This does not mean that the going was easy. In the key area of education, for example, the number of minority schools financially supported by the respective states diminished substantially in the 1930s. As early as April 1935, the new *Gauleiter* (Nazi Party Head) of Silesia, Josef Wagner, gave in a speech his understanding of how the (more congenial) relationship with Poland envisaged by the 1934 declaration would be interpreted in German Upper and Lower Silesia: "Everything that might point to anything Polish must disappear. Within ten years our Silesia will become quintessentially German ... In thirty years the whole Upper Silesia will know nothing about Poles."[9]

From the early days of Poland's resurrection at the end of World War I, the odds were heavily against the peaceful assimilation of national minorities (a third of the population) in what was an emerging national economy and a national state during an era of fervent nationalism, confrontational ideologies, close rapport of each nationality with religions that seemed never to have heard of ecumenism or reasonably courteous coexistence, and the presence of firmly embedded historical memories of wrongs done to each other since nation-states came into being.

Because of over a century (1795–1920) of occupation and domination by three foreign empires (Prussia, Russia, Austria-Hungary)—and much longer for Poles in Silesia—the integration problem had an additional intraethnic dimension. This was to overcome the effects of a long separation and become a functioning national community again within a framework of new social, political, and economic institutions befitting modern times—in short, to bring Poles together, rather than divide them into those who in the interwar years came from what was sometimes called Poland A (urban industrial west), B (the former Austrian Galicia), and C (the "far eastern" confines, marches, or *kresy*). Poland had a cultural DNA problem of sorts, or bloodless civil conflict in peacetime once national unity had been restored between three economically, and to an extent culturally, different parts of their country. Poles from areas of the country formerly under the relatively less oppressive, more "enlightened" Austrian suzerainty tended to look at their Silesian compatriots with a certain cultural hauteur due to their social graces (or lack thereof), syntax, grammar, and garbled pronunciation of the native language. However, since sizeable areas of Galicia/Nether Poland (Małopolska) were economically less developed than Silesia, their residents were not averse, once the country was reunited, to migrating in search of jobs in the more industrialized Upper Silesia. This also held true for those Poles who before 1918 were under harsh Russian dominance, except that in the perception of those Poles, the Russian occupiers and their Cossack nagaika-wielding enforcers had little if anything to teach them culturally, socially, politically, and economically.[10] In short, the Russians—the Whites and later the Reds—did not receive any respect. If there really was a problem about non-Silesians getting the best jobs after independence, it was accentuated by the Great Depression that affected the whole country after 1929 and had not been made easier by the combination of the tariff war waged by the Weimar Republic. It was also occasionally hampered by some domestic political philosophies and policies of the Polish government that left untapped a wealth of professional expertise of Poles officially considered not to have been Polish enough because of their geographic provenance. For all his real, semireal, and alleged faults of character and errors of policy, Michał Grażyński, the governor of Silesia (September 1926–September 1939), himself a Silesian import from Nether Poland, ignored this parochial disapproval of hiring "aliens" in the Silesian government sector (including education, cultural activities. and research) with generally positive results for the country and the province.[11]

The major challenge, however, was not absorbing in industrialized, relatively higher-income Upper Silesia Poles from other parts of the formerly divided country, but assimilating national minorities. The ideal would have been for the minorities to have embraced being so blended, like the people who in the nineteenth and twentieth centuries came to America seeking freedom. But this was not the case—neither at the beginning of Poland's independence, when Poland alienated them, and vice versa, by border-defining disputations, nor toward the end, during what is called here the "misgivings" period of the late 1930s.

At the beginning of 1939 the population of Poland was about thirty-five million. Of this number, close to twelve million (roughly 34 percent) constituted the so-called "national minorities": Ukrainians numbered about five million; Jews between three and three and a half million; Belorussians and Germans about one and a half million each, the former living in eastern/northeastern parts of the country and the latter in formerly Prussian-occupied western Poland. There were also other smaller national minorities—the

Lithuanians, Czechs, Slovaks, and Gypsies (Roma), for example. The national/ethnic minorities of interwar Poland resisted and rejected assimilation for a variety of reasons and traded with the majority mutual dislikes and antagonisms rooted in history, more as entireties than on the level personal relations. Neither would they settle for the federalism favored by Piłsudski with regard to Lithuanians and western Ukrainians, which accepted their national culture but required loyalty to Poland.

In the early morning hours of September 1, 1939, the German panzer war machine struck this young old country with all the power of coordinated air force, panzer (armored units), infantry, and navy. The Poles fought, as best they could, as a matter of honor, until their catastrophic defeat.

Redemption

It may seem easy to criticize the actions of others, especially when the results are less than positive and most of those responsible for them are gone, no longer able to explain and defend themselves other than through the occasional memoir they left. I must admit, however, that contrary to this view, I found writing the "Misgivings" section of this chapter difficult and painful, causing a temporary writer's block, which some of my Polish readers will, no doubt, wish had remained permanent on the premise that there are some things in life that should remain unmentioned. I understand the premise but cannot accept it as a social scientist and, more important, an American of Polish extraction. I understand it because of what the Polish people had suffered under the bestial Nazi German and Soviet communist occupations, and on top of that the forty-odd years of deprivation of liberty, freedom, and independence under the boot of Soviet lackeys, a gift from the Munich-type 1945 Yalta Agreement formed by Stalin, Churchill, and the ailing Roosevelt. I also sympathize with Poles' wish not to encourage the obloquy aimed at them from many sides, most of it undeserved. But such sniping, though still common, would not be much diminished by omission. I have chosen instead to balance the account by briefly discussing the various imponderable obstacles that confronted the reborn Poland during the infinitesimal time span of its independent existence and by listing some of the positive achievements that, despite some governmental fumbling and bungling of which the first generation born in restored Poland was aware, made them proud to have been born in that beautiful land.

First off, the enormity of the undertaking. For 123 years (1795–1918), Poland had been divided among three imperial powers, including two of the harshest. After World War I and some grudging reshuffling of borders, the country was put together again, contracted in dimension and different in shape. The three regions (or at least parts of each) formerly governed by Russia, Prussia, and Austria-Hungary were allocated by the victors to the reborn Poland. These three areas had a lot of national minorities but little commonality of legal, political, social, and economic institutions; the differences ran right down to varying widths of railroad tracks between Russia and the other two occupiers. People who over six generations had been brought up in very dissimilar cultural environments and (except for a handful of grandee families who through marriage accessed the occupiers' social strata,) were subjected to vilifications and debasement of their national origins and history, and reminded daily of their underling status, now had to be brought together again in one nation. This implied a monumental task of redesigning, fusing, and implanting concordant social systems to create unity, harmony, and agreement—and to find, through trial and error, appropriate strategies and produce modern arms to defend the process of national construction, in the event that one's neighbors (and former masters) had other ideas (which they did).

The colossal undertaking could begin in earnest only after the new contested borders of the reborn country had been defined and more or less secured, and the several local councils, camps, and committees aspiring to become *the* (or a part of the) national government sorted themselves out. It took another four years for the Wilsonian idea of Poland's self-determination to become Poland in fact, with recognized boundaries, unified territory, an army, and a government.[12] By then, because of the dustups on the frontier question, none of her neighbors were well disposed to her, with the exception of Romania.

Return to life of national entities by self-determination of their people takes time and money; Poland's rebirth had precious little of either. If 1923 is taken as a convenient base, her life span was not quite seventeen years, a short "season" by any count.

As for financial resources, it was the shortest of all. The provinces formerly under Russian mismanagement, particularly the eastern confines, allotted to Poland after a bloody war with the Bolsheviks (1919–21) had promising economic potential, but so far there was nothing to show for the promise other than backwardness, and poverty, and plenty of bison for Hermann in the future. On the other hand, most of Upper Silesia's industries now in Polish hands, courtesy of the Third Uprising (May 2/3–July 5, 1921), had lost the former domestic German and Russian markets for their products as well as many technical experts and CEOs who elected to relocate in Germany, a problem Lloyd George had once raised in his watch-and-monkey allegory. Much of Nether Poland, formerly under Austria, was not all that badly off, though it was hardly the Vienna Woods. True, Poland now had narrow access to the Baltic sea (via the so-called corridor), but if the free port city of Danzig –("free" in League of Nations terminology only) is excluded, the short coast (140 kilometers) mainly consisted of sandy beaches until Gdynia, the wonder seaport of the new Poland, arose from what as late as 1920 was a fishing village. Gdynia reached 127,000 inhabitants in 1939, then the largest and most modern port on the Baltic sea and the tenth largest port in Europe with transshipment of 8.7 million tons of merchandise (46 percent of Poland's foreign trade in 1938) compared to 10,000 tons in 1924. Even without the statistics, it was the pride and joy of the first Polish generation born in their self-owned country; citizens called it Poland's eye on the sea. The eye opened to the world in August 1923, and its vision expanded rapidly thereafter. The person principally responsible for the scheme's inception and fast progress through years of inflation and depression was Eugeniusz Kwiatkowski, a chemical engineer who was also a minister of industry and commerce (1926—30), a deputy premier, and a minister of finance in several governments from 1935 to 1939.

In 1925 expired the coal part of Geneva Convention about Silesia, signed by Germany and Poland in 1922, according to which Germany was obliged to import, tariff-free, six million tons of Polish (Upper Silesian) coal annually for three years. The Weimar

Republic promptly let it be known that it was closing its door to Polish coal. As such things go, Poland upped its tariffs on German goods, and Germany responded by raising its duties on Polish goods and for good measure prohibited the import of a whole slew of Polish products altogether. Before one could say "tit-for-tat," a full-scale tariff war was in progress. In the first quarter of the year Poland had exported nearly three million tons of its Upper Silesian coal to Germany, but they exported only eighteen thousand tons in the second quarter, with the result that unemployment in the country jumped by almost one quarter in four months. The Polish government made a long-term decision to redirect the country's coal exports to Scandinavian countries (Sweden, Norway, and Denmark). Three years later, on Kwiatkowski's initiative, Poland started the construction of a special railway line linking Upper Silesian coalfields with Gdynia. It was the largest ever state transportation investment in the second republic. Unfortunately, by the time the line was ready for use in March 1933, the world was at the height of the Great Depression.

Kwiatkowski was a proponent of the sea trade responsible for the development of Poland's merchant and oceangoing fishing fleets, and he was also the author of a project for the development of a centrally-located industrial region (COP) designed to both economically invigorate areas of the country lacking industry and to locate areas for new defense plants as far away as possible from the German border in Silesia without getting too near the Russian frontier on the other side. The main city was given the name *Stalowa Wola* (Steel Will), which began to grow around a steel mill in 1937–38. Kwiatkowski left Poland for Romania with other members of the Polish government on September 17, 1939. He returned to Poland in 1945. In 1948 he was removed from all official economic activities by Moscow's satellite Polish government and was banned by administrative decree from residing on or near the seacoast. He survived by writing math textbooks. He died in Cracow in 1974, at age eighty-five.

Overall however, professional attention given in Poland to economic construction (distinct from maintenance and repair during the four or so years after Versailles) was overshadowed at the highest levels by military urgencies and party politics that were

seen as a zero-sum game. This was due in some measure to the
scarcity of professional economists, both absolute and relative to
the numbers of professional politicians and army officers holding
positions for reasons other than expertise in the departments of
which they were in charge. It could also be attributed to the state
of economic science grappling at that time with novel aggregate
and monetary disturbances of catastrophic proportions brought
to the surface by the Great War, for which contemporary theories
were unable to provide satisfactory explanations or even just pain-
reducing remedies. Two notable exceptions were Edward Taylor
(1884–1964) and Oskar Lange (1904–1965), who were ideologically far removed. Taylor was a neoclassicist, a professor of political
economy at the Adam Mickiewicz University in Poznań, the founder
of the Poznań school of economics, and an author of several insight-
ful books. He was deeply involved in analyzing the Polish inflation
and published two works on the subject, both in 1926. Lange was
a socialist and the author of a political tract "The Road to Socialist
Economic Planning" (1934). His politico-economic views did not
make him a favorite of the ruling elite, and so from 1931 to 1934
he switched to statistics. In 1934–1936 he visited England and the
United States and wrote a series of analytical works in economic
theory and methodology, including the famous *Economic Theory of
Socialism*. From 1939 to 1945 he was a faculty member of the University of Chicago. After the war he cooperated with the Polish
communist government.

   Poland and some other European countries (notably Germany)
experienced two colossal economic breakdowns that put severe
constraints on what could be done in the way of growth, development, and improvement of public material welfare without adding
to political turmoil and ideological polarization. (Note Hitler's
aborted Munich putsch of November 8–9, 1923.) The first, a bud-
getary/monetary crisis, began right after the war, reaching its
apogee in Poland in 1923 in the form of mind-boggling hyperinflation that made one wonder whether in the absence of foreign
grants or loans there would be enough zeros left in the world to
compute the Polish mark's exchange rate against the U.S. dollar.
The Polish mark was tied to the German mark, which fell precipi-
tously in 1923. The man mainly responsible for finding and putting

into effect pragmatic policy remedies for the financial crisis that threatened the country's economy, and by extension its disintegration from within, was a moderate member of National Democracy, Władysław Grabski, twice premier and several times (including conjointly with his premiership) minister of finance in the first half of the 1920s. Above all, Grabski was a practical economic scholar and a strong-willed optimist. He was not a proponent of expanding the state-owned sector of the economy (banking excepted), and in that sense he was a liberal in the classical, Adam Smith meaning of the word. As was to be expected, he was bad-mouthed by political opponents for alleged mistakes and insufficiencies in matters of foreign policy going back to the July 1920 conference at Spa (Belgium) where, claimed his critics, he failed to obtain military assistance from the Allied Supreme Council in the form of arms and munitions for Poland's defense against the advancing Soviet armies, never mind the extreme unlikelihood of the Council giving such assistance.

The fact remains that Grabski's economic prescriptions worked—for a crucial while, anyway. They included the establishment of a central joint stock bank independent of government bureaucracy with exclusive right to issue legal tender on the English model (*Bank Polski*, Bank of Poland); the injection of 2.5 million U.S. dollars into the stock market to stabilize the exchange rate of the Polish mark against the dollar and thus restore confidence in the melting Polish currency; the reduction in nonessential expenditures by the government (primarily on administrative overstaffing and railroad subsidies); the cessation of printing money to cover governmental deficits; and the replacement of the old Polish mark by a new currency, the *złoty*, backed by gold and foreign currencies freely convertible into gold, with such (gold standard) reserves not to be less than 30 percent of the national currency in circulation. Polish marks were converted into złotys at the rate of 1.8 million marks to the złoty, the latter being made equal to one gold Swiss franc, equivalent to 5.18 U.S. dollars (compared with ten million Polish marks to the dollar on January 8, 1924). The conversion of marks to złotys was completed in July of that year.

Grabski was also instrumental in founding a national investment bank. Similar reforms were introduced during the same period in

Germany, Gdańsk, Austria, and Hungary with international assistance. The Polish reform was carried out entirely from domestic resources. By Fall 1923 in German Silesia, paper monies issued by local governments, railroad administrations, savings banks, and business enterprises were used to supplement the flat-on-its-back German mark. Earlier, toward the end of World War I, small stones were used in some parts to make coins. A similar situation was to be found in post-civil war Spain (July 1940) when in Madrid bus tickets (and, in parts of the countryside, postage stamps) were used to supplement the devalued peso. The bus tickets were made of thin, cheap, yellowish brown, strips of paper. When the bus doors opened, one had to hold the tickets tightly without crushing them, or one's fortune would fly away.

Beginning in 1925, just about the time Germany said paid to its tariff responsibilities under the Versailles Treaty and the Geneva Convention, Grabski's opponents in the seym, now wearing the hat of political economists, began to find Gruyère-sized holes in his reforms, especially those having to do with monetary stabilization through adherence to the gold standard's fixed exchange rates. Compared with what went before, a welcome measure of monetary stability in Poland was in fact achieved in the first six months of Grabski's' second government during which it had plenipotentiary power, reluctantly granted it by the legislature, to introduce its planned reforms. The cooling down of the economy relaxed the atmosphere both in the cabinet and the seym. Grabski took this opportunity to try and stabilize not only the economy but his government by bringing in professional experts who shared his economic and political philosophies. As fate would have it, at this time the Germans cut off their coal purchases, upended the Poles in the tariff war, and dumped massive amounts of złotys onto the Berlin and Vienna money markets, reducing the value of the Polish currency by half of its originally fixed gold value. Unable to stabilize and professionalize the government, Grabski's monetary stability showed cracks under outside pressures beyond his control. With prices rising, Silesian unemployment shooting up, and public disturbances spreading, he resigned from office on November 13, 1925, and retired from political activity after Piłsudski's May 1926 coup. He died in Warsaw in 1938 at the age of sixty-three.

A Question of Honor

With the ex post November 1938 consent of Germany, Great Britain, France, and Italy, Polish troops that entered Zaolzie on October 2, 1938, remained there. It was a Sunday. I remember as a boy watching history unfold from a hill on the Polish side of Cieszyn overlooking the bridge across the river, which defined the boundary between two countries. I also remember having mixed feelings about the whole thing. One was a child's pride in his country for being a winner. I looked at the sky looking for the Polish air force, but there was not much to see, just one or two small planes flying past. A rather short Czech officer came over the bridge, the top of his military cap covered in white for surrender. I felt embarrassed for him. It was general knowledge that the Czechs, with their world-class Škoda works, had a well-outfitted army of some one and a half million men, probably the most modern and best equipped in central Europe. It also had nifty fortifications on its border with Germany, much better than our Sławoj Składkowski's peasant out-houses painted camouflage green. I was sure that if Poland were ever faced with a similar predicament as the Czechs, she would not preemptively surrender but fight and, of course, win. A little later that day, toward the evening, we saw German soldiers with their huge helmets and armed to the teeth, staring at us from their side of the new Polish-German border at Bogumin.

On October 24, Joachim von Ribbentrop, the German foreign minister and former wine merchant, held a confidential meeting with the Polish ambassador in Berlin, Józef Lipski. The two men talked of a plan for the solution of what Germany called "the Polish problem." The German proposal was this: Gdańsk was to revert to the Reich, an extraterritorial highway and a railway line were to be built through Pomorze (the "corridor") for use by German traffic, and Poland was to join the anticomintern pact (that is, abandon its policy of equilibrium). In return, Germany and Poland would mutually recognize their national border, the German-Polish non-aggression declaration would be extended for another twenty-five years, Germany would agree to Poland's extension of its national territory to the east (at the expense of the USSR) and have a common border with Hungary, Germany would cooperate in the matter of

Jewish emigration from Poland and on the colonial question, and there would be mutual consultation (read: asking Germany for permission) on all decisions dealing with foreign policy. It has been alleged that the proposal was kept confidential within Beck's Ministry of Foreign Affairs and was not revealed to other branches of the Polish government for some months. The reason for this was presumably that the German proposal was thought to be Ribbentrop's diplomatic trial balloon rather than the official position of the Reichsführer.[13]

Any speculations that these proposals were diplomatic *tâtonnements* and not the official policy of the Third Reich were dispelled by early January 1939, when the cession of Gdańsk, the corridor proposals, and joining the anticomintern pact were repeated in Berchtesgaden by Hitler to Polish Foreign Affairs Minister Józef Beck, and then again during Ribbentrop's visit to Warsaw on January 25–27 as undeniably official German requirements, just short of an ultimatum. They were found unacceptable at a meeting held in Warsaw's royal castle by Polish civilian and military authorities, including the president of the republic and the commander in chief of the armed forces. To make sure that the Poles did not misunderstand the seriousness of what it was all about, on March 21, 1939, having already swallowed Czechoslovakia, Hitler put it in writing. He addressed a memorandum to the Polish government demanding the return of Gdańsk to the *Heimat*, as well as the highway and railroad construction. The Poles proposed to talk about changing the status of the city from controlled by the League of Nations to joint administration by Poland and Germany, a compromise which was dismissed outright. On March 26, the Polish side officially and unequivocally dismissed Hitler's *Hände hoch* (hands up) memorandum.

At the end of March, Britain, though militarily far from ready, moved away from appeasement and promised Poland assistance in case of aggression. A few days later Hitler ordered his military to speed up the preparation of *Fall Weiss*, the blueprint for his war on Poland, to be ready by August. On April 28, 1939, in his Reichstag oration, he renounced the German-Polish nonaggression declaration of 1934. Eight days later, in a speech to the Polish Senate, Józef Beck informed the nation of Germany's one-sided demands.

He declared the renunciation of the nonaggression declaration to be without foundation and offered to negotiate with the Reich the differences between the two countries regarding the status of Gdańsk on the condition that Poland's access to the sea, legitimated in international law by the Versailles Treaty, not be jeopardized. In practice this would have happened had Poland agreed to the Autobahn being built on its Pomorze Corridor. No high-level plenipotentiaries would be sent to Berlin in order to avoid the kind of bullying and programmed outbursts of Hitler's temper that were used on the sixty-six-year-old Czech President Emil Hacha in the early morning hours of March 15 in Hitler's Berlin chancellery, which made Hacha faint. Poland, Beck said, would not allow itself to be pushed away from the Baltic Sea. "Peace," he continued, was "a valuable and desirable thing … But peace, like almost all the things of this world, has its price, high but measurable. We in Poland, do not recognize the idea of peace at any price. There is only one priceless thing in the life of peoples, nations and states. That thing is honor."[14] Germany became enraged and consternated. Beck's statement caused a 180-degree turn in Hitler's strategy—not in his objective, but in the means of reaching it.

By end of May 1939 there were signs that Nazi Germany and communist Russia were seeking a rapprochement at the very time that seemingly endless, convoluted negotiations between the Soviets and Britain and France about Russia's position in the growing Polish crisis were going on in Moscow. In the event of Germany's attack on Poland, would Russia remain neutral, join the two Western powers in a war against the invaders, and at what price? The "Polish problem" for the negotiators was that the Poles, having learned a lesson from history, would under no circumstances allow Soviet troops to enter Polish territory, even with strong pressure by the edgy French. By early August, Hitler had decided to ask Stalin for his hand in a marriage of convenience that did not exclude divorce down the road once the convenience wore off. After all, Hitler's quarrel was with communism, not with Russia or Stalin, and in some important ways the two states and their leaders were very much alike. On August 19, Hitler sent a telegram to Stalin via the German embassy in Moscow, asking that Ribbentrop be received by August 22 or 23. Ribbentrop would be equipped with full negotiating powers, dowry and all, which included giving Stalin, if need be, anything he asked for: close to half of Poland, Latvia and Estonia, and a free hand in Finland, although Lithuania was to be kept within the German sphere of influence on the model of Slovakia. The trouble was that Stalin, the embodiment of distrust and paranoia, had so far been playing hard to get. Then, on August 20, he broke off his months-long flirtation with the British and French, which was going no place, largely by reason of Stalin's endemic duplicity. He dispatched a reply to Germany, agreeing to receive the Ribbentrop matchmaker in the Kremlin on August 23. The formal German-Soviet nonaggression pact was signed later that same day by Ribbentrop and Molotov, the Soviet commissar for foreign affairs. They also created a secret protocol defining the respective German and Soviet spheres of influence ("territorial-political reorganization of the Baltic states" as it was phrased) in the Baltic countries and Finland: Finland, Estonia, Latvia were to be in the Soviet sphere, Lithuania in the German one. The partition of Poland between the two robbers, along a demarcation line that went right through Warsaw, was shifted on September 28 to be nearer the so-called Curzon Line, proposed by the British Foreign Secretary George Nathaniel Curzon in 1920, as the eastern frontier of Poland (and which, on the basis of the Roosevelt, Churchill, and Stalin Yalta agreement, essentially became the actual eastern border of the country after World War II).

What the secret protocol amounted to was that Germany was to make it as tempting and easy for the Soviets to come into Poland to collect their share of the loot, with the high probability, given the German invasion plan, that Soviet troops need not do much, if any, actual fighting; they could just grab the spoils. Mussolini informed Hitler that Italy was not ready for war and would not be for at least three years. Having thought it over, and to show his regard for his ideological elder who had backed him up on the Austrian Anschluss, Hitler postponed the attack on Poland by five days.

The key idea of the *Fall Weiss* blueprint was speed; mobility of attack; and overwhelming superiority in numbers of men, firepower, and up-to-date military technology directed not only against the enemy's armed forces but its civilian population: *Blitzkrieg* (lightning warfare) and *Totalkrieg* (total warfare) that, together with mercilessness of the regular army and the unspeakable terror perpetrated by the special units (*Einsatzgruppen*, the death squads) would spread shock, confusion, panic, and paralyzing trauma in the victim's ranks.

On Friday, September 1, 1939, at 4.40 in the morning, the forces of destruction and savagery kicked in the door, and the terror of World War II began. Their Soviet co-conspirators waited in the backyard for sixteen days, pushed the back gate on September 17, and picked up their share of the territorial loot.

Notes

1.   Mark Paul, "Traditional Jewish Attitudes Toward Poles" (October 2007).   http://www.glaukopis.pl/pdf/czytelnia/TraditionalJewishAttitudes TowardPoles_MarkPaul.pdf

2.   As of the time of writing (2008), the law was still in force.

3.   Piłsudski hoped that Wilno and its region would be a state of its own, as Central Lithuania, which he saw as the best compromise with the Lithuanian demand for the city and territory, and a stepping stone to a Polish-Lithuanian federation. This little statelet did exist for a short while, but its Polish majority voted to be part of Poland, while the Lithuanian minority there abstained.

4.   I witnessed the event.

5.   Contrary to memories of my youth, although there was a "Colonial League" in Poland, Foreign Minister Beck never seriously thought of colonies. What he wanted was Polish access to raw materials via international trade agreements.

6.   The song was named after the author of the lyrics, one Horst Wessel, son of a Lutheran minister; protégé of the future minister of propaganda, Josef Goebbels; and member of the SA (*Sturmabteilung*), the party's brown-shirted storm troopers, street brawler, and player of medieval oboes who in 1930, at the age of twenty-two, was shot in the face by an assailant apparently for falling behind in rent payments. The murder was blamed on the communists. The song was outlawed after the defeat of Germany in 1945—and still is. In loose translation: "Raise high the flag ! Close ranks, now all together !"

7.   Personal recollection.

8.   In the Munich *Haus der Deutschen Kunst* (House of German Art, HdDK) designed by architect Paul Ludwig Troost and built on Hitler's order between 1933 and 1937, a porcelain vomitory large enough to accommodate Hermann's embonpoint was still in the early 1950s riveted to the walls of the men's room. It was reserved for Göring's use during or quickly after a banquet and generous doses of alcoholic beverages that followed his viewing of Nazi art on display at the Haus. Göring was shortly to become an avid collector of art stolen from all over German-occupied Europe. He committed suicide after being sentenced to death by the Nuremberg Tribunal in 1946. One piece of art he did not take as a keepsake was the very popular allegorical painting by Hubert Lanzinger of Hitler as a knight in shining armor on a horse with the flag raised high, called *der Bannerträger* (the Standard-bearer).

9.   Alicja Galas, Artur Galas. *Dzieje Śląska w datach* (History of Silesia in dates). Wrocław: "Cadus," 2004, 235.

10. Before Poland reemerged in 1918–1920 as an independent state entity, there had been some migrations of workers from Austrian Galicia to the more economically developed western region of Poland under Prussian control. Also, as we have seen in chapter 2, there had been movements of Polish intelligentsia political activists from Russian and Prussian occupation to Nether Poland administered by Vienna.

11. On September 17, 1939, with other members of the government, Grażynski left Poland for Romania and subsequently France. After the collapse of France in June 1940, he made his way to Britain where, probably on the advice of his political opponents in the Polish Government in Exile (headed by General Władysław Sikorski), he was interned together with many other former *Sanacja* officials in Rothesay, the main town on Bute Island off the west coast of Scotland. Released in 1942, he served in the Polish army in Scotland (1943–45) and was promoted to the rank of lieutenant colonel. After the war (1946–1960), he was a member of the exile government's National Unity Council, a body that for practical political reasons was no longer recognized by any Western country other than Ireland—and that only for a while. He was fatally injured by a car in a London street in December 1965 and rests in Putney Vale Cemetery with his wife, Helena, once actively involved in the development of the Polish Girl Scout Organization.

12. To recall, the first president of the republic, Gabriel Narutowicz, was assassinated on December 16, 1922. The national democrats tried to portray the assassin, one Eligiusz Niewiadomski, as a national hero. The cabinet resigned, and General Władysław Sikorski took over the presidency as well as the ministry of the interior, responsible for the preservation of public order. His government resigned in May 1923. After World War II, the crown was removed from the head of the white eagle (Poland's coat of arms) by the communists in deference to their selective populism and subservience to their puppeteers in Moscow. It was put back on again after the communist government was dispatched. in 1990.

13. Antoni Czubiński. *Najnowsze dzieje Polski, 1914–1983* [The Latest Polish History, 1914–1983], Warszawa: Państwowe Wydawnictwo Naukowe, 1987, 249.

14. Foreign Minister Beck's speech to the senate may be found in *Varia: Komendant, Naczelnik, Marszałek, Józef Piłsudski: jego czasy* (Chief, Commander, Mashal, Józef Piłsudski: His Times) at http://komendant.cal.pl/content/view/97/135. The video of the speech is available on YouTube. Later, after the destruction of Warsaw in September 1939 and August 1–October 2, 1944, the cynics would say, "We have our honor; the Czechs have their Prague." On Hacha's experience with Hitler in the cavernous Reichschancellery: Eugene Davidson, *The Unmaking of Adolf Hitler*. Columbia: University of Missouri Press, 1995, 343–359.

THE FOURTH PARTITION OF POLAND
(September 1939–1945)

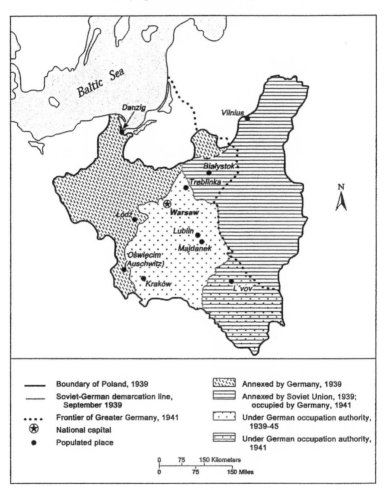

—— Boundary of Poland, 1939	Annexed by Germany, 1939
—— Soviet-German demarcation line, September 1939	Annexed by Soviet Union, 1939; occupied by Germany, 1941
•••• Frontier of Greater Germany, 1941	Under German occupation authority, 1939–45
✪ National capital	Under German occupation authority, 1941
• Populated place	

0   75   150 Kilometers
0   75   150 Miles

The Lights Go Out in Poland

September 1939 Defense War

The undermanned and insufficiently trained Polish armies designated in the High Command's defense plan "Z" (for *zachód*, "west")
to hold the several expected fronts were quickly splintered by
larger, better equipped, and more mobile German armies. Many
mobilized Polish soldiers never reached their units before it was
all over because the general mobilization was ordered just one day
before the German assault.

On September 6, the day German troops not only seized
Cracow—a city less than a hundred miles from their border that,
according to widespread prewar opinion in Poland, the aggressor
would never reach—they were on their way to Warsaw. At this
point Marshal Rydz-Śmigły, his general staff, and the government
headed by President Mościcki and Premier Sławoj Składkowski
shifted first to Nałęczów near Lublin, then to Lublin, then to Krze-
mieniec, and then to Brześć, the last within spitting distance of
where seven Soviet armies totaling more than half a million men
and five thousand tanks were waiting for Stalin to give the order to
cross the Polish border. On the day the two-week siege of the Polish
capital began (September 13), the Germans broke the resistance of
Polish forces along the Narew and Bug rivers and took Brześć the
next day.[1] Just before that, Rydz-Śmigły and the government moved
to Kuty on the Romanian border. By that time Poland was falling
apart under the German blows. A decision was made to make a
stand on a last defense line, the Romanian Bridgehead (southeastern marches bordering on Romania and Hungary). It could have
become a defense line, theoretically at least, if only the Soviets had

kept out of conflict. By then the fragile and mostly mute communications system linking military and civilian authorities, and the two with the citizens, had for all practical purposes collapsed, leaving a nerve-wracking, chaos-promoting news vacuum. Simply put, nobody knew what was going on.

On September 17, 1939, at dawn, the Soviets fulfilled their obligation under the Ribbentrop-Molotov pact, handing a note justifying their action to the Polish ambassador in Moscow at three in the morning. As they crossed the thousand-kilometer-long border, they often put on a show of comradeship in a common cause, waving white flags at the Polish border protection troops (KOP), shouting anti-German slogans (*Na Germanca!* Let's get the Germans!) and other such tripe to add to the confusion of the already disoriented Polish audience. This lasted only a few hours. Then they put on their helmets, slammed down their tank lids, surrounded the Polish soldiers, and took prisoner as many as 180,000 officers and enlisted men, including Jan Przybyła's wounded oldest son, the twenty-four-year-old noncommissioned officer Zbyszek. About twenty thousand men were killed or wounded in this socialist realist masquerade, an omen of what was to come.[2] Three hours after the Soviets had crossed the border, the news reached the ambulatory Polish supreme army headquarters. Before leaving for Romania, Rydz-Śmigły issued to the scattered armies his last-but-one order (general directive, *dyrektywa ogólna*), the last from Polish soil. It epitomizes the confusion at that time, not only of society at large but at the very highest echelons of national leadership. As if scribbled hastily on the knee, it read:

> The Soviets have entered. I order a general retreat to Romania and Hungary by the shortest routes. Do not fight the Bolsheviks unless attacked from their side, or if they try to disarm units. The task of Warsaw and cities that were to defend themselves against the Germans—unchanged. Cities which the Soviets will approach, should negotiate with them regarding exit of garrisons to Hungary or Romania.[3]

Then he and his civilian colleagues, the president, and cabinet ministers of the Second Polish Republic crossed over to Romania and were interned. Three days later (September 20, 1939), having reflected on the consequences of his departure on national morale and the judgment of history, he issued from the place of internment his last order—more an explanation, rationalization, and defense of his recent actions than a military command, although some prefer to call it an "extension" of his previous order. The "do not fight the Bolsheviks" order was, Rydz-Śmigły argued, intended to gain time (what would have been only a few hours at the most) for the withdrawal of as many troops as possible to Romania and Hungary:

> I wanted to do that so as to then take you to France and there organize a Polish army. My intention was that Polish soldiers continue to take part in such a way that at a victorious end to the war there would be a Polish army that would represent Poland and its interests.[4]

Of about a quarter million Polish officers, noncommissioned officers, and enlisted men from various eastward retreating armies who on September 17, 1939 had found themselves in the Romanian Bridgehead, several tens of thousands (including eight thousand airmen) managed by early 1940 to reach France from Romania and Hungary, sometimes in improbable, roundabout ways (for example, Silesians sneaking through Cilicia to French-administered Syria) that made Lloyd George's geography look normal. Among them were the remnants of the Tenth Motorized Cavalry Division commanded by General Stanisław Maczek, which in the course of five days' nonstop combat in defense of Nether Poland against overwhelming German forces, and then in screening operations, slowed down the enemy's advance at the cost of the lives of half of its men. After September 17, the division crossed to Hungary, where it was interned. Many of the survivors made it to France. Others, both former soldiers and civilians, came later, escaping from occupied Poland at enormous personal risk. Among these was Jan Przybyła's youngest son, seventeen-year-old Janusz.

While Rydz-Śmigły was composing his apologia, most of the other military and civilian internees in Romania and Hungary were unaware of the document and were by themselves figuring out ways to leave Romania and Hungary. They intended to head for what they still thought, despite troubling evidence to the contrary, was resolute, mighty France where, they heard through the grapevine, a Polish army was being reconstituted. Some made it through Italy, Germany's uncomfortable ally who seemed to look the other way when in the fall and winter of 1939–40, on the train platforms of Milano, it saw large numbers of men of military age dressed in what obviously had been army uniforms calling themselves "Polish tourists" and changing trains for the French border station of Modane.

In the meantime, in Craiova, President Mościcki was busy dealing with the constitutional consequences of the disaster that had befallen his country. On September 25, 1939, in a decree predated to September 17, 1939, he nominated to the presidency General Bolesław Wieniawa-Długoszowski, a Piłsudski legionnaire who was at that time Polish ambassador to Rome. The appointment, date and all, was intended to discourage Rydz-Śmigły—who on September 1 had been nominated by Mościcki to succeed him but apparently didn't get it—from even thinking about that job. The new nominee caught a train from Rome to Switzerland and from there proceeded to France only to find that the French government found him unacceptable for the position of Polish president, partly because of the opposition of the French ambassador to Poland and General Władysław Sikorski. Długoszowski agreed to withdraw, and the decree of September 17 was suitably changed on September 20 to nominate for this post Władysław Raczkiewicz, formerly minister of internal affairs, governor of several provinces, and speaker of the senate. Mościcki resigned from the presidency on September 30 and settled with his family in Switzerland.[5] On November 7, 1939, the role of commander in chief of the newly formed Polish Army in Exile—equipped with surplus, sometimes obsolete, French arms—was assumed by General Sikorski who had made it to France from Romania already in September.

Rydz-Śmigły resigned as commander in chief and inspector general of the armed forces twelve days earlier. He had been moved from Craiova on October 14 and had been housed in the residence of a former Romanian prime minister in Dragoslavele. On December 10, 1940, he escaped and clandestinely entered Hungary. The following year (October 25, 1941), he left Hungary and made his way through Sucha Hora in Slovakia to the Polish village of Chochołów near Zakopane and, five days later, reached Warsaw. He asked to be admitted to the underground armed resistance organization (ZWZ) at the rank of private. His request met with a frosty reception, and as far as can be established he did not take part in the underground struggle against the Germans in the few remaining weeks of his life. He died of *angina pectoris*, on December 2, 1941, and was buried in the Warsaw Powązki cemetery under the name of Adam Zawisza. In 1991, after the communists had been shown the door, the tombstone was changed to his own name. The causes and date of his death continue to be subjects of controversy. There are several phantasmagoric conspiracy theories based largely on anecdotes and fueled by old political and personal grudges that, even in the face of a deadly enemy, once divided valiant insurgents in the several branches of the resistance movement. As yet there is no peace in eternal rest.

Those facing the invader from trenches or across the river, with guns blazing, bombs falling, and fires burning, did not need to be reminded from near the Romanian border that "the task of Warsaw and cities that were to defend themselves against the Germans [was] unchanged." It was realistically self-evident to those on the spot that it was "them or us" until the last bullet, so the remnants of various Polish armies that had managed to reach Warsaw from whichever direction—sometimes having to fight their way *into* the encirclement—defended the capital from September 14–28, led by General Walerian Czuma and the city president, Stefan Starzyński, an economist, Piłsudski legionnaire, Sanacja man, former deputy minister of finance, and member of the BBWR. Starzyński refused to leave the capital with the president of the republic and the national government on September 6, when two German motorized panzer divisions were heading for the city. Thereafter, as civil commissioner of defense, he rejected repeated counsels to leave Warsaw, addressing the citizens by radio each day with calming broadcasts to keep up their spirits under bombardments by German heavy artillery and carpet-bombing. He was arrested by the gestapo on October 5, 1939, together with other eminent personalities to serve as hostages during the victory parade before Hitler. After the parade, he was released and rearrested shortly thereafter. It is believed that he was sent to the Moubit prison in Berlin and from there to Dachau concentration camp, where he was executed probably in 1943.

Modlin (*Forteca Modlin*), a place near Warsaw, defended itself against numerically and technically superior German forces from September 13–29. Troops on the Hel peninsula, opposite the port of Gdynia on the Baltic coast, put up fierce resistance from day one. After September 20 there were no Polish troops left anywhere that could have helped them. Despite that, they continued their resistance until they ran out of ammunition on October 1, when an act of surrender was signed in the Sopot Grand Hotel. The next day German forces took over the last sandbar of Poland's access to the sea. In the September 1939 "War of Resistance," as it has come to be known, the very last to surrender was General Franciszek Kleeberg's independent operational group "Polesie," which tried and failed to carry out Rydz-Śmigły's order of September 17 to break through enemy lines to reach the Romanian Bridgehead and then turned around and headed for Warsaw. On the way it fought a number of battles with the Soviets and German panzer divisions from October 2–5, when it ran out of ammunition and surrendered. General Kleeberg was put in a prisoner of war camp (Oflag IVB) near Dresden and died in a military hospital in Weiss Hirsch on April 5, 1941. His remains were brought back to Poland in 1959 and buried in a military cemetery at the place of his last battle.

To prevent being captured by an imminent German invasion, on August 30 the naval destroyers *Błyskawica*, *Grom*, and *Burza* received a central headquarters order requiring them to leave Gdynia forthwith and sail for Britain, with which five days earlier Poland had concluded an agreement of mutual military assistance. They did so, and in the evening of September 1, accompanied by British naval vessels, the ships entered the Scottish port of Leith near Edinburgh. They subsequently took part in the battles of the Atlantic and the North Sea.

Nightmare

In the 1921 Upper Silesian plebiscite, Chropaczów, a smoky, heavy industry and mining township, voted 66.8 percent for belonging to Poland and got its wish a year later. It lay next to the newly demarcated, tense, national frontier between Poland and Germany;

so that among other inconveniences in a densely populated area, the border line cut across a narrow-gauge trolley line. Given that this was contested Silesia, to deal with simple, everyday border-crossing procedures (IDs, customs, duties, and so on) for passengers going home from one side of town to another, required nothing less than a German-Polish, Upper Silesian Convention, which was duly signed on May 15, 1922 in Geneva, Switzerland, after much contrariness by hot-under-the-collar representatives of the two countries, with League of Nations people looking on. The customs duties part of the convention effectively expired three years later when Germany launched a tariff war on Poland. The national border itself was scythed by German troops in the early morning hours of September 1, 1939, and the name of the place was promptly changed to *Schlesiengrube* (Silesian Mine).

At that juncture Jan Przybyła, who since 1930 had been the chief administrator of Chropaczów, left for Cracow, the former Polish capital (1320–1596) and considered by many Poles at the time a "safe" town, beyond the reach of even the strong military power of Hitler's Germany. This was the second exile from his cherished "closer homeland," thirty-six years after his departure from Silesia for the same city. Marta also left for Cracow. She apparently returned to Katowice to look after "Przybyłówka," their Katowice-Ligota home on Kłodnicka Street where a year earlier they had celebrated the twenty-fifth anniversary of their marriage surrounded by their children and other members of the family. However, when she did not sign the *Deutsche Volksliste* (German people's appurtenance list), which she could have done by reason of the German origin of her maiden family name, she had to leave Silesia, and the Katowice-Ligota home was expropriated (January 22, 1941). She then settled in Cracow, the administrative center of the General Government, the part of Poland not formally incorporated into the German Reich or given away to the Soviets under the August 23, 1939, Ribbentrop-Molotov Pact. For the time being, people in Cracow were permitted to live and make a modest living under the watchful eye of the multifarious and ever-present German secret police. From June 1, 1940, until the end of the war in 1945, the gestapo issued, generally once a month, so-called surveillance dailies, listing up to thirty thousand names of people sought by the

Cracow gestapo. Jan's name was certainly on those death warrants, and for security reasons he, Marta, and Zbyszek lived separately. Marta resided in Borek Fałęcki, not far from Jan's shelter, where she found a job as teacher in a primary school, possibly a clandestine one, since by then all Polish schools had been banned. Maria (Marysia) lived in Warsaw, where she worked for a savings bank.[6]

With his memories of the relatively nonchalant occupation of Cracow on his first visit as a young man, Jan would not have been alone in hoping, perhaps dreaming, that this time too, while tragic and deplorable, the occupation would not descend into savagery. It in fact did. Jan was also resolved to do what he could, as he had done in his younger days, to preserve what could be saved of Polish culture and work against all odds for his country's second resurrection. He may have underestimated the wear and tear that time brings on a person, and being a moral man, the potency of pure evil.

The hope of decent people that the Nazi occupation of Cracow— while predictably harsh given its Prussian warrior culture's temperamental connections and the recruitment of its *ne plus ultra* from the criminal and sadistic detritus of Germanic society, would nevertheless bear at least a distant resemblance to that of the Habsburg empire so far as minimal civilized conduct was concerned—was thoroughly crushed two months after the entry of the Wehrmacht and its SS/gestapo helpers into the city.[7]

On November 6, 1939, SS-*Obersturmbannführer* (lieutenant colonel) Bruno Müller ordered the rector of Jagiellonian University to have all professors come to the Collegium Novum and hear a lecture on the Reich's policy regarding science and university education in the General Government. One hundred forty professors came, were screamed at by the *Obesturmbannführer*, and then were manhandled and arrested. For the sake of punctilious order and thoroughness (*Ordnung und Gründlichkeit*), anyone unfortunate enough to have been in the building at the time was also picked up, bringing the total to one hundred eighty-three people. After interrogation they were sent to the Sachsenhausen and Dachau concentration camps during the worst winter in living memory. The lecture trap went by the code name *Sonderaktion Krakau* (Special Action Cracow), and the "lecturer," Doctor of Laws (1935) Bruno

Müller, was chief of the Cracow SS security police and the leader of an *Einsatzkommando* (EK2 / 1), at that time one of twenty-five such "special task forces" staffed by what Poles in the region considered to have been psychopaths. The units became widely known during the 1941 German incursion into Russia as *Einsatzgruppen* (and their component *Einsatzkommandos*). The *Einsatzkommandos* in Poland were usually headed by the Nazi Party's intellectual elite. Of the twenty-five units operating in Poland in 1939 and the early 1940s, fifteen were led by men with doctoral degrees, and not just from the Hitler era.

There was an international outcry over the arrest, and it seemed to have had a (temporary) effect. Most of the older professors were set free by about February 1940, but fifteen died in the camps from maltreatment, and another five within days of their release. Three years later many of those who survived the ordeal (including the former Rector Tadeusz Lehr-Spławiński) formed an underground university in Cracow attended by eight hundred students, among them Karol Wojtyła, the future Pope John Paul II.

Bruno Müller was a nasty piece of work. Born in 1905 in Strassburg (Strasbourg, at that time under German rule), he held until 1945 a number of high SS, security police (*Sicherheitzdienst, SD*) positions wherever grisly work had to be done: in Cracow, Jarosław, Rouen, Prague, and Kiel. He was captured by the British in 1947 and tried by a war crimes court in December, which sentenced him to twenty years of hard labor. After being released in 1953, he became an insurance salesman in the Kiel area. In 1960 he died peacefully of natural causes in Oldenburg, where in 1935 he had begun his secret police career as head of the local office of the gestapo (*Geheimstaatspolizei*). During the Cold War, repeated attempts by the communist Polish government to have him extradited to Poland were unsuccessful.

The *Sonderaktion Krakau* was only the first step in something much larger, more gruesome, and longer-term in Hitler's plan for the final solution (*Endlösung*) of the "Polish Problem": the extermination of Poland as a nation and a culture, and the enslavement and eventual physical annihilation of its people (nationcide) and all "sub-humans" (*Untermenschen*) in Europe and the world. "Poland," Hitler said at a luncheon with Hans Frank and Martin Bormann, "must be treated as a colony; the Poles will be slaves of the greater German World State."[8] The name given to the opening act of this demonic tragedy by its executor-executioner Hans Frank, head of the general government in Cracow, was *AB-Aktion* (Special Pacification Operation). Having "registered" the Jagiellonian University professors in concentration camps, the *Volskstumkampf,* in all its violent brutality, was directed at Polish secondary school teachers—not in Cracow alone but all across occupied Poland. *Volkstum* (People's nationality) was an obfuscatory, pseudophilosophical, jingoistic, blood-and-soul-and-native-soil concept that had been knocking about in some German heads for a considerable time, including the head of Adolf Hitler, who in his *Mein Kampf* (1925–27) made it more racist and lethal by emphasizing the need for unrelenting and unforgiving struggle. Hence the Bismarckian *Kulturkampf* (*Mann muss die Polen aufs Maul schlagen*) was replaced by the *Volkstumkampf,* and the result was mass executions, mass annihilation; Germany's actions directly contributed to the decline of Western culture in the early decades of the twentieth century.

In the spring and summer of 1940, especially May and June, the *AB-Aktion* was expanded to include the entire intelligentsia, the educated elite of the Polish nation, their institutions, and their creative endeavors. Hans Frank put it simply: "What we have now recognized in Poland to be the elite, must be liquidated." The Poles were "to become a society of peasants and workers [with no] cultured class"—a variant of what the Prussian regime tried to do to Polish Silesians in the past, but this time without any legal or moral restraint whatsoever, and over a wider area, in a shorter time, at a lower cost (slave labor), and with higher efficiency.[9]

These horror hunts, juristically referred to as *AB Intelligenz Aktion* (AB's Intelligence Operation), were a preemptive cleansing action designed to strike terror in the heart of anyone contemplating to sabotage the New Order as it prepared to, and did, tear apart France. Within weeks, more than thirty thousand people were rounded up throughout the General Government; thrown in prisons (including Montelupi in Kraków and Pawiak in Warsaw); beaten and tortured during lengthy interrogations; and sent to Sachsenhausen, Mauthausen, and the still-under-construction Auschwitz (Oswięcim) concentrations camps, where most of them perished.

About twenty-five hundred of "those we [the Nazis] have recognized in Poland as the elite" were executed in the Palmiry forest and five other locations near Warsaw from December 1939 to July 1941. Among the butchered remains that could be identified were those of Maciej Rataj, two-term seym deputy and speaker of the seym (1922-1928); Janusz Kapuściński, an Olympic gold medalist; Jan Pohoski, vice president of Warsaw; Mieszysław Miedziałkowski, Polish Socialist Party activist and one of the founders of Centerleft; and Senator Helena Jaroszewiczowa, one of nearly two hundred women murdered in this *AB Aktion*. The victims were transported in trucks from Pawiak to the wooded place of execution and with their arms tied behind their backs,were lined up on the edge of an escarpment so that after being mowed down by machine gun fire, they would fall into deep pits. Those still showing signs of life were finished off. The graves, filled with several layers of bodies, were covered with earth on which pine trees were planted to conceal the deed.[10]

The *AB Aktion* came in many garbs. A favorite with the genocidal boys in black was the roundup (in Polish, the dreaded *łapanka*). The procedure was wildcat in nature, quick, simple, and random: SS men in their Opels, as well as regular soldiers in their olive green, appeared out of nowhere, blocking off a section of a street, an alley, a square or trolley car; grabbed all who happened to be there; forced them up against the wall of the nearest building; scooped them up into trucks and Black Marias; and swished them away to their fate— slave labor or death. Sometimes, by chance, the wildcatters would catch someone they were actually after and squeeze a confession out of him at the gestapo headquarters in Cracow. However, the main purpose was simply to spread dread.

Once in a while these roundups didn't work out quite as planned. Sometime in 1940, Zbigniew (Zbyszek) Przybyła paid a visit to Uncle Gustaw Deissenberg (his mother Marta's brother), who in the interwar years was the Warsaw representative of the Italian automobile firm Fiat and had an office in the hotel Bristol on the elegant Krakowskie Przedmieście. Deissenberg lived on long, narrow Kozia Street, not far from his office. Because Zbyszek was actively sought by the gestapo for his underground resistance to German occupation, his visit to Warsaw was not motivated so much by a desire to see his relative again as by the need to cover his tracks and find a less endangered hiding place in another city for a while. One day, several gestapo cars screeched to a halt outside the apartment house and adjacent buildings on Kozia Street, and the drivers and passengers jumped out with guns at the ready, ran into the houses, and began a search of all the apartments in the blocked-in area. They chased the inhabitants—Zbyszek and Gustaw among them—out into the street and lined them up against the wall, where they had to stand perfectly still, their hands raised above the back of their heads, the gestapos aiming their rifles at them from the opposite wall a few feet away.

Just when they thought that their life would end, a drawer came flying out of one of the windows of a house, evidently thrown by a frustrated SS gentleman turning someone's home upside down and not finding anything politically incriminating or materially cashable. The flying drawer hit one of the gestapo men in the street smack on the head. He fell to the ground unconscious, bleeding profusely. His companion turned to the hostages standing with their hands up against the wall and asked whether there was a doctor among them. Zbyszek, who was not a doctor but knew a thing or two about first aid from his brief exposure in Cracow to premed education, stepped out of the line saying that he was one. The SS men rushed a first aid kit from their car, and Zbyszek began to dress the wounded man's head but soon found that he could not manage it alone. He turned to the gestapo man and asked for a helper, pointing to his uncle, who stood terrified at the wall. The gestapo man allowed Gustaw to come and help the "doc" with the medical ministrations. When they were finished with the disinfection, bandaging, and such, the Germans having satisfied themselves that their man was alive and properly taken care of, ordered the two medics to carry the injured man to a car. This done, the gestapo man in charge told them they could leave. When later they returned to the apartment in Kozia Street, they learned that all the others had been taken away by the gestapo, most of them never to be seen again.[11]

While this was going on, the Soviets held massacre fests of their own that—in their ideological objectives, methodology, and numbers—bore close resemblance to the *Volkstumkampf*. National socialism was rooted in Hitler's obsessive racism, according to which only one race, the Germanic, was worth anything and was therefore appointed by destiny (*Schicksal*) to dominate and enlighten the world. Socialism found its equivalent in Stalin's Marxist-Leninist social racism, where the superior class (twin of the Nazi/Nordic *Herrenmensch*), the international proletariat (the have-nots in terms of property),led by the communist party, would inevitably prevail and expropriate—that is, liquidate—the rotten capitalist elite's property, its culture, and its very life by reason of Marx's historical necessity and revolutionary conflict (dialectical, "thesis-antithesis" *Kampf*).

But that is ideological mythology, grim fairy tales. As for the practical action needed to prod destiny and historical necessity so that they would be completed in all their glory within the life spans of the anointed Führer and the "Father of all Peoples," Russia had one advantage over Germany: space galore. Much of the available land was uninhabitable because of lousy climate, but it was just the thing for class enemies—the "people outside the people," the excludable people, the nonpeople as Chairman Mao Zedong put it in his dopey aphorisms. When one is endowed by nature with endless acres of Siberian taiga and permafrost, why not send the elite troublemakers—as a matter of fact, *any* troublemakers—there? Better still, make them walk there dressed in their summer rags just before winter sets in. By the time they arrive at their destination—the coal mines of Vorkuta, for example—most of them would be gone forever. Having the prisoners build the biggest extermination camp in the world, like Auschwitz, does not make dialectically materialist sense when one is fortunate enough to have nature take care of the problem by having the rascals starve and freeze to death in "the prison without a roof" at a temperature of fifty below zero Fahrenheit, not counting the chill factor. So in addition to tormenting the people's enemies in the KGB cellars of Lubyanka and Kharkhov and the slaughter house of Smolensk until they mercifully died, or shooting them in the back of the head in Katyń and other places, the Soviet communists, like their imperialist predecessors the Russian Czars, sent those they considered to be Polish intelligentsia, the bourgeoisie ("head of the nation"), to their death in the taiga.

But the Russians didn't stop there. In a virtual mirroring of the Nazi expulsion of Poles to the General Government from the part

of Poland directly incorporated into the Third Reich, Russian communists, assisted by resident Ukrainians, proceeded to ethnically /
nationally cleanse Polish peasants,workers, artisans, and clerks
from the rural areas of eastern Poland occupied by Soviet troops
as per the Ribbentrop-Molotov pact, appropriating their homes
and family possessions, looting their churches, and deporting their
churchmen. Beginning in the extremely cold winter of 1939–40 and
through the spring of 1941, the Soviets packed those they called
kulaks (rich-peasant class oppressors) to the brim in railroad freight
cars (the "white mortuaries"). Tens of thousands of rural Polish
families, including children, were transported to do slave labor in
camps (*łagry*) and collective farms (the distinction between the two
being narrower than the names would suggest) in the backward
depths of the Soviet empire.

Like German Nazism, the Soviet system was one of tight
secrecy and was rife with rumor, so the number of Poles deported
to the Soviet Union cannot be known to this day with the degree
of precision that statisticians prefer. At a conservative count, it was
several hundred thousand.[12]

On June 22, 1941, German armies attacked the Soviet Union.
Eight days later they took Lwów without much trouble. They were
received with bread and salt by local Ukrainians, now much more
numerous than they had been before the Poles lost the city to the
Soviets in September 1939. The army was followed by the *Abwehr*,
the army's military intelligence appendage, and the *Einsatzgruppen*
(death squads) under the command of an old Kraków hand, thirty-
eight-year-old SS-*Oberführer*, Dr. *juris* (Leipzig University, 1929)
Karl Eberhard Schöngarth, who was high up in the hierarchy of the
Nazi secret police and security services.[13] One of the brains behind
the formation of the murder squads, he brought his own special
Einsatzgruppe "Galizien" (including the zBV made up of Ukrainian
collaborators trained in the SS Sipo-AD Police School in Zakopane,
later in Rabka) to cleanse and liquidate in Lwów, a once-cultured
city. The *Einsatzgruppe* would get rid of those defying the Pan-Ger-
man New Order: the Polish intellectuals still hanging around the
universities poisoning young minds, as well as the remaining Jews,
many of them refugees from Nazi-occupied western Poland, who
after September 17, 1939, survived Soviet deportations and local

Ukrainian "special measures." There were one hundred twenty thousand Jews in Lwów when Schöngarth came on the scene. By the time he was reassigned, in July 1943, there were less than a thousand.

Schöngarth also brought along an improved *AB-Aktion* blueprint. After the arrest of the Jagiellonian University professors, Hans Frank complained to a meeting of SS and police officials that the way the business had been handled caused the Third Reich no end of headaches because of the international community's negative reaction. From now on, there was no dilly dallying. Those arrested were to be shot on the spot. Moreover, this way was cheaper and more efficient: no longer would prisoners have to be shuffled from one concentration camp to another before being executed. The new plan made the SS men happier in their job and it earned the improver, Dr. Schöngarth, an SS Reichsführer's Honor Sword and the Reich's Sports Badge. In recognition of his exemplary service, Dr. Schöngarth was invited to attend the Wannsee conference on January 20, 1942, at which the "Final Solution of the Jewish Problem" was discussed and the decision made to murder all the Jews in the rapidly expanding Germanic living space, preferably in gas chambers. After more dirty work in the Netherlands where he applied the experience and methods gained in Poland (*polnische Verhältnisse*, Polish analogy), Schöngarth was promoted to the rank of SS *Brigadeführer* (brigadier general). Captured at the end of the war and tried by a British military court in Burgsteinfurt on February 11, 1946, he was found guilty of murdering an Allied (probably American) airman who bailed out of his disabled plane and landed unhurt on the lawn of a villa, which as fate would have it, was the headquarters of the SS-AD security services in Enschede, Holland. Schöngart was hanged on May 16, 1946. Of the more than fifty *Einsatzgruppen* officers brought to trial after the war in Nuremberg and elsewhere, five received the death sentence. During the first 55 days of the war in Poland (September 1–October 25, 1939) the approximately 2,700 *Einsatzgruppen* criminals executed more than 16,000 people on the spot.[14]

Two days after Schöngarth's arrival in Lwów, during the night of July 3/4, 1941, the *AB-Aktion* was applied in its upgraded form.[15] The homes of Polish university professors were entered or broken into (locks were shot out if the door was not opened right away). The professors and all family members, as well as guests present in the house, were taken outside, walked in single files to trenches that had been dug to specifications just before at nearby Wulecki Heights, were made to stand four at a time at the edge of their graves, and were shot from behind by a firing squad. After they fell into the pit, new groups were lined up, and the executions continued. There were no coups de grâce even though at least two of the victims who fell into the ditches appeared to have been still alive. Earth was spread over the graves and stamped on with military boots. The massacre was witnessed by many neighbors, awakened by the shots and puzzled by the activity at the Heights this late. In the rising daylight they watched the unfolding scene of horror from the windows of their homes, several of them using binoculars. Thirty-eight persons (including four women) were murdered in the Wulecki Heights, and two at another location on July 11 or 12. On direct order of SS Reichsführer Heinrich Himmler, Kazimierz Bartel, chairman of the department of geometry at the Lwów Institute of Technology and a former prime minister, was arrested on July 2 by Schöngarth's *Einsatzgruppen* and executed at sunrise on July 26. The whole Sonderaktion was, as in all other SS murder enterprises, accompanied by tawdry robberies and looting whatever was at hand, from confiscation for personal use of housing, valuable paintings, and other art objects, diamonds, and gold coins for the big shots from *Obersturmbannführer* (lieutenant colonel) on up, to cigarette cases, bracelets, watches, fountain pens, cameras, cups, and saucers on down to the ranks at and below SS *Rottenführer* (corporal).

When the tide of war turned against Germany during 1943, and more so the following year, in the interest of hygiene, national reputation, and possible personal troubles if captured by the Russians or the Western Allies, the decomposed bodies were exhumed and disposed of in a sandy area in the Krzywczycki Forest on the outskirts of the city. How this was done defies and revolts the imagination. It has been told in exotic languages like Polish, but is not widely, if at all, known in the West. So let's retell it—briefly, for it is not pretty.[16]

As the Soviet armies were moving westward, it became clearer each day to the führers at all levels of the Nazi hierarchy that they would have to do two things: first, significantly accelerate the liquidation of the *Untermenschen* (subhumans) within their grasp, because otherwise all their previous efforts to leave the world sparkling clean for future Germanic generations would have been for nothing; and second, make disappear millions of decomposed carcasses all over conquered central and eastern Europe—not just because of the stench but to cover up evidence of actions (*Liquidierung,* or physical extermination) that other people who did not share the philosophy of the *Volkstumkampf* might consider uncivilized. In the worst-case scenario, the state-of-the-art gas chambers and crematoria would have to be blown up. In Lwów during their three years' presence (July 1941–July 1944), the Germans carried out massive executions of Jews, Russian prisoners of war, Poles, and Ukrainian nationalists (the last's earlier enthusiasm for the German liberators had substantially waned) using the upgraded Frank /Schöngarth template: quick, cheap, and on the spot, with no costly railroad transportation (needed for the troops on the eastern front) or lengthy construction of barracks and torture bunkers in concentration camps. All that was needed were guns, bullets, shooters, shovels, and a forest with sandy or marshy soil.

Such a place was the Krzywczycki Forest, conveniently accessible but not a tourist's first choice. There, an elementary camp was set up to which tens of thousands of Jews, Russian prisoners of war, Poles and other human beings were brought in trucks, They were stripped naked, shot, and immediately burned in huge pyres. Then the ashes were sieved to recover gold teeth and any valuables concealed by the victims in their intestines or vaginas. After that, bones that had not been fully burned were passed through a grinder and scattered together with the ashes in the forest. As many as 2,200 Jews were executed in a day and 3,000 exhumed bodies incinerated. But who would do the job of digging out, burning, sieving, pulverizing, and scattering the remains? Shooting is another matter: any self-respecting SS man would do it, and not a few Ukrainian gestapo helpers (*Gestapohelfern*), if only because they could pick up a gold tooth or two without anybody noticing or minding. Here a cruel tweak was slipped into the proceedings. In 1943 a unit called *Sonderkommando 1005* was formed for just this purpose.[17] It was composed of enslaved Jews, twenty of whom late in the evening of October 8, 1943 (the day before Yom-Kippur), under the supervision of SS men, were sent from the Krzywczycki Forest camp to Wzgórze Wuleckie with the order to dig up bodies buried there, which they brought to the forest. The next day, together with several hundred other human remains, they burned the putrefied corpses in a huge pyre, grinded the remaining bones, and scattered the ashes to the winds.

From the standpoint of an individual human trying to survive, as from that of a whole conquered nation, Cracow and Lwów were identical in the terror ethic imposed on them in September 1939 and June 1941 by their Nazi and Soviet masters. The cities were no longer the decent places they had been in 1903–1907 under the Austro-Hungarian empire's Galician administration, when the youthful Jan Przybyła migrated from the one to the other for personal security reasons. The second time around he chose Cracow, again in his attempt to evade the tentacles of an incomparably more bestial regime, using for that purpose some of the experience, a little dusty by now, and old connections acquired earlier in life. Lwów, as we shall see, while not directly involved, kept popping in and out of this danse macabre.

When he came to Cracow in early September 1939, Jan had to find a place to stay and register with the occupation authorities without divulging to them his true identity. Like decades ago, during his clandestine trips from Lwów to Silesia, he needed well-fabricated fake identity papers under an assumed name that would not prompt his pursuers to cross check with the lists of state enemies prepared for the gestapo by the more vigilant members of Poland's interwar German minority organizations and volunteer informers. Within a few days of his arrival, he had found a place to live, a job, and a new name with professionally made and certified personal identification documents, all thanks to his longtime friend from Katowice, Tadeusz W. Dobrowolski, an art historian and former director of the Silesian Museum in Katowice who later that fall was swept into a concentration camp by Bruno Müller's Special Action Cracow, but later released. He and his wife, Agnieszka, were at one time teachers at the Municipal Middle and Senior High School for Women, in which Przybyła's daughter Maria (Marysia) had been a student before beginning her higher studies at the Warsaw Main School of Commerce. Another relative involved and residing at the house was Maria Mitera Dobrowolska.[18]

The speed and quality with which the papers were produced reveals the advanced state and graphic artistry of the Polish underground resistance network at that early time, as well as the courage and nobility of Jan's friends. Their work in this case had been made possible by a loophole in the Cracow ID regulations. Because of heavy bombing, many people who ended up in that city had, with everything else, lost their original identity cards. The Cracow municipal government announced that these could be replaced by new documents, provided another person possessing valid original ID papers would guarantee the veracity of the applicant's answers to the questions on the application form for replacement. This is what the Dobrowolskis did by certifying that the applicant's name was Jan Midowicz from Lwów, a close acquaintance of Dobrowolska's brother. It was, at any rate, how Maria Mitera-Dobrowolska remembered the genesis of the name Midowicz that Jan used until June 11, 1942, when he was betrayed. In the remembrance of his daughter Maria, her father borrowed the name from his wife Marta's cousin Mieczysław Midowicz, owner of some landed property in the Cracow voivodship, whom Jan liked and in whose house he had stayed shortly before the war in 1939, together with Marysia and his brother-in-law Gustaw Daisenberg, a major in the Polish army. (The spelling of the name was elastic over time as the family became Polonized: von Deissenberg, Daissenberg, Daisenberg. The founder, Ignacy Deissenberg from Bavaria, came to Poland with Napoleon's armies, eventually settling near Tarnowo in Nether Poland, roughly two hundred kilometers from Lwów). Whatever the exact provenance of the name, Jan moved in with the Dobrowolskis at their single-story, garden-encompassed house on 13 Łagiewnicka Street in Kraków (43 Zamoyski Street in 1991) as a high school teacher from Lwów.

The place was fairly crowded, for in it resided already another refugee from German and Nazi revenge, Miłosz Sołtys, Jan's coworker at the Polish Plebiscite Commission in Bytom (Beuthen) from 1920–21, his predecessor as regional inspector in Silesia of the Polish Scouts Organization, and in 1932 for a very short period—because the post-plebiscite German administration in Beuthen would not confirm his nomination—the first principal of the first-ever private Polish high school on German soil. Jan was also known as Professor Midowicz to his employer, Adam Ronikier, at the Main Welfare Council (RGO), the only Polish charity organization, that was approved by the German occupation authorities for the General Government (largely as a result of the efforts of Cracow Archbishop Adam Sapiecha). It did its social welfare work under Nazi supervision and control. Already in February 1940 the organization distributed food; monetary help; and American gifts of medicines, clothing, blankets, shoes, and other basics to more than a million needy persons, thus bringing a little light into Poland's darkness. As always, the system's slightest glimmer of humane action was accompanied by its opposite—in this case the unleashing in the fall of 1939 and spring of 1940 of the *Sonderaktion Krakau* and *AB-Aktion*, when being a "professor" of anything was the last thing one would want to be.

The precise area and purview of Jan's work at the RGO, other than the distribution of general welfare assistance, is not known. According to Mrs. Mitera-Dobrowolska, it included the salvaging of Polish cultural heritage, such as books banned by Nazi book burners. He disseminated among trusted acquaintances the contents of French and British news broadcasts passed on to him by his contacts—another activity forbidden and severely punished by the occupiers, as radio sets were confiscated from Polish residents. He wrote a few poems—politics through poetry. The only surviving poem from those dark times was "Wawel," written shortly before his arrest in 1942, with its ray of hope in its last two lines. It is reproduced in his handwriting in the Annex.

But distributing material aid to those desperately needing it (something he had done in 1919 during and after the First Silesian Uprising), saving books from destruction by latter-day vandals, and spreading information about what was happening in the world (untainted by the lies dispensed by Dr. Josef Goebbels' monopolistic propaganda machine) was only part of the clandestine life he led in Cracow.[19] Already in mid-September 1939, the trio Dobrowolski-Sołtys-Midowicz set up an underground resistance group named simply "Silesia," which on the nineteenth of that month, two days after the Russian stab in the back, published the first number of a news sheet called *Poland Lives,* later changed to *Voice of the People.*[20] They also edited leaflets in fluent German addressed to German soldiers, an idea that fell flat when it was applied in the 1921 plebiscite as the "Free Speech for Upper Silesia" but worked when the British tried it in the form of personal, often juicy, tabloid broadcasts, curses and all, allegedly originating in a German military radio station, the *Soldatensender Calais* (The Soldiers' Radio Station Calais), but really coming from the BBC in Dover, England, and directed in 1944 at German soldiers after the D-day landing. The Cracow flyers were scattered about passenger train compartments by Polish railroad guards. Midowicz did not lose contact with his friends, former fighters for a Polish Silesia. One of them, Józef Korol, active before the war in the Polish Scouts Organization (ZHP) and at the time hiding in Silesia, paid a short visit to Cracow in December 1939. The problem was that Korol was wanted by the gestapo not only for his past but for being involved in present rebellions, in the formation and leadership of several successive Polish partisan and armed resistance organizations in Silesia. Midowicz arranged for him to meet another Silesian ZHP activist and prewar mayor of Chorzów then hiding in Cracow, Jan Grzbiela, who thus became active in the Silesian resistance while continuing to reside in Cracow. Korol was shot dead by the Germans in a confrontation on August 28, 1940.

It is highly probable, and supported by the testimony of his daughter Maria, that Jan's direct involvement in clandestine resistance to German occupation during his eighteen-month sojourn at 13 Łagiewnicka Street (early September 1939 to April 12, 1942) resembled what he had done in his youth. He fought with pen rather than gun and tried to make people's oppression, hunger, poverty, and grief more bearable by distributing material help and giving the solace of hope. His participation in producing the news sheet and leaflets intended for German soldiers testify to the first, his welfare work at the RGO to the second.[21] But such distinctions and humane impulses meant nothing to the Nazis; it was disobedience punishable by death. For a time, at any rate, his conspiratorial activities were not discovered despite several gestapo visits at 13 Łagiewnicka Street, including at least one during which the house was as good as torn apart. The absence of weapons other than pens, the persuasiveness of the fictitious identity papers, the constant vigilance of the relatively small group of old and trusted friends postponed—but because of an unforeseeable concatenation of circumstances did not prevent—what was to happen. For Jan, treachery dealt the final blow.

Not long after the Soviet invasion of Poland, Marta Przybyłowa learned that her eldest son Zbigniew (Zbyszek), a noncommissioned reserve infantry officer, had been wounded and was held prisoner by the Russians in the Lwów area. She left Kraków and reached the river San, which separated the German and Soviet occupation zones. After crossing the river in a boat under the cover of night, she found the camp in which her son was held, obtained his release—how, nobody knows—and brought him to Cracow on Christmas Eve 1939.[22]

Marta's achievement was all the more remarkable because at about this time the NKVD was preparing the execution of Polish officers and NCOs who had been taken prisoner after the Soviet invasion of Poland on September 17, 1939, and had been labeled as "class enemies" in Marxist-Leninist eyes. These fifteen thousand men were held in three POW camps: Kozielsk, near Orel (today in Belarus); Starobielsk, near Kharkiv (in today's Ukraine); and Ostaszków island on Lake Seliguer. The prisoners were treated in accordance with the barbarian ethics of the Golden Horde. Four hundred or so prisoners from the three camps escaped death by being transferred to another camp about a hundred miles from Kozielsk before the massacre in early 1940. These were carefully chosen either for their pro-Soviet stance, their informer work, their personal usefulness to the Soviets, or Italian and German intervention—none of which were applicable to Zbyszek. He was released only due to Marta's courage and ingenuity. The Russians, of course, refused to admit the responsibility for the collective Katyń murder for more than half a century. In the democratic West, public interest in the crime was marginal at best.

Back in Cracow, Marta discovered that the previous day (December 23, 1939) her youngest son, seventeen-year-old Janusz, set off for the Tatra Mountains with a friend to traverse the border through Slovakia to Hungary, an act punishable by death if caught by the Germans, and not without risk of repatriation by Hungarian authorities under pressure from Berlin.[23] Once on the other side, he was detained and placed in the Buda citadel in Budapest, from which he escaped and made his way to France (his intended final destination), where a Polish army under French command was being cobbled together by recruitment of refugees (Sikorski's "Polish tourists" mentioned earlier) and émigré residents of Polish descent—a process in which his uncle, Wiktor Przybyła, was involved in Paris in the early 1940s. He underwent training at Coëtquidan, a Morbihan township (Brittany) where the new Polish army's training facilities (and the French Army's War College, Saint Cyr) were located. He was assigned to a heavy machine gun squadron of a battalion in a Polish Motorized Cavalry Brigade formed by General Stanisław Maczek, a distinguished veteran of the September 1939 campaign in Poland. In June 1940, after France fell to the Germans, some Polish army contingents, including the one in which Janusz served, were evacuated to Britain; Janusz's group left on the Polish ship *MS Sobieski* from Saint-Jean-de-Luz, just down the road from the pricey seaside resort, Biarritz.[24]

Other Polish soldiers and civilians tried to make their way to England through Franco's Spain. A slippery ally of Germany, Francisco Franco did not want to be drawn into the war on either side, even though he owed a sizeable debt for his victory in the Spanish civil war to the Fascist axis. To achieve this goal without bringing down Hitler's wrath on his ravaged country that had emerged just about a year before from that fratricidal war, he had to be careful. Being careful meant, among other obligations, that Polish and other soldiers (French and French-Senegalese) who crossed the frontier from France were detained at Miranda del Ebro, the infamous detention camp for foreigners where conditions were not much different from those in Nazi concentration camps. One should add in fairness that the food situation in Spain was critical at that time. But we are not talking here only about feeding the detainees.

After the fall of France, in June 1940, Wiktor Przybyła and his family made their way on foot through the Pyrenees frontier crossings at Fos (France) and Les (Spain), not far from the Principality of Andorra. Then they travelled by bus and train through Lerida and Zaragoza to Madrid. After a week or so, armed with transit

visas for French Morocco, they proceeded to Lisbon, Portugal—
one stretch in a sealed carriage guarded by gun-toting nationalist
soldiers taking Spanish Republican civil war prisoners to Spanish
Morocco. In Lisbon, a British ship, the *Hilary*, loaded with green
bananas and other stuff from Manáos in Brazil's Amazon Basin,
picked the family up after a couple of days and zigzagged its way
through German submarine-infested seas near the Bay of Biscay
and around Ireland, depositing them seven days later in Liverpool,
England. The ship, as I recall, had a wooden antiaircraft gun on its
foredeck for decoy.

Four years later, Corporal Janusz Przybyła, after more training
in Scotland (during which time he also passed a matriculation exam),
served in the Polish Motorized Cavalry Division, commanded by
General Maczek. The division went into action at the very time
that the Warsaw Uprising against the German occupiers was in
progress (August 1–October 2, 1944). It took part in the Falaise
battle, during which fourteen German army and SS divisions were
encircled and destroyed in the Chambois forest pocket. The division
also participated in the capture of Wilhelmshaven and its entire
garrison, including some two hundred ships of the German navy,
and on October 28, 1944, freed the Dutch city of Breda from four
years of Nazi occupation. The city fathers awarded their liberators
honorary citizenship. One hundred sixty of those honorary citizens,
including the commanding officer, repose there.

At first the Germans refused to recognize the Polish participants in the August 1944 Warsaw Uprising as combatants. This
meant that the insurgents, if captured, were not protected by the
Geneva Convention on the Treatment of War Prisoners from
instant death. Britain and the United States finally recognized the
Polish Home Army (the insurgents) in late August 1944. They had
waited for Soviet agreement, which never came. However, there is
reason to believe that the presence of Polish troops on the western
front gave the Germans reason to seriously rethink their initial
decision, which they did. After the end of the war in Europe (May 8,
1945), Maczek became the commanding officer of all Polish forces
in Britain. Many British wanted—but did not force—the Poles to
go back home to what was soon to become a communist country
run from the Kremlin by proxy, with Polish law adapted to Soviet

law, and the Office of Public Safety (SB) replacing the gestapo and NKVD. Some did go home, but others for equally cogent reasons did not. General Maczek was stripped of his Polish citizenship by the communist regime of People's Poland. Maczek was not in strict legal terms an "Allied" soldier, probably because in 1945 Britain withdrew its recognition from the Polish Government in exile in London and switched it to the Warsaw communist government imposed by Stalin, and so he did not have combatant rights and could not receive a British war pension. To earn a living he found a job as a bartender in an Edinburgh hotel, where he worked until the 1960s. He died in December 1994 at age 101 and is buried with his soldiers in the Polish Honor Cemetery at Breda, the Netherlands.

Janusz returned to Poland in 1947. He spent those two years in England attending lectures on Polish law at Oxford University. On his return his studies were certified by the Jagiellonian University in Kraków so that theoretically he could have pursued a career in law in his own country, were it not for the inconvenience that by 1949 Polish law became prostituted by Stalinism, and anyone who had spent the war years in the capitalist West, especially in the Polish exile army, and would not bend with the wind became persona non grata so far as practicing the law and many other sensitive professions was concerned. He found out what had happened to his parents only in the summer of 1945 during a visit to his sister Maria (Marysia) Stangel in Bolzano, Italy.

Janusz's elder brother (Zbigniew) Zbyszek's arrival in Kraków on Christmas Eve 1939 and his hectic undercover life (both before and after), introduced an additional dimension into his father Jan's endangered existence, and also into that of Marta who—like a true mother, without giving a thought to possible side effects—saved her son from what she felt would have been certain death at the hands of the Soviets by bringing him to Cracow. The problem for the chronicler is that Zbyszek's life is known only in fragments because much of it was spent hiding from the gestapo.

The Polish Scouts Association (ZHP) played a major role in Zbyszek's life and in that of a multitude of young and middle-aged people in the interwar and war years. It was, together with the (Polish) Catholic Church, a repository of patriotism with only one commandment: "Give your all to your country." In the course of the

September 1939 campaign, as during the Silesian plebiscite in the
1920s, scouts played a symbolically uplifting, if often ineffective and
tragic, role in many David-Goliath confrontations with the enemy
in different locations. In Katowice, for example, when the "Kraków"
army pulled out of Silesia on September 3 as fast as its horses would
allow to avoid encirclement by German panzers—the "sea of iron."
After the defeat, the scouting community went underground and
continued its struggle against the occupiers, doing auxiliary work
and eventually more for the clandestine network of armed resist-
ers who by 1943 had become the Home Army (AK) responsive to
the Polish Government in Exile in London and who after the war
and until 1989 were bullied and discriminated against by Moscow's
lackeys in charge of the government. The bulk of the work in
question was not of the pen-and-paper or welfare-and-charity type,
but one involving guns, hand grenades, bombs, and similar explo-
sive means of bilateral communication. Zbyszek was an activist who
marched to his own drummer in education as in other pursuits, with
two years of military training behind him, one who took the patriotic values of his scouting youth seriously. He was surely involved
in the growing underground resistance network, but precisely how
is not possible to say. What we do know is that as early as 1940 the
gestapos were after him, which, of course, made them connect the
dots with the rest of the Przybyła family within their reach.

In the spring of 1942, in addition to the upgraded *AB Aktion,*
the Germans unleashed in Cracow a wave of arrests connected with
the subversive activities of Wacław Smoczyk, son of a watchmaker,
an army second lieutenant (military engineer) during the September 1939 campaign and the leader of sabotage and guerrilla attacks
in Silesia by armed organizations he and others created, among
them "Polish Armed Forces" (SZP) and later (early 1941) a second
network of the "Reprisal Group" of "Armed Combat Association"
(ZWZ).[25] Betrayed by a co-conspirator in the pay of the German
secret police, Smoczyk was caught off-guard by the security police
in Katowice on March 28, 1942, and committed suicide by putting
a bullet through his head. He was twenty-four. The reward offered
by the gestapo for information leading to Smoczyk's arrest was
ten thousand marks. The gestapo found no materials that would
have enabled them to break up the network. Nonetheless, as was

their standard procedure, they arrested his whole immediate family, interrogated them, and sent them to Auschwitz, where they were murdered. Several other people were quickly arrested and met the same fate.

Fearing that he would be snarled up in the tightening dragnet, Zbyszek, who had been somehow involved, in the resistance network, found a hiding place in a small village near Cracow and used the name Franciszek Rosa. In the fall of 1943, he was arrested reportedly for smuggling and ended up in what was regarded as an unconquerable, high-security prison located on the top of a steep hill in Wiśnicz Nowy, near Cracow.[26]

When early in December his sister Marysia heard about it through the grapevine, she and her future husband, Jerzy Stangel, drove to Wiśnicz to see what could be done. This was incredible courage on her part since fifteen months earlier, on release from a couple of months' imprisonment in Cracow, she had been warned not to meddle in politics. However, Marysia had unstinting resolve and was fluent in high German with a trace of Viennese tonal elegance. She also possessed irresistible charm, thespian sensitivity, stunning good looks, and, yes, a little good luck. Details like this lets one begin to understand the otherwise incomprehensible. She walked into the Wiśnicz prison by herself and explained that she was the prisoner's fiancée, Maria Przybylanka. She managed to gain access to the director of the prison (a nearly impossible thing), and more than that, to persuade him after many polite requests to let him see her "fiancé." One must add in fairness that the commandant, a high-ranking officer with a doctorate, of course, seems to have been a rara avis (a rare bird, a "good German" as the saying went) among German officials in those days, especially at grim places like this, for he showed a flicker of humanity, a spark of good.[27]

Once in the waiting room, Marysia got permission from the guard who accompanied her to greet her brother for a few seconds during which she whispered in his ear, "I am your fiancée." She then chatted with him in the guard's presence about his health (appendicitis perhaps) and the need to be admitted to hospital for treatment. She extracted another audience with the commandant and asked him to please allow her fiancée into the prison hospital because he was sick, the bonus being that he was also a competent male nurse and surgeon's assistant who could help the short-handed and no doubt overworked prison physician. When she left, the director escorted her beyond the door of the prison building, once a convent of the Order of Discalced Carmelites and next to a palace once owned by Polish nobles. She later received a letter from her "fiancé" informing her that he had been admitted to the hospital for treatment, and since he was knowledgeable in medical matters, the prison doctor (probably a Polish prisoner) requested that he be transferred to the infirmary as his adjunct, which was granted.

About eight months later, on July 26, 1944, a group of thirty-two Home Army (AK) soldiers under the leadership of captain Józef Wieciech (nom de guerre "Tamarow"), acting on intelligence that the Germans were about to transport to Auschwitz 120 Polish political prisoners held in the Wiśnicz jail, raided the SS battalion stationed on the hill. Within forty-five minutes the AK freed the prisoners, locked up two score guards in their dormitory and three German officers, including the commandant and four guards in a small munitions store room, warning them that if by chance they managed to get out before 6:00 AM, they would sorely regret it. The officers were freed around four in the morning by guards returning to the prison from a drinking session in a tavern downtown. Years later, one of the participants in the raid wrote that only the commandant, after being released by the revelers from the munitions store room, asked that a chair be brought, and sat on it in a cupboard until 6:00, as ordered by the AK intruders.[28]

Zbigniew survived the rest of the occupation and the war. It is not known whether he was among those liberated by the AK action on July 26, 1944. Neither can one be sure that the commandant who sat on his chair in the cupboard was the same person who had talked to Marysia eight months earlier.

Intensively investigated after the Smoczyk affair, Marta did not disclose her son's whereabouts. However, in their newly energized search for Zbigniew Przybyła, son of an elusive, long-time foe high on the list of persons wanted by the Reich as far back as 1903, the indefatigable secret police began to become curious about Marta Deissenberg-Przybyła's social life, including her frequent calls on 13 Łagiewnicka Street, where a professor Jan Midowicz happened to stay.[29]

Aware of the danger, Jan sought advice on what to do from his friend Jan Grzbiela, who urged him to immediately move out of his current residence to an address in Batory Street. But it was too late. He was arrested as he was getting ready to retire on April 12, 1942, was mercilessly interrogated at No. 2 Pomorska Street, was imprisoned and tortured again in Montelupi, and was sent to Auschwitz two months later on June 11, 1942. Marta was arrested on the same day, interrogated, imprisoned in the Helclów women's prison near Montelupi, and then sent to Auschwitz-Birkenau on July 11, 1942, exactly one month after her husband.

Summoned by Mrs. Maria Mitera-Dobrowolska, Marysia came to Cracow to see what she could do to help her parents and walked into the beast's lair.

Notes

1. On September 22, 1939, the Germans handed over Brześć to the Soviets as part of the Ribbentrop-Molotov dowry, and the two armies held a joint victory celebration downtown. On June 22, 1941, they took it away from their erstwhile allies and held onto it until July 28, 1944, when the Soviets took it back after considerable bloodletting on both sides. It now belongs to Belarus, a member of the Russian Federation of Independent States.

2. *Z bolszewikami nie walczyć* (Don't fight the Bolsheviks) by Przemysław Mandela, http://www.obiektyw.net/artykul-z-bolszewikami-nie-walczyc-13. html

3. *Kampania wrześniowa* (The September Campaign). http://wikipedia. org/wiki/Kampania_wre%C5Bniowa, 22. Poland had a mutual aid treaty with Romania dating back to 1921, but only in the event of a Soviet attack. The part of Hungary to which the troops were to retreat was a part of Czechoslovak Transcarpathian Ruthenia before Czechoslovakia had been wiped off the map on March 14–16, 1939.

4. *Ostatni rozkaz Wodza naczelnego Edwarda Rydza-Śmigłego* (The Last Order of the Commander in Chief Edward Rydz Śmigły) http://wikisource. org/Ostatni_rozkaz_Wodza_Naczelnego_MarszC%82ka.Edw

5. Mościcki died in 1946 in Versoix near Geneva. His remains repose in the vault of the archcathedral of St. John the Baptist in Warsaw.

6. Jan's brother Wiktor, my father, sent his wife and children to Cracow a few days before the outbreak of the war because he was convinced, I am sure, that the Germans would never get that far. He left Bielsko just before the occupation of the city on September 3. A member of the staff who stayed behind informed us later that within hours of the entry of German troops into the city, gestapo men were in Villa Sixt looking for the mayor.

7. On the Prussian connection: chapter 1 above and Debórah Dwork and Jan van Pelt, *Auschwitz*, New York and London: W. W. Norton & Company, 2002, chapter 2, 18–65.

8. *Hans Frank in Polen* (Hans Frank in Poland). http://alien.mur.at/ rax/KUN_POL/POLITIK/ORG/frank/poll.html

9. Both citations are from Mark Sroka, *The University of Cracow Library under Nazi occupation, 1939–1945*. http://gslis.utexas.edu/landc/fulltext/ landC_34_Sroka.pdf

10. On Palmiry: http://ww.czosnow.com.pl/infor.pha?nd=palmiry_2

11. Letter from Elisabetta Stangel-Grifoni (daughter of Maria Przybyła-Stangel,), June 15, 2008.

12. For a discussion of the number of Poles deported to the USSR: N. S. Lebedeva, "The Deportation of the Polish Population to the USSR, 1939–41," *The Journal of Communist Studies and Transition Politics*, vol. 16, no. 1–2, 2000, pp.28–44. Ms. Lebedeva is a Russian scholar and an editor of Katyń documents. Polish historians put the figure of Polish deportees in that period at about four hundred thousand. Ukrainian historians claim that 20 percent of the deportees were Ukrainians.

13. He was assigned to occupied General Government Poland as head of the SS Sipo-SD in Cracow on January 30, 1941. *Kripo* stands for Criminal Police. After his bloody stint in Greece (July 1943–July1944), he became the Head of the Sipo-SD in the Hague, and from March 10 to April 1945 replaced Hans Albin Rauter as commander of the SS in German-occupied Netherlands. http://wikipedia.org/wiki/Karl_Eberhard_Sch%C3%B6ngarth.

14. http://www.holocaustresearchproject.org/einsatz/

15. Wacław Szybiński, *The Murder of Polish professors by German Authorities in Lwów in July 1941*. http://www.lwow.com_profs.html. Edited and partially translated from the Polish of Zygmunt Albert's *Kaźń profesorów lwowskich— lipiec 1941* collection of documents, Wrocław: University of Wrocław Press, 1989, ISBN 8322903510.

16. Drawn from Zygmunt Albert, *Mord Profesorów Lwowskich w Lipcu 1941 roku* (Murder of Lwów Professors in July 1941) in *Kaźń profesorów lwows-kich, w lipcu 1941 roku* (Wrocław, 1989), 60–62.

17. Zygmunt Alberts, 61–62.

18. The information on Jan's time spent in hiding in Cracow is drawn from accounts contained in Tadeusz Czylok's *Powstanie i Geneza Katowick-iego Harcerstwa: Inspektor harcerski Jan Przybyła—Informator Historyczny nr. 3*, Katowice: Komenda i Komisja Historyczna ZHP w Katowicach 1991, 38–44 ; and based on information provided to the author of that work by Maria Mitera-Dobrowolska on June 28, 1987, and Jan's daughter Maria Przybyła-Stangel in 1988, and researched by her daughter Elisabetta Stangel-Grifoni in 2008. Maria Mitera-Dobrowolska may have been the wife of Kazimierz Dobrowol-ski, a professor of sociology and ethnography at the Jagiellonian University, but this is not certain.

19. Goebbels's doctoral dissertation was on the eighteenth-century German Romantic novelist Wilhelm von Schütz. Doctorate in Romantic literature from Heidelberg University (1921) notwithstanding, Goebbels did not have any of his literary output published, not for lack of trying.

20. According to information given by Mrs. Mitera-Dobrowolska on June 28, 1987, in Czylok, chapter 5, 39.

21. Elisabetta Stangel-Grifoni (Maria's daughter), email to the author, August 8, 2008.

22. Czylok, 39–40. Also http://www.katyn1940.info/258.xml

23. An old Polish rhyme: *Polak-Węgier dwa bratanki / Tak do szabli jak do szklanki*; loosely translated: "A Pole and a Hungarian are two brothers / As much in arms as in liquor." The rhyme had to be taken cautiously in those days, given the Hungarians' obligations and proximity to Nazi Germany. Still, even then, with the Germans huffing and puffing down their necks, there was temperamentally and historically more than half-truth to the saying. Nevertheless, Janusz was imprisoned in the Buda citadel. He got away—no easy task without a helping hand of someone familiar with the place.

24. Janusz Przybyła. *Wspomnienia 1939–1945: Francja* (Memoirs 1939–1945: France). *Więź* (Bond), no. 7–8, July–August 1976, 184–202. An account of his six months service in the Polish Armored Cavalry Brigade in France, including the catastrophic collapse of French resistance in June 1940. His perception of the French army's lack of will during the debacle is strikingly similar to Irène Némirowsky's view of demoralized French civilians in her *Suite Française* (New York: Vintage Books, 2007).

25. The creator of the first Silesian network of the reprisal group was Franciszek Kwaśnicki, a military engineer who was captured in early 1941, his network destroyed by the gestapo. Smoczyk formed a second network, which extended its activities to the territory of the prewar Reich, including Berlin.

26. The Montelupi prison in Cracow was overfull. Smoczyk is known to have traveled through what was then known as "old" Germany (*Altreich*) choosing his targets, and through the General Government to find the means for his retaliatory actions: parts of bombs, for example, which he assembled in Katowice. It is possible, but still only a guess, that Zbyszek's arrest for "smuggling" could have had some connection with all this.

27. Also, on a macro level the belief in the inevitable invincibility of the German armies was put to question about ten months earlier, on January 31, 1943, when General Paulus' 6th Army surrendered at Stalingrad with a loss of 146,000 lives. Of the 90,000 German war prisoners taken by the Russians in that battle, only 6,000 returned home after the war. The tide had turned, and some few Germans in the know began to have inklings of doubt about the Führer's infallibility in matters of faith and policy, They also began, ever so slowly, to reexamine their personal future and present attitudes as a form of insurance.

28. J. Kaczmarczyk. "Akcja Wiśnicz." *Dynamit* [Dynamite]. Cracow, 1967, part II, 20. Cited by: Jerzy Ślaski, *Polska Walcząca* [Fighting Poland]. Warszawa: Oficyna Wydawnicza Rytm, vol. 2, third enlarged edition, 718–20.

29. Elisabetta Stangel-Grifoni. Email August 10, 2008, to the author based on information obtained from her mother Maria (Marysia) Przybyła-Stangel. Also Czylok, 42. As has been noted before, Marta's residence was not far from

Jan's. According to the death certificate of the Auschwitz German authorities (*Sterbebuch*, Band 13/3/1942, page 1463 of August 16, 1942), Marta's last address before her arrest was *Krakau* (Cracow in German) *Lagiewniki* (Łagiewniki) *Hauptstrasse* (Main Street), 426. Jan, it will be recalled, lived in Cracow at 13 Łagiewnicka Street.

Corporal Janusz Przybyła (Polish Army in Exile), Holland November 1944.

Roundup (Łapanka). Photo from Centralna Agencja Fotograficzna in: Jerzy Piotrowski (1957), Miasto Nieujarzmione (The Unsubjugated City), Warsaw: Iskra. Transferred from pl. wikipedia. Original upload and description by Andros 64.

Death

Marysia's Diary
(1942)

This chapter contains the surviving pages of a diary (translated from Polish) kept by the Przybyłas's daughter Maria, the indomitable Marysia (after 1963 Maria Przybyła-Stangel). I am indebted to her son, the late Krystian Stangel and daughter Elżbieta (Ela, Elisabetta) Stangel-Grifani for the original manuscript (pp. 59–70). The translation and notes are mine. I use the city's name Kraków in the text rather than the better known abroad Cracow, wherever it appears in my cousin's manuscript.

I stayed in Kraków. I moved in with my mother's friend, Zofia Krauzowa, on Prądnicka Street. I began to take action. On the one hand, discreet and undercover efforts to find my father; went several times to RGO, to its chairman Ronikier and many other people. I clung to them like a drowning man clutching at straws. On the other hand, I knocked on all doors looking for mother. I was sending parcels to my mother and father. In this I was helped by the devoted and fearless Mrs. Zazulowa, who handled all aid to prisoners in the Montelupi and Helclów jails.[1] Oh! How miserable

---

1   Two high-security prisons in Cracow. The first is located on Montelupi Street and named after a sixteenth-century Italian family who had owned the original building. From 1940 through early 1945, it was a Nazi prison for about fifty thousand political prisoners, mainly Polish and Jewish, most of whom were either executed in the prison after savage interrogations or sent to the extermination camp in Auschwitz-Birkenau and Płaszów. From 1945 to 1956 the jail was used by the communist secret police (*Urząd Bezpieczeństwa*) and its Soviet prototype, the NKVD. Several thousand Polish anti-German underground fighters of the war years—former members of the Polish Home Army (*Armia Krajowa, AK*) and Freedom and Independence (*Wolność i*

my heart was. To free father; father first of all, before the gestapo[2] finds out that "Professor Midowicz" is Jan Przybyła from Silesia.

One day, I came back home from town around two in the afternoon. The entry to the room was through the kitchen. The door from the hallway to the kitchen was open ajar. As soon as I stood in it, Mrs. Krauzowa's daughter Muszka whispered to me that a gestapo man was waiting for me in the room. I thought she was joking, winked at her, and pulled some stupid face of disbelief. She pulled me to the open door; really! Muszka wasn't joking. The gestapo man sat in an armchair. His head hang down; he was asleep. What a mess! I opened my purse and dropped my notebook, with all its notes and many names in it, into a pot in the kitchen. I checked the contents of the purse. Looked. Still asleep.

"Listen, what did he say?"

"He said that he has to search through your stuff."

"And what—tell me quickly—did he do?"

"The other one did."

"What other one? You must be crazy! There's only one here."

"The other one, tall and dark, his whole pate covered with

Niezawisłość, WN)—were incarcerated there. Some 180 were executed, 126 of them between the ages of eighteen and thirty, and many more deported to the Soviet gulag. These massacres began as early as April 11, 1945, very shortly after the so-called liberation. Helclów was an institution for the elderly and for physically or mentally disabled people. The Nazis later converted the institution to a prison for Polish women, many of whom were sent to extermination camps such as Płaszów, a hard-labor camp near Cracow established at the end of 1942 primarily for Jews and Gypsies (Roma), with a section for Poles and other nationalities added later. In 1944 it was transformed into a concentration camp. As Soviet troops approached, corpses of prisoners killed from 1942 to 1944 and buried in mass graves (about eight to twelve thousand) were disinterred and burned on pyres in an attempt to erase forensic evidence of the crime. Maria Zezulowa became in 1942 the chairperson of *Patronat* (*Towarzystwo Pomocy nad Więźniami*), a prewar organization offering help to prisoners, which was revived with German permission in March 1940. Her total devotion to her work was described by all prisoners and their families as a symbol of humanity at its very best: extraordinary solicitude, understanding, empathy, strength, and courage in confronting barbarity at its worst.

2   *Geheime Staatspolizei* (State Secret Police), which in 1936, under Heinrich Himmler, became an important branch of the *Schutzstaffel*, the SS.

tousled hair. He was furious that you weren't there; he cursed and ordered this one to wait here."

"All right, and what next?"

"He ordered him to bring you in, and just kicked the door and left. It was a good thing that Mom wasn't here; she would just worry again

"I'm terribly sorry that you have unpleasantness because of me. Don't be worried about your mother; everything will be all right."

I sat down in the kitchen and lit a cigarette. They can't find anything there. I cannot run away. They would take Mrs. Krauzowa, Muszka, or Janek hostage. No. I must give myself up into his hands. Quite simply, there is no other way. I stood in the doorway.

"Good morning, sir."

The gestapo operative jumped to his feet, blushed, and quickly looked around the room. He was an older man, perhaps in his sixties, grey-haired and obese. He gave the impression of being very tired, and now just simply confused.

"Don't worry about it at all. I fully understand it. It's the heat. But at least you took a little rest."

The German was looking at me with astonishment.

"You see, I come home and am told that I have a guest. Please, sit down. What can I do for you? Perhaps you'd like to smoke a cigarette?"

Yes. That was me speaking. I heard my voice. It was calm, controlled, and somehow very cheerful.

"Well, yes," he said. "Very gladly. Only, you see, I must do my duty and take you to the gestapo."

"Duty isn't a bird; it won't fly away. You must give me a little time to enjoy freedom. Besides, I have to, after all, get ready: a toothbrush, soap, blanket."

"Well, yes. That might be useful ..."

We walked slowly. Somehow my companion was not in a hurry, and I needed a lot of time to think. Quiet down, heart! Calm down now. Maybe they won't put me in jail right away. But perhaps they'll interrogate me. How did they manage to get my address at Mrs. Krauzowa's? They must have followed me, but where and

when? Yes. Ewald[3] informed them. He took two parcels for Mom;
perhaps he never delivered them ... Letter! I wrote a letter to Mom,
after all, it's allowed to write a few words through the committee.
I didn't give a return address. They were surely looking for me
ever since they got the letter. Maybe they will ask me about my
brother, for whom they've been searching. Yes. For sure. I saw him
a few days ago in a field, in Prądnik. No! Nobody could have seen
us there ... My God! Perhaps they know that professor Midowicz is
my father. Perhaps they will bring him down to Montelupi[4]? Yes.
They will certainly confront me with him. I swear to myself that
even if I were to die, I will disavow him. I don't know him. But
what if he himself has confessed? Something tugged at my heart;
but I have a wallet in my pocket and in it a postcard from prisoner
Midowicz, who is asking for a truss. Yes. I must destroy that card.
I still have some jelly beans in the pocket.

"Would you like some candy?"

"Aber, wo![5]

"No, then I'll eat them." I took out the bag of candies, crumpled
the stiff card in the palm of my hand, and chewed it up together
with the jelly beans.

"Nice city, your Kraków."

"Of course it is. And have you already been at the Wawel?"[6]

"No. The governor is there.[7]

---

3   Oswald (Ewald) Jűrgen was from mid-1942 to the end of 1943,
frequent supervisor of day guard shifts at the Montelupi prison. Besides acting
occasionally as an information conduit for some prisoners, he has also been
identified as having taken part in executions of Montelupi prisoners. Wincenty
Hein, Czesława Jakubiec, *Montelupich*, Kraków—Wrocław: Wydawnictwo
Literackie, 1985, 93, 141

4   The high security prison, see note 1.

5   A negative in Silesian dialect.

6   Royal castle on an escarpment over the Vistula river in Cracow dating
back to the Midle Ages.

7   Hans Frank, SS *Obergruppenführer* (rank equivalent to general in the
army), doctorate from Kiel University (1924), personal legal adviser to Adolf
Hitler, former minister of justice and head of the National Socialist Jurists
Association. From October 26, 1939, to January 1945, when he fled from the
advancing Soviet troops, he was governor-general of those occupied Polish
territories not directly incorporated into the German Third Reich, the position

We came onto Pomorska Street. The whole place was teeming with gestapos and SS men. Without a word I entered the building at number two. My companion asked me to sit on a nearby bench. I sat down and waited. Five, ten, fifteen minutes. Yes. I clearly remember being here before the war. It was some kind of academic residence for students from Silesia. In fact, Zbyszek lived here.[8] And now! The gestapo men looked at me attentively as they passed by, and I at them ... Suddenly I heard my name. I got up and followed my tourist guide. First floor, second. Suddenly. What's that? A dreadful, long scream tore through the entire floor. No! Not a scream! A howl, the howl of a person being tortured somewhere in a distant room. It stopped, died down.

I walked into the room. Three gestapos stood at a desk. They gave me a cold look that said nothing.

"Good morning, gentlemen," I heard my voice saying, calm and determined. Silence.

"Heil Hitler!" replied the older, perhaps fifty-year-old gestapo man. "Call in Noak!" he said to one of his younger colleagues.[9]

A moment later a young, very tall, black-haired man came in. Yes, that's the one Muszka spoke about. His whole pate was shaggy,

---

Rudolf Wiesner (see chapter 4) had aspired to. Caught by American soldiers at Tegernsee (Bavaria) on May 3, 1945 (coincidentally the Polish National Day), he was tried by the International Military Tribunal in Nuremberg; sentenced to death by hanging on October 1, 1946; and executed on October 16, 1946. In an interview with the Nazi organ *Völkischer Beobachter* (June 6, 1940), he commented in the following way on red posters that were plastered in German-occupied Prague after seven Czechs had been shot: "If I had to put up a poster for every Pole shot, the forests of Poland would not be sufficient to supply the necessary paper." His wife, sharing their residence in the Wawel castle, called herself *Königin von Polen* (Queen of Poland).

8   The building at No. 2 Pomorska Street, constructed in the interwar years (1931–36), was to be a home for Silesian students studying in Cracow and accommodated short-term tourists from Silesia. During three years of its operations, it also contained offices of the Western Poland Association and a cinema. On September 13, 1939, it became the Cracow district headquarters of the gestapo.

9   Noak, actually spelled Noack, was a gestapo interrogator at No. 2 Pomorska Street, Department III 2B.

his face insolent and arrogant with cold, ruthless eyes. The others left the office.

꩜

My interrogation lasted from four in the afternoon to nine in the evening. He asked me for personal details, about my mother and brother. Yes. It was about my brother. He wanted to get his hands on him. For five hours we played cat and mouse. Sometimes he spoke harshly, at other times calmly. He smiled Judaslike, as if trying to inspire my trust. He banged his fist on the table, contorted his devilish face, yelled for the whole floor to hear. He offered me a cigarette and cursed when I refused. He jumped up from his desk, ran around the room, powerfully banged his cane on tables and desks, stopped afar, gave me a loathsome look, approached me slowly, brought his sweaty face and mad eyes close to my face and, with all this, from time to time, he repeated his question: "Where is the brother?"

"I don't know," I replied probably for the hundredth time. "I don't even know if he's alive. Anyway, I'm from Warsaw; how can I know where my brother is, who lived in Kraków?"

"You stupid Polish swine!" he yelled. "I'll show you." He leaped to the desk, took out a handgun from the drawer, approached me, and putting the gun to my temple, said:

"You Polish swine. Do you know what this is and what it is used for?"

"I know. This is a gun, and it is used to kill Polish swine." I heard my voice calm and cold. "But you will not frighten or kill me with a gun, Mr. *Scharführer*[10] Noak. You were only told to interrogate me; somebody else will shoot me; in any case somebody else will give the order. Why do you lose so many hours for nothing? It's a beautiful May evening. It would be better if you went for a

---

10   SS *Scharführer*, a rank equivalent to sergeant in the army. In Stanisław Czerpak's and Tadeusz Wroński's *Ulica Pomorska 2: O Krakowskim Gestapo i jego siedzibie w latach 1939–1945* (No. 2 Pomorska Street: On the Cracow Gestapo and Its Headquarters in the Years 1939–1945), Kraków, Muzeum Historyczne M. Krakowa, 1972,109. Noack's rank (spelled with a "c") is given as SS *Hauptscharführer* (Criminal Division), equivalent to master sergeant. It is possible that this reflects his promotion since 1942.

walk with your girl. Send me back quickly to Montelupi, and that will be it."

Silence. And then a loud outburst of laughter, a dreadful, long guffaw as of a demented person. He threw the gun back in the drawer and laughed, laughed...

The *Oberscharführer* [11] stood in the door.

"So, what's so funny in here?"

Noak fell silent. He submitted the report signed by me, which showed that I didn't know where my brother is.

"You didn't like the interrogation, what?"

"Of course...Only this gentleman is needlessly wasting his time...He could have done all this in half an hour. Too bad that you didn't interrogate me."

The *Oberscharführer* squinted, narrowing his eyes to the thinnest of slits, and I couldn't tell whether he would strike me in the face with the whip he held in his hand.

"All right. You can go home. You will report to us every week until you go back to Warsaw."

"Fine, which day of the week?"

"It can be Friday, the day of the Lord's Passion."

"All right. Goodbye."

I was just crossing the threshold when I heard the Sharführer's voice.

"Ein Moment. Do you know a certain professor, one moment, what's his name?" Here he glanced into his files. "Ja. A certain Professor Midowicz?"

"Midowicz?" I looked him straight in the eye. "Midowicz? Yes, I know this name. He's some distant cousin of my mother's."

"Stimmt!" [12] I hear. "You can leave."

---

11   SS *Obserscharführer*, a rank equivalent to sergeant major in the army. The person in question was probably a man by the name of Schulz in charge of Department IBL. (The L probably stands for the German *Lager*, as in "concentration camp"). In Czerpak and Wroński's book, Schulz's rank is given as SS *Obersturmführer* (and inspector of criminal matters), a rank equivalent to lieutenant, four grades above SS *Obsrscharführer*. One cannot expect the subject of a five-hour gestapo interrogation to remember the finer distinctions in the authority grades of SS bureaucratic excrescence.

12   Correct!

I left the room and walked slowly. My legs refused to carry me. Does he know that Midowicz is my father? No. It's my frightened heart that's anxious. "A guilty person doesn't act normally."[13] I said that he was my mother's cousin because, anyway, we had all agreed that if some day something were to happen, we would say that. No. He probably knew. Why did he ask me about it? Yes. When I get downstairs, they won't let me out of the gate, he's probably already now giving the order by phone. They played cat and mouse with me. I went downstairs on wooden legs. On the right side I passed the doorman's lodge. I walked out. I felt the breath of May evening air. Someone, somewhere was playing the piano. I walked slowly. Have I really aged so much? I dragged myself along like an old woman. So I am free. So I can still do something to help my father and mother. Careful, because I'm right in the lion's mouth, and one false move can ruin everything.

Every week I sent parcels to my mom. I disguised my writing when addressing parcels to the professor.

One day in June a parcel sent to my father was returned with the note: "Prisoner Midowicz unknown." Dagger into the heart. Did they send him to a camp?[14] Or else... My God. Don't let me finish the thought—there are bunkers in Montelupi, and there... After a few days I managed to determine that my father had been sent to Oświęcim.[15] My tormented heart was driven to despair. I had been under the illusion that with the help of the RGO they would let him out of prison. I believed that so much. So many intercessions, so many endeavors, and all this for nothing! And now that they have taken him there, to the death camp, what am I going to do? Oh! I can't even officially ask for you anymore.

I sent parcels to mom. All my resources were completely exhausted. I decided to go back to Warsaw.

On Friday, July 10, I reported to Pomorska Street and notified the *Obserscharführer* that I was leaving for Warsaw. On Saturday morning, having packed my things, I decided that with my last

---

13   Approximate English equivalent of a Polish saying: *"Na złodzieju czapka gore."* Literally: "The thief's cap burns" (or "is hot").

14   Concentration camp. In German: *Konzentratsionslager* (KL)

15   Polish name of Auschwitz

pennies I would buy some fruit for mother and deliver them through Ewald, who before twelve was to pass by on the agreed-on route.

It was hot. I stood on the corner of Długa Street and [Słowacki] Avenue wearing a flowery dress and a straw hat with a very broad rim. Suddenly. What's that? A frightful grating, engine noise of a long, black limousine. Instinctively I turned my back and stood with my face to a hardware display window. Slamming of car doors, steps ...

"Gnädiges Fräulein ! Ich habe die Ehre."[16]

Right next to me stood Noak, eyeing me ironically and offering his arm like in a ballroom.

"Kommen Sie mit."[17]

I got into the car. The doors were slammed shut. It was a long. six-passenger limousine. They ordered me to sit in the middle. Noak sat beside me, some other gestapo man on my other side, in front of us two gestapos, guns pointing in my direction.

"Wo ist Ihr Vater?"[18] I heard the voice of the gestapo man on my left.

"Mein Vater?" I repeated. "I don't know. I, too, would very much want to know."

After a while I found myself in a room, which, so I thought yesterday, I had left once and for all. Behind the desk stood my by now acquaintance, the older *Oberscharführer*. Next to him a few other gestapos who were joined by those who brought me here. They stood in front of me forming a tight wall. I leaned against the room wall; at least they won't surprise me from the back. I stood there with my wide-brimmed straw hat, and in my hand held a large box of cherries wrapped in paper.

"Where is your father?" asked the *Oberscharführer* in a calm but firm voice.

"I don't know, sir. I have not seen my father since the beginning of the war. He left for somewhere in the direction of Lwów. I know nothing since then, although I would very much like to know."

"Well, you'll find out," yelled Noak.

---

16 If you please, miss. It's my honor.
17 Come along.
18 Where is your father?

"Ruhe!"[19] the *Oberscharführer* shouted.

"And do you know this person?" asked the *Oberscharführer*, showing me a clip of three photos of my father. My God! Father. In a striped prison uniform, head shaved, emaciated face. And on the third picture, those terrified, horrible eyes. Probably at that time they were . . .

"If you'll permit me to look at it closely, Mr. *Oberscharführer*. *Ich bin kurzsichtig*, I am shortsighted. No, sir. I don't know this man."

"Have a good look. Who is it?"

Silence. All the gestapos are looking at me.

"This is your father!"

"What! My father? But Mr. *Obserscharführer*! You'll forgive me if I laugh. You're making fun of me. This is some old man, bald and thin. But I know my father perfectly, and I would recognize him at once."

Consternation. Silence.

"So this is not your father?"

"No. I don't know this man."

"What is in this parcel?" Noak hollered, pointing his finger at my box.

"Why don't you answer?" said the *Oberscharführer*."

"Because Mr. Noak is yelling at me like at cattle, and a cow doesn't know how to speak."

A whip swished, intended for my head. My straw hat fell to the floor. The whip missed my face; it flew out of Noak's hand, pushed high up by the *Oberscharführer*'s hand. Some sort of brief order was given, and I began to follow two gestapo men.

Suddenly I heard:

"Halt! Give her her hat," the *Oberscharführer* told Noak. Noak bent down and, with a beastly look, threw the hat at me.

A few minutes later the heavy gate of the Montelupi prison closed behind me. I entered the registration office with my hat on, wearing gloves. In the office, for a split second they thought I came to visit one of the SS men. Ewald was standing close by. "What are you doing here?"

"I've been arrested." He lowered his eyes and said nothing

---

19 Quiet! !

more. They took my watch and purse. I was led to a cell on the first floor.

Peace at last, I thought. So my father was here for over two months. They took him from here. Oh my! So they already know that this is my father. Is it possible that he admitted who he was? Could it be that my mother admitted it under interrogation? Calm now. I'll do whatever can be done to get in touch with her. It certainly won't be easy. However, perhaps I'll be put somewhere near her cell when they switch me from here to Helclów.[20] Perhaps I will manage to see her, if only from a distance. Oh! How I would weep my eyes out on her shoulder. No. She surely is broken. It is I who must be strong. She must find consolation in me.

Silence. Or perhaps someone screaming somewhere? Perhaps they are beating someone? This is, after all, the Montelupi prison. No. Saturday afternoon. Someone is singing. Yes. Someone is singing in the next cell. Be cheerful my heart! I should go to sleep. Those three photos of father. Dreadful.

"Pst! Pst!"

What's that? Somebody is below the window. I climb up the wall, am already at the window. Ewald!

"Hören Sie."[21] You will be here only three days. Here it's the quarantine, and later you will go where your mother was."

"What do you mean "where my mother *was*? Where is my mother now?

"So you don't know? This morning at eight they took her away from here ..."

"Where to?"

"To Oświęcim."[22]

"That's impossible, that's impossible ..."

"But yes. It's certain. I saw her myself."

"Thank you." My God ! What am I thanking him for ...

He saw my mother! And I? I was packing my things for departure. I could have seen her, if only from afar. No. Even so I wouldn't have been able to see her. Probably the whole transport went in trucks. It's too much for me. I am persistent, but I don't have any

20 A nearby women's prison.
21 Listen.
22 Auschwitz.

strength left. I have to cry. It's a good thing that nobody can see me. It's good that the gestapos can't see me cry.

The next day I found out from the guard that there is a physician in the prison, in fact a prisoner himself. They gave me permission to see him; I said that I had liver failure. I was left alone with him for a moment. Yes. He knew Professor Midowicz. He had given him some medications.

After three days they moved me to No. 11 Helclów Street. It was here that my mother had been held before. A young woman approached me. It was Mirka Kościelniak from Katowice. She recognized me. In this cell my mother had been imprisoned. They had talked together for hours. She had been receiving parcels. I asked her if she knew whether it came out that Professor Midowicz was someone else. No. My mother said nothing about it to her. She had not been interrogated about this matter at all.

Mirka's parents were already in Oświęcim. Her brother had been killed. The Germans executed her other brother by firing squad. Mirka was completely down and seemed not to care about anything anymore.[23]

I spent two months in the prison. During that time I underwent seven interrogations. They were always asking me about my father. I always answered the same thing. One day a gestapo man came for me. He told me to take my things and said that I would be transported elsewhere. When I arrived at the Montelupi registration office, "my" *Obersrcharführer* was standing there. He told me that I was free. He read me a commitment, which I had to sign, to the effect that I would never, and to no one, divulge what I had experienced and seen in the prison, and about what I had been interrogated.

I hid all my trifles in the cherry box. I put on my hat and gloves and without a word headed for the door. In the corridor the *Oberscharführer* came up to me.

"Hören sie mal.[24] I was in Auschwitz. Your father is very ill. Perhaps he won't survive all this. He has a … yes, a heart condition. You will probably now say again that he is not your father. Well, I

_____

23   Mirka had been arrested in connection with the Wacław Smoczyk debacle (see chapter 6).

24   Listen a minute.

am not surprised, I also have a daughter about your age, but if it came to me, she would not be so stubborn as you. Leave quickly, one never knows. Things may again get complicated, and then I will have to arrest you."

"You don't have to release me at all. You can send me to Auschwitz."

"Come on! You are young, you still have life before you, you speak such good German. Only don't play at politics. I wish you well."

I returned to Warsaw. The commissioner in charge of PKO,[25] Loessl, would not give me a job. In October I began to work for a private timber firm.[26] In mid-October I received a telegram from Auschwitz informing me that my father died from heart failure.

---

25   Polish Savings Bank

26   The firm with an office in Warsaw and furniture factory in Zwierzyniec in the Zamość area was owned by Jerzy Stangel, a mechanical engineer. Born in czarist Russia, he left that country after the Bolshevik revolution of October 1917, stayed first with an aunt in the Ukraine, and then moving to Poland, first to Wilno and later to Warsaw. A stateless person, his Nansen passport (refugee travel document) enabled him to conduct his furniture business in German-occupied Poland after September 17, 1939. Marysia worked in his firm as accountant after she lost her job at the PKO following her release from the Helclów prison in Cracow. They were married in December 1943. During the Warsaw Uprising of August 1944, Marysia was caught in one of those ad hoc roundups (*łapanka* in Polish). Seeing that she spoke German and Polish fluently, they ordered her to go into buildings in which the insurgents were hiding in cellars—and which German tanks were ready to level in a matter of minutes—and persuade them to come out. At this time the insurgents had been granted recognition as combatants. She was subsequently sent to a temporary concentration camp in Pruszków, and from there a forced labor camp in Austria. She and her husband eventually managed to escape to the American zone of occupation in Austria, and returned to Poland in 1948.

Maria (Marysia) Przybylanka; after December 1943, Maria Przybyła-Stangel

Reports from Hell
Words

There are hundreds of thousands of words in the English language. Even the Germans, with their affinity for numbers and decimal points, are not able to tell precisely how many. It is certain, however, that there are not enough words, in English or any other tongue, to convey the monstrosity of the crime the German Third Reich committed against life, and not just because of numerical dimensions. The process of transitioning people from human to subhuman to nothingness has been coldly, scrupulously, neatly, and dishonestly recorded by the prison and concentration camp authorities, with the help of slide rules and fine penmanship, in the surviving documents (though the most revealing ones were destroyed by the perpetrators at the last minute). They deal with arrest, interrogation, jailing, transportation, reception, registration, processing, housing, food rations, daily activities, work, punishment, and death These give the cold, bare, largely accounting, distorted facts. They are followed here and there with corrections based on testimony of surviving inmates and admissions of the torturers whose most common defense when tried for their crimes was that they just carried out orders.[1] A broader picture of the diabolical reality that hovers behind the bureaucratic lies will be the subject of the next chapter: lives demeaned, humiliated, deprived of the last vestiges of human dignity, tortured, shot, gassed, incinerated, and hurled into foul pits.

Bureaucratic Elevens: The Lethal Symmetry

Jan Przybyła (alias Midowicz)

SUNDAY, LATE EVENING, APRIL 12, 1942, KRAKÓW

Arrest by gestapo in his bedroom at 13 Łagiewnicka Street.
Interrogated at gestapo Headquarters, 2 Pomorska Street.

MONDAY, APRIL 13, TO THURSDAY, JUNE 11, 1942.

Imprisonment and questioning at Montelupi prison.
Interrogation at 2 Pomorska Street and Montelupi continued.

Putting aside the assumption that this was done simply to satisfy the gestapo men's perversities, the brutal, relentless questioning would suggest that the Germans were not 100 percent sure that Jan Midowicz was actually Jan Przybyła. From a nearby avenue the prisoner was spotted by Maria Mitera-Dobrowolska as he was being taken to and from questioning at 2 Pomorska Street; according to her testimony, his head was bandaged, his face severely bruised.

Transport of the prisoner on June 11 in railroad cattle car with numerous others to Auschwitz. Arrival at Auschwitz, *Kasernenstrasse* (Barracks Street, named by the Germans after the former, mostly single storey brick barracks used before the war by the Polish army). Arriving prisoners were disembarked and taken to a bath facility in Block 26. They surrendered all their clothing, underwear included; all personal belongings; and identity documents. In return they received a camp number and proceeded to a barber, who removed all their body hair, rubbed them with disinfectant, and dispatched them to a shower. They then received a striped camp uniform made of coarse cloth.

Reception: Identification and registration consisted of the prisoners' filling out a personal form and verbal questioning. Detailed information on next of kin had to be given. The forms were kept in the camps' gestapo office.

Discomfited by not knowing for sure who it was that they had in their hands, other than a senior high school teacher (and this despite all the beatings since the arrest), the Germans pulled a surprise on

him that, given his physical condition and mental exhaustion, could
cause him to stumble. At the reception building registration they
had waiting for him a Silesian lout from Katowice, probably a camp
guard. When the prisoner was asked to give his name and occupation and answered "Jan Midowicz, professor," the man interjected:
"What do you mean you're professor Jan Midowicz? I know you.
You are Jan Przybyła, who lived on Kochanowski Street, near my
parents' store, where your wife used to buy meat." Jan broke down
and admitted his identity.[2] He told his friend Dr. Szkudlarz, former
vice president of Katowice, who was a prisoner at Auschwitz and
worked in the stables, of his breakdown at registration. Szkudlarz,
who saw Jan during the last two months of Jan's life, related this to
Jan's daughter, Maria (Marysia) Stangel, after the war.

Jan received serial camp number 39217, which from now on
became his only name. It was stamped on a strip of canvas and
sown onto the uniform in a precise place, just above the left breast,
together with a red triangle (the color signifying "political"), the
vortex pointing downward, and the letter "P" for Pole within it.
After that, three ID photographs were taken from three angles.[3]

Housing: in a numbered barracks block.

In 1940, the twenty brick buildings in Auschwitz I, forty-five
meters by eighteen meters each, were used to house prisoners. In
February 1941 three-tier wooden bunks were put into the blocks
equipped with three straw mattresses, each mattress and a single
blanket shared by at least two inmates. Sanitary facilities on the
ground floor consisted of twenty-two toilet seats and urinals and a
washroom with earthenware gutters and forty-two faucets.[4]

Work: in stables and elsewhere as ordered.

Awakened at four in the morning by gong, curses, and beatings
by the capos. Lined up for breakfast that consisted of half a liter of
ersatz (artificial) black "coffee" made of chestnuts or whatever other
substitute for caffeine was available—that is, if there was any of the
vile stuff left when one got to the head of the line. To spill any of
it was a crime punishable with more beatings, kicking, and curses
by the trustees. Following breakfast, there was morning roll call
in rows of ten so as to make it easier for the SS men to count the
prisoners. This done, work squads were formed and marched off to
their various work assignments. Once outside the gates, SS guards

took over, guns at the ready. The workday, initially performed at
the double, normally lasted twelve hours with a half-hour break
for a midday meal consisting of a quarter of a pint of turnip soup.
Those who died on the job were carried back to the camp by their
fellow prisoners. The evening roll call followed. Then came supper:
three hundred grams of bread, supplemented by a bit of sausage
or margarine and occasionally a little spread of cheese. The con-
vergence of malnourishment, maltreatment by the guards and
capos, and the backbreaking nature of the assigned outdoor tasks
meant that "work" did not bring freedom, as the sign on the camp
entrance promised, but was a method of extermination under the
bureaucratic rubric of "death of natural causes." But there was also
a particular punishment known as "execution by starvation." It was
used when a prisoner escaped (or tried to escape). During a roll call
the commandant would pick out ten or more prisoners who lived in
the block in which the escapee had lived. They were put in one of
the punitive cells in the basement of Block 11 and left there to die
without food and drink.

JUNE 12–AUGUST 10, 1942

Daily activities: morning, noon, evening, and emergency roll
calls; stable duties; and any other assigned labor.

The roll calls often lasted hours on end, in summer heat and
freezing winters. Standing at attention, the prisoners had to watch
the lashing or hanging on portable or permanent gallows of prisoners accused of various transgressions.

Food rations: Officially, the theoretical daily allocation per
person doing hard labor was said to have been 2,150 calories; 1,738
for the rest.

These figures were never realized—they were consistently much
lower. One source puts the average daily calorie intake per emaciated laborer at 1,250–1,400 calories. A surviving prisoner (1943)
puts it this way: "Hunger was the most frightful, the most hateful
incubus, hanging over the prisoners ... Only the gas chambers were
more effective."[5]

MONDAY, AUGUST 10, 1942

Punishment: Public lashing. Reason unknown.

In the camp there was no why. The flogging took place on the *Appelplatz* (roll call square) in front of all inmates standing to attention. If rules were followed, Jan would have been stretched on a bench especially built for this purpose, his hands tied behind his back, unable to move his legs. The usual number of strokes with a stick or a whip was twenty-five. But upward variants were permitted. Thus, for example, the prisoner could be ordered to count each stroke aloud in German. If he—or she, for women were whipped too—made a mistake, the whipping started all over again, until the prisoner got it right, or expired. What was left of Jan was tossed back into the stable. His fellow prisoners found his condition very grave. They helped him as much as they were able. They believed they could save him. But this was not to be.

Tuesday, August 11, 1942

Death: Camp guards dragged the prisoner out of the stable, threw him into a truck, and drove off toward the main camp gate to his place of death exactly two months after his arrival in Auschwitz and one month after that of his wife Marta. The memory of the bookkeepers fails them when it comes to specifying the exact place where the crime occurred. Possibly in one of the cottages turned temporary gas chambers. Or perhaps he was tossed into a sand or gravel pit. The Auschwitz death certificate (dated August 16, 1942) specifies that "Landowner (sic) Johann Przybyla, Catholic, born in Schierakowitz, county Gleiwitz, on October 18, 1884, died in Auschwitz on August 11, 1942, at 11:50 AM. Cause of death: heart failure [in agglutative German, *Herzmuskeldegeneration*, degeneration of heart muscle]." Degeneration yes—not of Jan's heart muscle, but of Germany's heart.[6]

Marta Przybyłowa

Sunday, April 12, 1942, Kraków

Arrested by gestapo at her residence 425 *Hauptstrasse* (Main Street, today Armia "Kraków" Street), Łagiewniki, Cracow.

Interrogation at gestapo headquarters, 2 Pomorska Street and/or Montelupi prison.

Imprisonment at Helclów Women's Prison, cell no. 11

Interrogations continued.

Interestingly, Mirka Kościelniak had been in the same cell at
Helclów as Marta, and the two "had talked together for hours."
Kościelniak later told Marysia, who was put in that cell a few days
after Marta's transfer to Auschwitz, that Marta had not told her
anything about whether or not the Germans had found out that
Professor Midowicz was someone else. In fact, according to Marta,
"she had not been interrogated about this matter at all."

SATURDAY, JULY 11, 1942

Transportation of the prisoner by cattle train from Kraków to
Auschwitz, *Kasernenstrasse* (substantial price discount given to the
SS by German railroads for the correct wholesale number of pas-
sengers). Prisoner ordered into the reception center.

Reception: identification and registration of prisoner Marta
Przybyla, no. 8561; removal of all personal possessions; disinfection, delousing, shaving; given concentration camp uniform with
red triangle and P (Pole) put on; three ID photographs taken.

Housing in women's barracks Block I in Auschwitz-Birkenau.

Daily activities: roll calls, hard labor.

FRIDAY, AUGUST 28, 1942

Marta was allowed to send a censored postcard to her daughter,
addressed to Marysia's workplace at the PKO bank in Warsaw. The
seven rules (*Anordnungen*) governing this privilege were brought to
the potential writer's attention on the left side of the postcard's face
by the camp commandant, a creature by the name of Rudolf Höss
(more about Höss in Chapter 9).

"Auschwitz 28. VIII. 1942

I am in good health and work. I feel quite well and am
very glad that you are free. I'm asking you to try and see
your father again soon.[7] Please write soon to let me know
whether all are in good health; what is our Janka doing?[8]
Please send me 50 marks. What happened to our home? I
am constantly with all of you in my thoughts. I pray much
and ask you to do the same. I send you and all of you my

good wishes and heart-warmest kisses my dear child. Your loving Mother."

SUNDAY, OCTOBER 11, 1942.

Death: Marta Przybyła, Catholic, born von Deissenberg, on April 27, 1885, in Skawina, died at Auschwitz[-Birkenau] on October 11, 1942, at 2:40 PM [precisely two months after the death of her husband]. Stated cause of death: influenza.[9] [More likely, she was killed in a gas chamber.]

Notes

1. In filling in the empty spaces absent in the official reports, regarding what went on after arrival in the concentration camp, I have resorted, among other sources, to the Holocaust Education & Archive Research Team's (HEART) "Auschwitz Concentration Camp—The Basics."
http://www.holocaustresearchproject.org/othercamps/auschwitzbasics.html.

2. Czylok, 43

3. Beginning in the spring of 1942, when Auschwitz's primary function became mass extermination, Jews were no longer photographed or registered. Just in case a prisoner trying to escape would rip off his blouse, the whole thing was also sewn on the outer seam of the right trouser leg. A green triangle indicated "professional criminal," the source of many of the camp's trustees, or *capos.* Black meant "asocial;" for example gypsies, plus the letter Z (*Zigeuner,* gypsies in German). Purple was for the Catholic clergy; outside the camp it denoted the rank of cardinals. Pink was for homosexuals. Jews were marked by two triangles superimposed to form the Star of David, the bottom one yellow and bearing a letter that indicated the country from which the prisoner had been deported (e.g., F for France). Violet was reserved for Jehovah's Witnesses. Soviet prisoners of war, whose first transport arrived in Auschwitz in July 1941, were treated with exceptional savagery and were identified by the yellow letters SU, for Soviet Union, painted right on their camp uniforms. Before execution all prisoners, men as well as women, had to strip naked. Their discarded uniforms were used for new arrivals.
Marek Kucia, "Jews—The Absence and Presence of a Category in the Representations of Auschwitz in Poland, 1945–1985," http://www.studiajudaica.pl/sj18kuci.pdf.

4. HEART, "Auschwitz Concentration Camp: The Basics," p. 2.

5. Józef Garliński, *Fighting Auschwitz: The Resistance Movement in the Concentration Camp* (Greenwich, CT: Fawcett Publications, Inc., 1975, 41). HEART, "Auschwitz Concentration Camp: The Basics," p. 3 for the actual average daily calorie intake figure.

6. Information obtained from a copy of the *Sterbebuch* (*Book of Death*), volume 13/3/1942, p. 1463, No. 19491/1942. Received from the Archival Documentation Division of the National Museum Auschwitz-Birkenau, Oświęcim, 27.8.2008.

7. Jan had been murdered in the camp seventeen days before.

8. Refers to the youngest son Janusz, by then in General Maczek's First

Armored Cavalry Division in Britain. To distract the censor's attention, the name given on the card is female, like "Joan."

    9.   Obtained from *Sterbebuch* (*Book of Death*) volume 24/2/1942, p.825, No. 35339/1942 (dated October 17, 1942). Archival Documentation Division, National Museum Auschwitz-Birkenau, Oświęcim, 27.8.2008.

Montelupi prison in Kraków

Guard tower at Montelupi

Gallows at Auschwitz I

Jan Przybyła Polish Political Prisoner, June 11, 1942, Auschwitz 39217

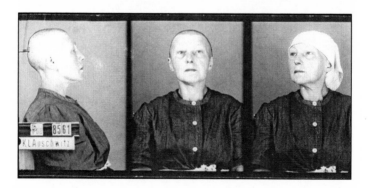

Marta Przybyła Polish Political Prisoner , July 11, 1942, Auschwitz 8561

Death pit at Auschwitz-Birkenau

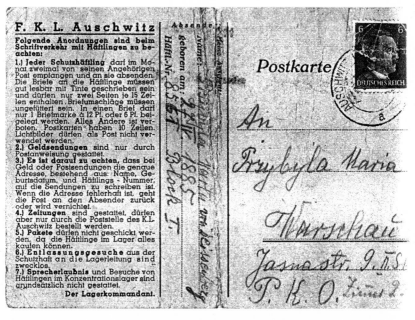

Marta's postcard from Auschwitz, August 8, 1942 (front and back)

Auschwitz: The Thousand-Year Shame of the Third Reich

The Auschwitz concentration camp was conceived on a freezing day in January 1940 at a conference in the Breslau office of SS general and Silesia police head, Erich von dem Bach-Zelewski. The meeting was attended among others by SS colonels Arpad Wigand (Bach's right hand man) and Richard Glücks (inspector on Reich territory of concentration camps, of which there were then six, including Dachau, which was activated on March 21, 1933) less than two months after the ascendance of Hitler to supreme führership. The camps' population just before the war was between twenty-five and twenty-seven thousand. The number of those who died there before the war is not known. The proximate reason for the urgency of the conference was that Silesia's jails could not accommodate the large influx of Poles arrested by the German security forces as individual and organized underground resistance to the occupation grew in Poland, both in the part absorbed by the Reich and in the General Government. Jews were rounded up and herded into barricaded reservations or overcrowded urban ghettos—when they were not dealt with by the death squads.

After some back and forth that included sending three commissions to search for the right place, it was agreed to propose that the new ten-thousand-capacity camp be built in Zasole, a suburb of the somewhat run-down town of about fourteen thousand people by the name of Oświęcim (*Auschwitz* in German), which had been in the late 1800s an important railroad junction between the three occupying powers. During the interwar years, the Polish army used and then abandoned a few one-floor brick buildings dating back to the Austro-Hungarian Empire, as well as other dilapidated structures in need of fixing. The land was marshy, and the climate unhealthy, with mists sticking close to the ground and causing frequent cases of malaria. The agreement was approved by Himmler on April 27, 1940. That was the day Auschwitz concentration camp, the eighth in the German Reich, came into being—eighth, because the camp at Oranienburg near Berlin, opened in 1933, had become in the meantime the administrative headquarters of all German concentration camps.

A week later, Rudolf Höss—a forty-year-old Baden-Baden native, totally amoral but for once not a splenetic maniac, "more like a grocer," as one of the Nuremberg War Crimes Trial prosecutors put it, a member of one of the Auschwitz-vetting commissions—was appointed by Concentration Camps Inspector General Glücks to be the commandant of the new camp, a position he held until November 25, 1943. A member of the Nazi Party since 1922 and a volunteer of the Freikorps, Höss fought against the French in the Ruhr and Polish insurgents in Silesia in the early '20s. At the suggestion of Himmler in 1934, he joined the SS, quickly graduated to the elite SS Death Head units, and got a job as block supervisor in Dachau. Within four years at Dachau, he rose to the rank of administrator of prisoners' property, a sinecure because prisoners would never see their belongings again. In 1938 he became administrative assistant to Hermann Baranowski, the commandant of the two-year-old Sachsenhausen concentration camp, and was promoted to the rank of SS captain. A year later he joined the ranks of the *Waffen-SS*, a military limb of the Schutzstaffel (SS) originally formed from members of the paramilitary groups of the Freikorps and street brawlers of the Nazi Party, like the SA storm troopers. Under Himmler's direction it became, both as regards fanaticism and atrocities, a Nazi elite military formation.

Höss set off for Oświęcim in the company of five SS men. He had a noncommissioned SS officer by the name of Gerhardt Amo Palitzsch bring down with him from Sachsenhausen thirty German prisoners, most of them common criminals, to be the first trusties of the camp, who were also the first Auschwitz prisoners numbered

1 to 30. These trustees wanted to survive, so with few exceptions, to earn brownie points from the authorities, they were brutal to excess to Polish political prisoners. Höss had the German town council send him three hundred Jewish residents of Oświęcim to clean up the muck from the military barracks and other abandoned structures, which were now SS property. He put Palitzsch, "the terror of the prisoners ... hated by them to the utmost," in charge of discipline.[1] In his capacity as camp marshal, Palitzsch was responsible for seeing that executions were carried out in death block 11 and at the death wall in the block's adjacent courtyard. He sought to do this in person, whenever possible, with a small-caliber gun placed at the back of the victim's neck.[2]

Clearly, if only for security reasons, the tidied and patched-up twenty or so buildings sitting on a few acres of woebegone land could not, even in the sick imagination of the most callous SS men, contain the allotted ten thousand Polish political prisoners transported from Katowice, Kraków, Tarnów, Warsaw and other places, no matter how emaciated they were. The size of the camp had to be expanded and the perimeter better guarded by more than just electric barbed wire, a few watchtowers, the guards, and a sprinkling of foul-mouthed trusties. It took some prodding of the higher-ups, but eventually they agreed. On July 18, 1940 von dem Bach happened to inspect the facility, two days after the escape of a young Pole who had still not been found, presumably protected by Polish farmers in adjoining villages. Höss received permission to evict the farmers from what came to be known as the camp's jurisdictional "zone of interest" of twenty-five square miles thenceforth patrolled by SS guards and gestapo units but otherwise left uninhabited other than by SS personnel and their families, who were given the houses of the expelled Poles. The cleared zone in the fork of the Vistula and Sola rivers started with the town of Zasole but soon comprised the village of Brzezinka about three kilometers from Zasole and covered a wide area around the hamlet that the Germans renamed Birkenau.

By the end of 1943 when Höss left the Auschwitz complex (though he returned for a three-month stay the following May to straighten out some logistical loose ends), Birkenau had more than three hundred barracks of all types. Most of the barracks were wooden and of the horse stable type, without ceilings or windows. Meant to accommodate fifty-three horses, they instead housed a thousand prisoners crammed into sixty-two three-tiered bunks. Also constructed were four large crematoria equipped with gas chambers disguised as shower rooms.[3] The crematoria were able to consume more than four thousand human bodies a day. So as to be able to lodge a projected two hundred thousand inmates (at least temporarily, since most of the prisoners were scheduled to be gassed to death as soon as possible after debarking from the cattle trains), plans were made to add many more sheds and aux- iliary buildings arranged in an enormous rectangle and divided into smaller sections insulated from each other by high-tension electric wires and guard towers. The whole constituted a single administrative unit called Auschwitz I (the original camp, 1940) and Auschwitz II (Birkenau, 1941). In late October 1942 a third camp was added some seven kilometers to the east of Auschwitz I at the emptied town of Monowice (Monowitz). Monowice was near Dwory, where the German consortium I. G. Farben, the largest European corporation and fourth largest in the world, had built a synthetic rubber factory using the slave labor of eleven thousand prisoners. The company housed the prisoners in Monowitz so as not to lose precious production time transporting prisoners back and forth.

The German motorized armies badly needed synthetic rubber. Nearly forty slave labor subcamps were added in the area over time, thirty of them working for German industry. Only three of the closest to the central camp were directly administered from Auschwitz. The total slave labor force of the satellite camps in 1943 came to thirty-three thousand, and the monthly profit to the Auschwitz administration was two million marks.[4]

Coming from a land of great composers and musical virtuosos, if not subtle humor, Höss was not indifferent to the power of music. In January 1941 he organized an orchestra from among prisoner musicians and instructed them to play light-hearted tunes when notables such as Himmler visited the camp; Höss wanted to show that things were just fine and that culture was not lacking in this jewel of a penal institution. When there were no official tourists to entertain, the orchestra stood at the main gate at daybreak playing

military marches as columns of prisoners were leaving to do excru-
ciatingly hard labor in the zone of interest. It also played again late
in the evening as the prisoners returned to camp dragging their
murdered comrades.[5]

    The idea of "music as you kill" was not original to Höss. Several
other German concentration camps used prisoner orchestras as a
kind of heavy-handed joke when, for example, men were led to the
gallows. There was also a women's prisoner orchestra in Auschwitz-
Birkenau promoted by the music-loving chief warden of women's
barracks (October 8, 1942–November 25, 1944) Maria Mandel,
locally known as "the Beast." Her orchestra played at arrivals of
transports, roll calls, selection for gas chambers, and executions. It
is estimated that she signed orders to send half a million women and
children (including Marta Przybyłowa) to the Auschwitz-Birkenau
gas chambers. After the war she hid for a while in her birthplace
in Műntzkirchen, Austria. Found by American soldiers, she was
turned over to Poland, tried by a court in Cracow, sentenced to
death, and hanged in a Cracow jail on January 24, 1948, at the age
of thirty-six.

    Last but not least, Hőss found a three-floor villa for himself
and his family just outside the watchtowers and barbed wires on
the road to Oświęcim. It had been built in 1937 for his family by a
Polish army second lieutenant named Soja, who had been stationed
in Zasole. The house was requisitioned, and Soja was relocated to
a block in Auschwitz I—a few yards from his former house. He
survived, but when freed, he understandingly did not elect to return
to the area. He sold the house to some people who still lived there in
2007. From one of their windows they had a view of an abandoned
watchtower, and from another of the crematorium adjacent to the
former gestapo "political department" headed by SS Second Lieutenant Maximilian Grabner, in front of which Camp Commandant
Rudolf Hőss was hanged on April 16, 1947, from gallows built spe-
cially for the occasion.

    In case all this might seem heartless, it should be added in his
memory that after leaving Auschwitz at the end of 1943 to become
deputy to Richard Glűcks, by then the head of SS Economic-Admin-
istrative Central Office (WVHA), Hőss went back to Auschwitz on
May 8, 1944, to supervise "Operation Hőss," in the course of which

430,000 Hungarian Jews were gassed and buried in three months. The logistical problem was this: the recently built, state-of-the-art incineration facilities (big, five-muffle crematoria furnaces) of the largest concentration camp in the world could handle only 4,756 corpses a day if they didn't break down from overwork, which they invariably did, and also assuming that no one other than Hungarian Jews was killed in the camp during the ex-commander's sojourn in Birkenau (May 8 to the end of July), which was not so. Gassing was faster than incinerating and so blood-, vomit-, and excrement-smeared cadavers, hanging onto each other piled up in the morgues each day. These had to be pulled out from the gas chambers by a Jewish prisoners' special commando, *Sonderkommando* 1500, and disposed of, under the watch of SS men, the old fashioned way: by pulling them apart, one by one, from their deathly embrace, shoving them onto huge pyres, setting the pyres on fire, and, when it was all over, shoveling what remained of innocent human beings, the little ones too, into dirty ponds or filthy pits—the same way the corpse storage problem was solved in the mini-Auschwitz of Krzywczycki Forest.

The first transport of prisoners arrived in Auschwitz I on June 14, 1940, the day the French capital fell to the Germans. Sent on orders of the SS headquarters in Kraków, it consisted of 728, overwhelmingly Polish political prisoners and many of them youngsters of Janusz Przybyła's age who tried but failed to cross the border on their way to France to join the Polish army being formed there. There were also a few priests, some school teachers caught in the net of the *AB Aktion*, and several dozen Jews. They were given camp numbers 31 to 758. The first transport from Warsaw on August 15 brought 513 Polish political prisoners from the Pawiak jail and 1,553 men caught in street roundups and sent directly to Auschwitz. On December 31, 1940. a Pole brought to Auschwitz from Katowice received the number 7879. Camp mathematics not being a hard science, this does not mean automatically that there were at that point in time that many prisoners in the camp because no account was taken of those who had died. Other estimates put the number of prisoners in the original camp (Auschwitz I) between May 20, 1940, and March 1941 at ten thousand, most of them Poles. The forty-six Death Books in the Archives of the Auschwitz-Birkenau

Museum covering the period July 27, 1941–December 1943 contain
sixty-nine thousand death certificates, including those of Jan and
Marta Przybyła. After Auschwitz reached its second historical
stage, that of accelerated mass extermination (around the time of
Jan's and Marta's death), camp numbers were no longer given to all
those designated to go from the railway ramp straight to the gas
chambers; most of them were Jews from all over Europe.

From then on, the rate, volume, ethnic/national composition,
and mechanics of murdering people underwent a change. More lives
were extinguished each day, the absolute number of Jews murdered
increased exponentially, and there was relatively less liquidation of
life by means of deliberately created hunger and exhaustion, torture,
individual floggings, and executions by guns, and more death by
poison gas on a scale unmatched by Imperial Germany's use of it
on the French front in World War I. The change did not exclude
the continuation, unabated and unabashed, of the previous horrible
ways of ending life, with the expansion of pseudoscientific experiments on adults, children, and infants by execrable SS doctors such
as Josef Mengele, who was sent to Auschwitz-Birkenau in 1943,
the year when 106 castrations and experiments on sterilization of
women began. Mengele specialized in selecting prisoners for gas
chambers on arrival, and performing surgery on about 1500 sets
of child twins without anesthetics. If they did not die during these
and other proceedings, their hearts were injected with phenol. He
got professional backing from the German scientific firmament
and sent prisoner body parts (including skulls for measurement
of racial hygiene, *Rassenhygiene*) to one of his former professors
at the division of anthropology, human heredity, and eugenics of
the Kaiser Wilhelm Institute (KWI) in Berlin-Dahlem. Mengele
evaded capture after the war, and in 1958 he escaped to Buenos
Aires, Argentina, and later moved to Brazil. He died in 1979 from a
stroke while swimming.

It is true that over the years the Auschwitz concentration
camp's dimensions and methodology of killing underwent wholesale expansion and perverse modernization. The relative shares of
different ethnic groups put to death were changed so as to remain
at once rigidly faithful to static National Socialist ideology and keep

pace with the dynamic historical reality that was rapidly unfolding all around the mighty Third Reich—a challenging assignment.

In that reality, first came a succession of staggering German military victories in central, western, northern, southeastern (mostly to bail out Mussolini), and eastern Europe, and in North Africa (to prop up Mussolini again). By November 1942, Greater Germany had reached the peak. The swastika was driven into prostrated peoples from the French Pyrenees in the west to Caucasus in the east, where it was planted on Mount Elbrus, the highest mountain in Europe, and from Norway in the north to Greece in the south. On the other hand, what this meant was that in the east this Greater Germany now had a nearly three-thousand-mile front with the Soviet Union, from Murmansk in the north to near Grozny in the south. On the west was Britain and America preparing to pull down the Nazi flag. In other words, there was the distinct probability that Germany would have to face a war on two fronts. Then came the Russian winter; Kursk, the greatest tank battle in history; and the calamity of Stalingrad. The rest, as the saying goes, is history: two fronts, defeat, and final unconditional surrender, and with it the death of Auschwitz, the very residence of death.

While all this was happening, the Nazi belief system remained static because it was meant to last a thousand years unblemished, and only the supreme dictator, Hitler, could substantively alter it—which he had no intention of doing at any time, right down to his last breath. Those army officers who on July 20, 1944, tried rather late in the day (and failed) to remove him by concocting a plot code-named Operation Valkyrie were, on Hitler's orders, "hung like cattle," one by one, in Berlin's Plötzensee prison, a wire tied to the neck and attached to a slaughterhouse meat hook hung from the ceiling so they would die by slow strangulation, while Goebbels' cameraman recorded their death agony on sound film, knowing that the Führer, liked to relax by watching movies at the end of a hard day's work when he was not soliloquizing. The movie was developed at once and rushed to him. He watched it that very evening, again and again.

Earlier we touched on Nazi ideology and its inspirational forbears and outgrowths such as the *Volkstumkampf* (chapter 6), at the core of which was the immovable racist dogma of Germanic genetic superiority over the rest of humanity. It asserted that through the ages, Germanic peoples had evolved by some neo-Darwinian process of survival to be the fittest and brightest; they allegedly reached the status of *Übermenschen*, with the best "blood" and highest culture, a people to whom one would not hesitate to give a watch (chapter 3). The opposite of these supermen and women were the millions of nonpersons, the subhumans, infecting and dragging humanity's trailblazers down. They had to be hated, mercilessly combated, stripped of what little semblance of humanity they had left, and permanently removed.

The removal, however, could not be done all at once. Allowance had to be made for time ranges, for short and longer runs. In the short run, departure of the expendables from the unjustly truncated, post World War I Germany could be by emigration perhaps. When, as predicted by Hitler's chancellery, Germany regained its rightful living space in Europe and beyond, the ideologically correct blood would risk being diluted or, worse still, contaminated due in part to "differential reproduction" (despite official calls for large families) but mainly because huge numbers of racial undesirables would be added to the future Germania's population. Because of this, the intruders would have to be removed in a more permanent way.

German officials established a ranking of the severity of preconceived discrimination based on race and interpreted in the compound sense to include ethnicity, language, national origin, religion, hereditary mental and physical disabilities, and other hatred-based differences. Longstanding and widespread anti-Semitism in Germany and elsewhere being readily to hand, the Jews were given the pride of place. On September 15, 1935, the Law for the Protection of German Blood and German Honor, and the Reich Citizenship Law—the so-called "Nuremberg Laws"—were promulgated at a Nuremberg mass rally of the Nazi party and unanimously passed by the Reichstag.[6] They stripped Jews of German citizenship and more broadly of nationality by restricting their political, social, and economic rights; banning marriage and extramarital relations between German citizens and Jews; and, implying Jewish built-in moral turpitude, prohibiting Jews from employing in their households women under the age of forty-five. Next in line were the Poles, who were always more or less quietly discriminated against, but the negativity was more open, loud, and aggressive after Hitler lost his patience with Danzig and the "Corridor" Then came the Russians, whether communist or not, and other Slavs, whether friendly like the Slovaks and Croats, peacefully inclined like the Czechs, or militant like the Serbs. Farther down were the French, and scattered all about were gypsies, dwarves, anyone with the wrong color of skin or eyes, anyone with an unapproved shape of face or skull, homophiles, cross-dressers, and vagrants, "asocials," degenerate artists, the "morally feeble"—essentially those who would not tow the line on National Socialist Realism as exhibited in the House of German Art. On November 24, 1933, a Law Against Habitual and Dangerous Criminals was passed. It allowed beggars, the homeless, and the unemployed (i.e., "work shirkers") to be sent to concentration camps. In 1937 an exhibition of "degenerate art" opened in Munich and subsequently traveled to eleven German and Austrian cities. It showed 650 paintings, mostly by expressionists, out of 20,000 works that had been so decreed, many of which were burned.

What was needed (if only for appearances) and easily obtained was professional legitimacy to be conferred on this nationalistic, terminal narcissism and equal-opportunity racism by known, reputable, and respected professor-doctors and scientific researchers of established stature in the "applied science" of eugenics, genetics, anthropology, biochemistry, and neuropsychiatry, some associated with the prestigious Kaiser Wilhelm Society and with visible university hospitals.[7]

The Auschwitz monstrosity carried out the injunctions of this devilry and, to remain in good graces with the highest authorities, anticipated their wishes and added twisted innovations to the prisoners' punishments and other daily activities. It can be said that the camp went through two parallel phases reflecting the highest level of ideological corrections. The aim was to reconcile the belief system with what was actually going on in the real world, mostly on the battle fronts, when things were going well (or the never publicly admitted opposite). These adjustments were abrupt, made by one man when he felt like it, but he never adjusted the ultimate aim of annihilation. The fact that from now until further notice the

Germans were going to enslave and eventually put to death people
of group B did not mean that the group A people to whom they had
done this before were going to be treated better than before or let
go; group B were simply added to the more crowded equation. The
change was in emphasis and in numbers. How this was done in all
its appalling ways was up to Höss and Dr. Mengele, as were other
details (for example, output per oven). But the oral roots of the
ordeal of those branded had long been around:

> and she [the witch] got up and put her head in the oven.
> Then Grethel gave her a push, so that she fell right in, and
> then shutting the iron door she bolted it. Oh! how horribly
> she howled, but Grethel ran away, and left the ungodly
> witch to burn to ashes.[8]

The first functional phase of the Auschwitz concentration
camp's existence was dominated by Polish political prisoners and
randomly picked-up people. It started at the camp's 1940 opening—its gate had the inscription *Arbeit macht frei* (Work will set
you free), a shibboleth of nineteenth-century German nationalist literary origin—and merged, not ended, with the addition of
Russian POWs beginning in June 1941. The rapid German advance
and early disarray of Soviet forces resulted in huge numbers of
Russian soldiers surrendering, thus creating for the German army
a problem of human storage. To the relief of the Reichswehr's High
Command, Auschwitz offered to help take care of the Russian war
prisoners. And they did. All the soldiers in the first two transports to Auschwitz (July and September 1941) were murdered on
arrival without even receiving a camp serial number or getting a
photograph taken, a time- and money-saving practice also useful
in keeping things under wraps; the practice was later extended to
all those selected for instant death on the railroad platform. In the
following months other trains arrived with Russian POWs, most of
them conscripted peasants, as the communist political commissars
had already been put to death. On Himmler's order these peasant-
soldiers were assigned to build prisoner barracks in Birkenau. They
were "housed" three kilometers away in nine blocks of the original
camp, which was surrounded by electrified barbed wire and other

isolating devices. Each day at the crack of dawn, they marched out of Auschwitz I on their way to a building site at Birkenau Section B I. Designed by Fritz Ertl, a graduate of the famous *Bauchaus* school of architecture, to hold twenty thousand prisoners, the camp was a rectangle 2,300 feet long and 400 feet across. It was divided into two areas: (a) one containing brick barracks, and (b) the other horse stable-type huts. Every evening as darkness fell, fewer builders shuffled back, followed by carts loaded with corpses. By November 1941, the total of Russian war prisoners was about 12,000. When on March 1, 1942, they were transferred to Birkenau, 945 remained alive.[9] Given the inhuman burden of their work assignments in late autumn in the marshes, abominable treatment of them by the trustees, and their meager food rations, it was unlikely that those still living would survive long. When they could not work any more and thus became totally useless to their masters, they were reassigned to one of the unfinished barracks they had built with others in the B I "quarantine" camp and were killed.

There is a sad endnote to this. It is about those unfortunate "Russian" prisoners of war, including Ukrainians, Belorussians, and other national minorities of the Soviet empire, who survived the war, if not necessarily Auschwitz, and were handed over to Soviet authorities by the Western Allies. One must hope that this was done not to gain favor with Stalin but because of ignorance that at that time the Kremlin had decreed the conflict a "Great Patriotic War"—and a soldier's surrender to the enemy was considered high treason against the Russian fatherland, a crime instantly punishable by prolonged death.

Then there were the gypsies, who like other wanderers never stayed in one place for long, engaged in begging, and were accused of redistributing wealth by relieving passers-by of their wallets. According to Nazi ideology, they posed a hereditary genetic danger to healthy humanity and had to be eliminated for racial hygiene, the sooner the better—no need to give them numbers or photograph them. From the same perspective, alcoholics and the homeless were simply work shirkers: useless weaklings disposed of instantly inside the gates. Those diagnosed by politically reliable medical doctors as suffering from genetically inherited physical or mental deformities and disabilities were as good as dead on arrival at Auschwitz.

The transformation of the largest concentration camp in Greater Germany into the largest mass extermination machinery in the world occurred shortly after a top-secret conference at Wannsee in Berlin, convened by the second in command of the SS, Reinhardt Heydrich, on January 20, 1942, and authorized by Hermann Göring, who had been appointed by Hitler to be in charge of the "Jewish question" in 1938. It was a major functional phase in the existence of the Auschwitz-Birkenau camp, which was soon to be assisted by other mass death camps in occupied Poland, including Majdanek and Bełżec, where an estimated six hundred thousand Jews were murdered before the camp was closed in December 1942; Sobibór with 250,000 deaths, Treblinka with 870,000, and Chełmno (near Łódź) with 300,000 deaths, the early ones by carbon monoxide piped in from engines into sealed mobile vans, the later ones by more modern gassing methods. The Wannsee conference was attended by fifteen top Nazi officials, including Karl Eberhardt Schöngarth. It lasted ninety minutes and ended with glasses of cognac raised to celebrate a constructive achievement, unanimously approved.

The Jews had to go. Every one of them. Forever. No exceptions. No longer was sending them abroad acceptable, for the "abroad" (at least the European one), was rapidly becoming part of the Greater German Reich. However, with the seemingly unending expansion, the Reich was getting more Jews every day, potentially eleven million by German count—an intolerable problem. Of these eleven million, two and a quarter million were held in ghettos in the General Government, but five million were in the Soviet Union, including three million in the Ukraine alone. Then there were the Jews in Vichy France, Slovakia, the Baltic States, Belgium, Holland, Norway, Greece, and so on. Looking ahead, there were also those in enemy England, a country on the future absorption list, as well as neutral Switzerland and Sweden. Europe, Heydrich explained, would be "combed of Jews from east to west." Those from the west would be sent east. But in the east the result of the combing— physical elimination—could no longer be left to "natural causes," the euphemistic code phrase for death by hard labor and starvation, nor by "special treatment," code for death by beatings, kicking, flog-gings, firing squads, lethal injections, or suffocation in Auschwitz's block eleven ("standing cells" in which up to four prisoners were squeezed standing up for days or weeks on end, unable to bend, turn around, move their feet, or stretch their arms).

Fortunately for the Wannsee conferees, German chemists and engineers were making progress in the mechanics of formerly retail "special actions"—that is, gas-induced killing—and in the construction of larger and more input-output efficient ovens. Gravel pellets saturated with twenty percent hydrogen cyanide ("Zyklon B") and improved post-carnage ventilation of the gas chambers replaced carbon monoxide as the key constituent of the preferred industrial-scale, life-destruction line.[10] The first application of this advanced technology was in May–June 1942 in two temporary gas chambers called Bunker 1 and Bunker 2 in Birkenau. They were once cottages that belonged to Polish farmers before being dispossessed by the "special zone" operation. They were known respectively as "the little red house," and "the little white house." Until four large, state of the art gas chamber/crematory facilities came online in Birkenau between mid-March and mid-May 1943, the bunkers did their best to "process" the prisoners whose remains were buried in a mass grave in a nearby grassland, a procedure that contaminated the groundwater being sent to Silesian cities. After protests from the governor of Silesia, the bodies were disinterred and burned in open pits. The new crematoria had an impressive but insufficient daily capacity of 4,756 bodies, an inconvenience that, as we have seen, brought Rudolf Höss back to the camp a year later in a consulting capacity.

It was in 1942 that a second railroad ramp came into use exclusively for the unloading of Jews brought to Auschwitz for extermination. It was called the "Jewish ramp" (*Judenrampe*). Beginning in May 1944, all transports were unloaded at a platform within the Birkenau part of the camp where the modern gas chambers and crematoria were located within easy reach.[11] One would have thought that as the Soviet armies drew nearer, the murder frenzy would subside somewhat. That was not so in Auschwitz; the pace of gassing people and burning their bodies in modern ovens and primitive open pits sped up. There was so many more to kill and so much to hide. Large boxcar transports kept coming daily from all over Europe.

The last time the gas chambers were used was on October 30,

1944. On November 26 Himmler ordered the crematoria to be destroyed. That job was done by the end of December by prisoners of a special kommando who knew that they were going to be liquidated once they had finished their task. Crematorium IV had been blown up by a special kommando revolt on October 7, 1944. Crematorium V continued to be used to incinerate the remaining dead bodies until mid January 1945. All kinds of plumbing and other fittings were sent beforehand to Gross Rosen and Mauthausen concentration camps. Incriminating documents of the gestapo political department were burned, as well as records of hospitals in the central camp and Birkenau. All but six barracks of the so-called Canada in Birkenau, in which the clothing and other personal belongings of the inmates were stored, were burned, but not before half a million articles had been removed and sent to Germany. For some months before the Soviet troops entered the camp, thousands of prisoners were transported by rail boxcars to camps in the west. The final evening roll call took place on January 17, 1945, five days before the first Soviet reconnaissance units reached Auschwitz-Birkenau-Monowitz. There were no more trains, the German army having requisitioned them for its retreat. Of the roughly 67,000 prisoners left, about 16,600 were women. The next day a column of 20,000 left the main camp, heading southwest. Other death columns from Birkenau and the subcamps did the same. Those who fell behind or tried to escape were shot, the bodies left by the wayside. Those too ill or unable to walk remained in the camp: 1,200 in Auschwitz I; 5,800 in Birkenau; 70 percent of them were women. The Soviet army took the camp area on January 22, 1945.[12]

By then an estimated two million people, including one and a half million Jews, had perished in Auschwitz.

Somewhere in this desolate graveyard of human misery and anguish repose Jan and Marta, two among two million, lost but not forgotten.

Notes

1.   Józef Garliński [an Auschwitz Polish political prisoner]. *Fighting Auschwitz: The Resistance Movement in the Concentration Camp.* Greenwich, CT: Fawcett Publications, 1975, 285.

2.   Garliński, 44.

3.   Garliński, 110.

4.   Debórah Dwork & Robert Jan van Pelt. *Auschwitz.* New York: W.W. Norton & Company, 2002, 334–335. Garliński, 114–115.

5.   Józef Garliński, *Fighting Auschwitz.* Greenwich, CT: Fawcett Publications, Inc., 1975, 92.

6.   The previous year's (1934) rally in Nuremberg was recorded for posterity on film by Leni Riefenstahl. The name of the spectacular propaganda movie was *Triumph of the Will.* Albert Speer, Hitler's favorite architect and a member of his inner circle, designed the Zeppelin field stadium in which the rallies were held. He was also the architectural director of the 1934 event and was later minister of war production, for which he used slave labor. Speer got twenty years in Berlin's Spandau Prison (since demolished) and served them all. Riefenstahl, a personal friend of Goebbels, was not tried for war crimes. She pleaded "Art" and died in 2003 at age 101.

7.   William E. Siedelman, MD, "Medicine and Murder in the Third Reich." *Dimensions: A Journal of Holocaust Studies.* http://www.adl.org.Braun/dim_13_1_med_murder_asp. Also his "The legacy of Academic Medicine and Human Exploitation in the Third Reich." *Perspectives in Biology and Medicine,* 43.3 (Spring 2000), 325–334.

8.   Jacob and Wilhelm Grimm. "Hansel and Grethel." *Grimm's Fairy Tales.* New York: Barnes & Noble 2003, 62.

9.   Garliński, 112–113: "During working hours, the Capos had special orders to murder them on the slightest pretext."

10.   Dwork and van Pelt: 175–176 (standing cells); 305-306 (Zyklon B gas chambers).

11.   Holocaust Education & Archives Research team. "Auschwitz Concentration Camp." http://www.holocaustresearchproject.org/othercamps/auschwitzbasics/html.

12.   Garliński: 341–342 (the end of Auschwitz's 1,688 days); 325–327 (Sonderkommando).

The death wall next to Block 11 Auschwitz I

The death wall next to Block 11 Auschwitz I

Ruins of gas chamber and crematorium at Auschwitz-Birkenau

Birkenau (Source: Auschwitz-Birkenau State Museum www.auschwitz.org.pl)

Camp orchestra (Source: Auschwitz-Birkenau State Museum
www.auschwitz.org.pl)

Gas chamber and Crematorium (Source: Auschwitz-Birkenau State Museum
www.auschwitz.org.pl)

Bodies being thrown into pits for burning
(Source: Auschwitz-Birkenau State Museum www.auschwitz.org.pl)

POST-WORLD WAR II POLAND

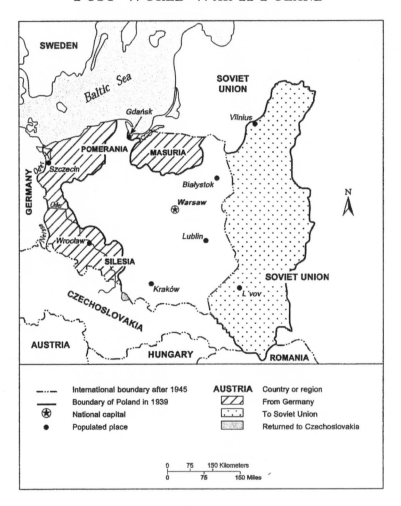

SWEDEN

Baltic Sea

SOVIET UNION

Gdańsk

Vilnius

POMERANIA   MASURIA

Szczecin

GERMANY

Oder

Białystok

Warsaw

Oder

Neisse

Wrocław

Lublin

SILESIA

Kraków

SOVIET UNION

L'vov

CZECHOSLOVAKIA

AUSTRIA

HUNGARY

ROMANIA

N

– – – – International boundary after 1945	**AUSTRIA** Country or region
———— Boundary of Poland in 1939	From Germany
⊛ National capital	To Soviet Union
● Populated place	Returned to Czechoslovakia

0   75   150 Kilometers
0   75   150 Miles

POST-WORLD WAR II POLAND
(Regional Map)

• Łódź

Lower Silesia

• Wrockław

• Częstochowa

• Opole

Upper Silesia

Gliwice • • Bytom
Katowice • • Sosnowiec
• Rybnik
Oświęcim •
(Auschwitz)   • Kraków

Bohumin •   Małopolska
Ostrava •   (Nether Poland)
Cieszyn •
      • Bielsko-Biała

Chech Republic   Krynica
                              •

                        •
                  Zakopane

Slovakia

Annex

The little poem, "Wawel," glorified the royal palace in Cracow overlooking the Vistula river. It was written by Jan Przybyła shortly before his arrest and subsequent murder in the Auschwitz-Birkenau concentration camp. It is the only verse of his many compositions that has survived in his handwriting. It ends on an upbeat note: "A cloud is still passing over it / But behind it, the sun is already shining!"

Wawel

w. IV. 1942

Wieki długie nad nim przeszły,
~~Lata~~ chmurne i słoneczne -
Wielkości do grobów zeszły
Te z pół chwały i stołeczne -
A On trwa w swym majestacie,
Dumny w swej królewskiej szacie.

Ileż ócz go podziwiało!
Ileż myśli się zrodziło!
Ileż serc tam zapłakało,
Ileż dusz się obudziło!
A On dalej trwa dostojny
W łaski swe królewskie hojny.

Tam Katedra ~~świątynia~~ piękna chowa
Święte szczątki Stanisława -
Zdąża Polak do Krakowa,
Bo ~~tam~~ Wawel, a w nim stawa!
Jeszcze nad ~~nim~~ chmura leci,
Lecz za nią już słońce świeci!

Bibliography

Addison, Paul. *The Road to 1945: British Politics and the Second World War.* London: Pimlico, 1994.

Blanke, Richard. *Orphans of Versailles: The Germans in Western Poland, 1918–1939.* Lexington: University of Kentucky Press, 1993.

Blobaum, Robert, ed. *Antisemitism and Its Opponents in Modern Poland.* Ithaca and London: Cornell University Press, 2005.

Davies, Norman. *God's Playground: History of Poland (Revised edition, vol 1 & 2).* New York: Columbia University Press, 2005

_____. *White Eagle, Red Star: The Polish Soviet War, 1919–1920.* New York: St. Martin's Press, 1972. London: Pimlico (New edition), 2003.

Deighton, Len. *Blitzkrieg: From the Rise of Hitler to the Fall of Dunkirk.* London: Pimlico, 1996.

Desbois, Patrick. *The Holocaust by Bullets:a Priest's Journey to Uncover the Truth behind the Murder of 1.5 Million Jews.* New York, Palgrave Macmillan, 2008.

Eatwell, Roger. *Fascism: A History.* London: Pimlico, 2003.

Fisher, David, and Anthony Read. *The Deadly Embrace: Hitler, Stalin, and the Nazi-Soviet Pact, 1939–1941.* New York: W. W. Norton & Company, 1999.

Garliński, Józef. *Poland in the Second World War.* Houndmills, Basingstoke, Hants, England: Palgrave Macmillan, 1985.

_____. *The Survival of Love: Memoirs of a Resistance Officer.* Cambridge, MA: Basil Blackwell, 1991.

Gregor, James A. *Phoenix: Fascism in Our Times.* New Brunswick,NJ: Transactions Publishers, 1991.

Lancorońska, Karolina. *Those Who Trespass Against Us: One Woman's War Against the Nazis.* London: Pimlico, 2006.

Lerski, George; Piotr Wróbel; Richard J. Kozicki. *Historical Dictionary of Poland, 966–1945.* New York: Random House, 2001.

Macmillan, Margaret. *Paris 1919: Six Months That Changed the World.* New York: Random House, 2001.

Mahlendorf, Ursula. *The Shame of Survival: Working Through a Nazi Childhood.* University Park, PA: Pennsylvania State University Press, 2009.

Paczkowski, Andrzej. *The Spring Will Be Ours: Poland and the Poles from Occupation to Freedom.* Translated by James Cave: University Park, PA: Pennsylvania State University Press, 2003.

Petersen, Michael B. *Missiles for the Fatherland: Pennemünde, National Socialism, and the V-2 Missile.* New York: Cambridge University Press, 2009.

Rieber, Alfred J. *Forced Migrations in Central and Eastern Europe, 1939-1945.* London, UK and Portland, Oregon, Frank Cass Publishers, 2000.

Watt, Richard M. *Bitter Glory: Poland and Its Fate, 1918–1939*. New York: Simon & Schuster, 1979.

Weinberg, Gerhard L. *The Foreign Policy of Hitler's Germany: Starting World War II, 1937–1939*. Chicago: University of Chicago Press, 1980.

Zamoyski, Adam. *Warsaw 1920: Lenin's Failed Conquest of Europe*. New York: Harper Collins, 2008.

Zubrzycki, Genevieve. *The Crosses of Auschwitz*. Chicago: University of Chicago Press, 2006.

Index

Note: Page numbers followed by a *"p," "n,"* or an *"m"* refer to photographs, notes, or maps, respectively.

A

Auschwitz-Birkenau
    accelerated mass
        extermination, 194–195
    aerial view of, 205*p*
    body disposal, 193, 207*p*
    camp orchestra, 206*p*, 191–192
    camp trusties, 189–190
    construction, 190–191
    death certificates, 193–194
    death pit, 186*p*
    death wall next to Block 11,
        204*p*
    first prisoners, 193–194
    founding of, 188–190
    functional phase, 198–202
    gallows, 185*p*
    gas chamber and crematorium,
        206*p*
    gas chambers, last use of,
        201–202
    Gypsies in, 199

    Jews, extermination of,
        199–202
    Polish political prisoners, 198
    prisoner dress, 182*n*
    Przybyła, Jan
        Auschwitz photos, 185*p*
        Auschwitz prison records,
            176–179
    Przybyła, Marta
        Auschwitz photos, 185*p*
        Auschwitz prison records,
            179–181
    removal of prisoners from, 202
    ruins of gas chamber and
        crematorium, 205*p*
    Russian entry into, 202
    Russian war prisoners in, 199
    and slave labor camps, 191
    transition from concentration
        camp to death camp, xii

217

LaVergne, TN USA
04 March 2010
174913LV00004B/11/P